444 DAYS

MEMOIRS

OF A

HOSTAGE
WIFE

MARGE GERMAN

STORY MERCHANT BOOKS
LOS ANGELES
2020

STORY MERCHANT BOOKS

ISBN-13: 978-1-970157-17-8

Story Merchant Books
400 S. Burnside Avenue #11B
Los Angeles, CA 90036
www.storymerchantbooks.com

Cover & interior formatting by IndieDesignz.com

TABLE OF CONTENTS

INTRODUCTION...I

PROLOGUE...III

CHAPTER 1 1

Preparing for Change..2

CHAPTER 2: SHOCK AND DENIAL: MY REACTION TO THE EMBASSY TAKEOVER...8

Learning to Cope with the Crisis..10

Family Meeting at the Department of State with President Carter 12

Church Services at Washington National Cathedral............................16

CHAPTER 3 18

The Militants Threaten to Execute the Hostages................................18

Thirteen Hostages Released 18

First Letter from Bruce Arrives, Written by the Militants....................21

CHAPTER 4: VERY DISAPPOINTING MEETING WITH THE CLERGY 30

Television Broadcast of the Christmas Services...................................32

Unexpected Mail from the Men of the USS KITTY HAWK 34

The Phone Call: My First Conversation with an Iranian Militant 38

CHAPTER 5: A SURPRISE VIDEO TAPE ARRIVES................................42

Packages for the Hostages 42

A Totally Unexpected Phone Call from Dad 44

CHAPTER 6: THE NIGHTLINE INTERVIEW, DAY 100......................47

CHAPTER 7: INTRUSION BY THE MEDIA CONTINUES....................50

Film Clip of Bruce...51

Ben's Phone Call to Me..51

CHAPTER 8: PHONE MESSAGE FROM THE INTERNATIONAL RED CROSS
....56

Discussing Bruce's concerns with Sheldon Krys 57

CHAPTER 9 62
   Memorial Services and Feelings of Guilt..............................64
   FLAG Meeting...64
   International Red Cross Meeting in New York.........................65
   Father's Day...67
   A Day at Kings Dominion..68
   The Family Meeting in San Francisco 69

CHAPTER 10: COMMUNICATING WITH THE MILITANTS.............72
   Free the Hostages-Unite the Families 72
   Psychiatrist Dr. Hauben to See Bruce 74

CHAPTER 11: IRANIAN MAKE THEIR DEMANDS KNOWN..............76
   Meeting with Dr. Ewalt of the Veterans Administration Office 77
   Frank Sinatra's Invitation to the Inauguration Rehearsal 81

CHAPTER 12: NEGOTIATIONS STILL GOING ON...........................82
   Jan. 20, 1981 – Inauguration Day – Day 444........................82
   Our Stay at West Point Military Academy 85
   White House Reception 86
   Parade in New York...86
   Speaking at the Children's Schools.................................87
   Home Coming in Wilkes-Barre, Pennsylvania 89
   March 15, 1981, Freedom Day at Peary High School..................90

CHAPTER 13: WHAT IS "GETTING BACK TO NORMAL?" 93
   June 11, 1981 Debbie's Convocation and Graduation 94

CHAPTER 14: THE FALL OUT 96
   Bruce's Behavior Becomes Nasty and Devious.........................97
   More Disappointments for the Children..............................98
   Appointment with Dr. Ewalt 101
   First Anniversary - Freedom Party.................................101
   Phone Call from Bruce's Boss 102
   Palm Sunday Letter 105
   Another Weird Phone Call 106
   Our Meeting to Talk..107

CHAPTER 15: NOT HAPPILY EVER AFTER 120

CHAPTER 16 135
    Finding the Right Lawyer 137
    Getting Rid of Hurtful Reminders...138
    Our All-Savers Certificate 139
    A Date that will Forever be Etched in my Mind.......................144

CHAPTER 17: LEARNING TO FIGHT BACK...............................148
    A Matter of Trustworthiness 150
    A New Year – A New Beginning?...151
    Bruce's Love Interest Revealed 154
    The Psychologist Visit 156

CHAPTER 18: WHO IS THIS DEVIOUS PERSON? 159
    Elaine and I Become Detectives...162
    Hiring a Detective 164

CHAPTER 19: THE HEARTACHE AS MY MARRIAGE ENDS.............167
    Depositions and Accusations 169
    Bruce goes to the Far East Leaving Us Without Money for Food 170
    Bruce Wants to Meet to Talk, Mostly About Him...................171
    His Feelings of Guilt..174

CHAPTER 20: THE AFTERMATH 179
    Going to Court for the Divorce..180
    Ben Called me about his Mother's Illness.................................183
    Hostages Twentieth Mini Reunion Jan. 2001..........................185
    Christmas 2003 189
    Theresa's Death and Funeral, February 21st, 2005 190

EPILOGUE...196
Looking Back 35 Years...196
    Matt's Graduation, Commissioning, and Wedding..................199
    Debbie's Graduation, Wedding and Children 200
    Chris' High School & College Graduation, his Marriage and Fatherhood
   201
    Time Heals All Wounds...202

INTRODUCTION

O n November 4, 1979, Iranian students/militants seized the American Embassy in Tehran, taking its diplomats hostage while demanding that the deposed Shah, Mohammad Reza Pahlavi, who had been admitted to the United States for medical treatment, be returned to them for trial and probable execution. **It was a demand of blackmail** Washington refused, and thus began one of the ugliest, most frightening and confounding incidents in American history.

Marge German and I met during that first terrifying week, when families of the hostages living in the Washington area were invited to the State Department to meet with President Jimmy Carter. Marge's memory of that meeting is clearer than mine—I don't recall speaking with the doctors or State officials—-but I do remember looking into the earnest blue eyes of the President, as he tried to reassure us that our loved ones would soon be released. Not only did diplomatic laws of immunity demand it, he said, but the Ayatollah Khomeini was a "religious"—and therefore "compassionate"—man.

I wasn't about to contradict the President of the United States—after all, I was a diplomat's wife—and yet, having lived and traveled for seven years in Pakistan, Afghanistan, and Iran as a white, Western, Christian "infidel" woman, I had been made fully aware of our religious and cultural differences. I had also witnessed numerous incidents of Islamic extremism, including the murder of a young, unveiled schoolgirl at a bus stop outside our front gate in Kabul, who was shot in the stomach by a mad mullah from Herat. Thus, "compassionate" was not a word I would have used to describe the Ayatollah Khomeini. He may have been charismatic to the Iranian mobs, but to me he was a radical, militant, Islamic fundamentalist, who would be ruthless in his revolutionary zeal.

Sure enough, a day or so later, Khomeini condoned the actions of the student/militants by calling them "the rosebuds of the Revolution" and encouraged them to break every law of international diplomatic immunity. They obeyed him, confiscating embassy property, stealing cars, commissary goods and household effects of American personnel, rifling through files and piecing together shredded documents, threatening to put the hostages on trial as "a nest of spies," and submitting their prisoners to fourteen months of brutal treatment which included beatings, solitary confinement, and mock executions. Indeed, the Iran Hostage Crisis has since been called the first act of modern Islamic terrorism.

Marge and I soon found we had several things in common: We were Foreign Service wives, each with three children, living in the state of Maryland, and both of us were married to men named "Bruce." We drew closer as the crisis continued, becoming trustworthy and supportive friends who could call each other at any time to discuss the latest turn of events, to cry, complain, commiserate, and compare notes. As the months dragged on, we learned a great many things about ourselves, about our strengths and weaknesses. Loyalty to each other was slow coming at first, though once achieved, it was very rewarding.

In March of 1980, we established the Family Liaison Action Group (FLAG). Marge was the Secretary of FLAG and I was a Vice President. One of my duties was to put out the FLAG Bulletin in an effort to keep everyone united and informed. We had the pro bono services of a distinguished lawyer and our own bank account. We organized candlelight vigils, church services at the Washington National Cathedral, wrote letters to the Secretary General of the United Nations, Kurt Waldheim, and hung yellow ribbons across the country. We organized meetings with psychiatrists who taught us how to cope with stress and fear, how to care for our children in such a public arena, and how to persevere in our daily lives in school, at home, and at work. We learned to exploit the media before they exploited us. Our churches, as Marge relates, were particularly supportive. By the time the ordeal was over, 444 days later, we could all have written (and some of us did) manuals for the handling of families in crisis. I am convinced that John Milton said it best when he wrote, "They also serve who only stand and wait."*

The Homecoming in January of 1981 was beyond glorious. As one hostage described it, "We were bathed in love." But sadly, not everyone lived happily ever after.

Penne Laingen
*from John Milton's sonnet "On His Blindness."

PROLOGUE

◆━━━◆

In 1958, a coworker introduced me to one of her former high school classmates, Bruce German. We were immediately attracted to each other and began dating. After three years, we married on May 27, 1961. While on our honeymoon, Bruce had a job interview at the Central Intelligence Agency in Washington, D.C. and was hired immediately. I had been employed at the Bell Telephone Company of Pennsylvania for six years and was up for a supervisory position but gave that up to move to Arlington, VA. I transferred to Chesapeake and Potomac Telephone Company in Washington, D.C. where I worked in the accounting office.

Bruce was told he would be due to go overseas within the next year, which meant I would have to leave my job again, so I decided I would apply to work at the CIA with my husband, and to my delight, I was hired! In February 1963, we left for Frankfort, Hesse, Germany, arriving there on my birthday, February 11. Lucky for me, the individual who worked as a travel voucher examiner in the Finance Department was reassigned to the United States, so that position was open, and I was chosen to fill it. It was one of the most rewarding jobs I'd ever had. I sincerely enjoyed dealing with the logistics of our agents' travels to various regions around Frankfurt, calculating their per diem, and converting drachmas, pounds, liras and other foreign currency to German marks.

It was just nine months later that our daughter, Debbie, was born on November 23rd, the day after President John F. Kennedy was assassinated. At that point, I just wanted to go back to the United States, but it was financially impossible. I decided to give up my career to become a full-time mother, and allow Bruce to take over my position, which put him on the more upwardly mobile path of a budget officer.

After a few years, Bruce transferred to the Department of State, Foreign Service and in 1976 we had our first overseas tour to Honduras, Central America. By that time, we had three children - Debbie, Matthew, and Christopher—who were excited to experience a new culture and Embassy life. It was a big adjustment to see television programs like *The Three Stooges* in Spanish. Their enthusiasm lasted for four or five months. After that, homesickness prevailed. We returned to the United States in 1977 and settled in Rockville, Maryland.

Bruce's next assignment took him to Tehran, Iran due to the revolution that occurred in February 1979. On November 4, 1979, the unimaginable happened. Bruce was taken hostage when militants overran the American Embassy. He had only been there five-and-a-half weeks. Although he was the direct victim, the children and I were indirect victims during those 444 days because what affected him, affected us.

To understand life in 1979, one must step back in time when television channels stopped broadcasting at 1:00 am. There were no cable television stations, only the three Network TV stations and a few local ones. Telephone answering machines were just coming into being, email was non-existent, and except for telephones, the U.S. Postal Service was the most important way to communicate.

During those 444 days, our daily lives revolved around what was happening to Bruce. We worried about his well-being: was he being starved, or tortured? Was he being kept warm enough in winter and cool enough in summer? Since I knew he was a very impatient person, I worried that he was being beaten for saying or doing something the militants didn't like. My prayers constantly asked God to protect Bruce and to guide us through this situation.

444 DAYS:

MEMOIRS
OF A
HOSTAGE WIFE

The 444 days of the 1979 Iran Hostage Crisis changed my life as well as the lives of every American who now must deal with the constant threat of terrorism, not only overseas, but also here in the United States

ALL INQUIRIES TO:
Marge German <u>mgerman1@verizon.net</u>
301-460-0773(h)—301-642-3175(c)
14102 Chesterfield Road,
Rockville, MD 20853-2052

444 DAYS

MEMOIRS

OF A

HOSTAGE
WIFE

Chapter 1

June 1979. "This is the place for you," read the note attached to a memo from the Personnel Officer at the State Department. Bruce read the attached memo that said budget officers were needed in Tehran and Tel Aviv. The memo also said that no other overseas position anywhere else in the world would be filled until someone was assigned to the Tehran position. All non-essential personnel at the U.S. Embassy there had been evacuated the previous February during the Iranian Revolution, when the Shah had been overthrown. Replacing those Embassy personnel was the top priority. Our last overseas assignment had ended in 1977 and Bruce was due for another overseas post. It was the career he had chosen as a Foreign Service officer with the Department of State.

The Tel Aviv assignment would be a regular two-year tour with the family, while the Tehran assignment would be an 18-month tour excluding family. However, two stateside visitations during the tour at six-month intervals would be allowed.

Bruce brought home the *Post Reports*, which described the living conditions, schools, etc. and we listed the good and bad points of each post. I preferred going to Tel Aviv as a family rather than being separated for 18 months, but timing was a problem. The Department of State wanted the budget officer to be there within two months, which meant that we would have to get passports, buy clothes, obtain school records, and put our household items into storage. We'd also have to find someone to rent the house in our absence. It would be a tremendous undertaking in that short a period of time. In 1976, we'd had just three months to prepare for our tour to Honduras, Central America and I didn't ever want to do that again. Our experience with renting out our house had been a nightmare since the tenants had done a lot of damage.

Bruce applied for both posts. He waited impatiently for the Board to meet to find out if he was accepted to either one. The Tuesday after he submitted his applications, Bruce went to his career counselor and declared he'd rather go to Tehran or not go at all, reasoning that it would be easier for him to go there by himself than for all five of us to go Tel Aviv. Economically, it would be more advantageous. He would receive a post differential due to the hazards of the area; I would receive a separate maintenance allowance because we would be supporting two households, and we wouldn't have to rent our house.

The Board was scheduled for Friday and we were told we'd know their decision by 5:00 p.m. When that day arrived, I waited nervously by the phone, hoping he wasn't accepted. Five o'clock came and my anxiety continued to build. The minutes slowly passed and with each one's passing I grew more hopeful. By 5:20 p.m. I was delighted—he hadn't been accepted! At 5:25 p.m. the phone rang.

"Hi, I'm on my way!" Bruce exclaimed.

I felt as if the bottom had fallen out of my nice, cozy world. This would be the first time in more than 18 years of marriage that we would be separated. That in itself would be traumatic. I prayed that if this was not meant to be, God would close all doors leading to Tehran. But everything seemed to fall into place that much more rapidly.

PREPARING FOR CHANGE

Bruce began the process of getting his passport, required immunizations, and signing out of the State Department. Meanwhile, I focused my energies at home on preparing for the move: making lists of items he was taking with him, getting clothes, and taking care of other last-minute details. Since he was only allowed airfreight and personal luggage, packing for him proved easier than it had been during our move to Honduras. It wouldn't involve emptying the whole house down to the last nail.

September 24th, 1979 Bruce's departure day came much too quickly. While he was packing his suitcases, Debbie (age 15), Matt (age 13), Chris (age 8), and I made little notes to put in among his clothes. Whenever he left the room, we tucked the notes into his socks, shirt pockets, underwear, and even the side pockets of the suitcase. When we were done, I still had one note left from Chris, which I slipped into Bruce's passport. Chris, in his childish scrawl, had written, "Dear Dad, I miss you already. I don't have anyone to pinch my toes. Love, Chris."

I knew Bruce would be delighted to find this message when he showed his passport upon arriving in Tehran. The rough housing that Bruce did with the children every evening after dinner was a special time for them. Chris would put his foot out in front of Bruce and squeal, "Don't pinch my toes, Dad!" all the while inching his foot closer to Bruce's hand hoping that he would.

I slipped a few more items into Bruce's suitcase and called to him, asking if I had forgotten anything. He didn't answer. He had been out of the room for about 15 minutes and I looked around but couldn't find him. I couldn't imagine where he was. Finally, I happened to look out on the Florida porch, off the dining room, and there he was. I went out by him and found him sobbing.

"Are you having second thoughts?" I asked.

He said, "Yes."

Until now, I had been the one in a very blue mood for the past week and he had been telling me not to worry. I reasoned time would go by quickly and that before I knew it, he'd be back home for his first visitation. As I stood beside him, I reminded him of this, and he replied, "When you say it fast, it doesn't sound long. But when you're living it, that's something else." I told him it wasn't too late to cancel. "If I did that, my career would be over," he said.

Bruce would visit his Aunt Mildred in Long Island first before flying to Germany. When we arrived at Washington National airport, we discovered that new security metal detectors had been installed right near the ticket counter and we would not be allowed to walk any further with him. He hugged and kissed each of us and held us close with tears running down his face, then turned and walked through the security arch and down the hall. As he started up the escalator, he turned and waved to us. I thought I would die of heartache. We waited until we couldn't see him anymore, then walked to the car.

As we walked back to the car, I was sobbing uncontrollably, and Debbie tried hard to console me. "This is what Dad wanted," she said, trying to sound upbeat. "You shouldn't be upset."

"No, this was not what he wanted, but what he felt was best for us," I cried.

"Well, he'll be home in only six months," she responded. I knew she was trying to be positive, but I said, "Deb, so much can happen in six months!"

The trip back was horrible. I dropped the children off at school and drove home. After crying the rest of the morning, I mentally reprimanded myself, telling myself that I had many things to do. I just had to get out of the house.

On the way home from running errands, I happened to look up in the sky. The clouds formed a huge cross as far as I could see, beginning on the upper left and stretching all the way to my lower right. My first thought was that it was a foreboding omen and that I would have a cross to bear. I shrugged it off as the result of an overactive imagination because I was feeling so depressed. Bruce had been gone only a few hours and already I missed him very much.

He called me later that evening from his aunt's house just as he was leaving to catch his 8:00pm flight to Frankfurt, Germany. He, too, was feeling the effects of the separation, especially since he had found Chris's note in his passport

"Why did you look in your passport?" I asked.

"My aunt wanted a recent photo of me, so I opened my passport. When I saw that note from Chris, I couldn't talk. I had such a lump in my throat and tears just rolled down my face."

"I had hoped you would discover the note when you went through customs. It would have been a little reminder of home upon your arrival in a strange country," I answered. After we hung up, I wrote him a letter, knowing it would take at least a week for the mail to get to him in Tehran, and that he would be very homesick by the time it reached him.

The first week without him was emotionally traumatic. It was hard for me to do the normal things such as grocery shopping, cleaning, and laundry. I tried to adjust to the role of both mother and father to the kids and to having total responsibility for the house and car.

Bruce always wanted me to be a stay-at-home mom, but I had decided that once I adjusted to the new responsibilities, I'd get a job. I had an excellent work record at Chesapeake and Potomac Telephone Company, who had an office in Maryland, and I figured I shouldn't have a problem getting rehired. Having a job would help the time to pass more quickly while Bruce was away.

I waited for word that Bruce had arrived in Tehran safely, which he said he would add to the end of a cable to the State Department. About one week later, I got a call from Pat Lee, who identified herself as the wife of Gary Lee, a man who was in Tehran with Bruce. Gary periodically checked the phone lines from Tehran to the U.S. and would call Pat as part of the test. He had asked her to call me to let me know that Bruce had arrived in Tehran safe and sound. I felt relieved.

After that, Pat and I would call each other periodically. I had met Gary once, about one week before Bruce left for Tehran, and had asked Gary how things were in Iran. He responded that they were pretty quiet since the Iranians were ignoring Americans at the moment. That was good to know, since it had only been a little over six months since the Iranian revolution.

The first letter from Bruce arrived about three weeks after he left. It was dated October 4, 1979. He was so terribly homesick and regretful of his decision to take the assignment. Bruce described his apartment as being quite large with a lot of closet space but he also said that it felt so empty. To make matters worse, he hadn't yet received any of my letters. I later discovered that my letters were taking about three weeks to get to him. I began taking my letters to Maria Melchiorre, a co-worker of Bruce's who lived near us, to hand carry. Since the mail could only go through the diplomatic pouch, this saved three or four days off the delivery time.

On Friday, **November 2nd**, Pat Lee called to inform me of a small article in the *Washington Post* in the section called "Around the World." The article stated that the Iranians were demonstrating in front of the American Embassy in Tehran to protest the Carter Administration's decision to admit the Shah into the United States for medical treatment. Pat told me that she had called the State Department and a few other people she knew, but no one seemed to have any information about the demonstrations. I was very concerned and decided to call Bruce that night. With the time difference, I'd have to wait until nearly midnight to reach him at the office since I didn't have the phone number for his apartment yet.

I called that night but couldn't get through. The phone lines were constantly busy. I tried again on Saturday night. This time the call went right through. A man with a deep accent answered on the third ring. I asked to speak to Mr. German and immediately Bruce was on the line. It was so good to hear his voice and he was really happy and surprised to hear mine.

He exclaimed, "Hi, What a surprise! I've been feeling down this week because I haven't had any mail. This is so much better."

"I've been writing at least every other day, so you should be getting mail very often." I asked about Tehran and what the city was like.

"There is a lot of construction going on here and all you see in the skyline are cranes. The Americans here have named them the national bird."

When I asked about the demonstration, he said, "Oh, they've been going on for a couple of weeks. The demonstrators chant, scream, and pray in front of the Embassy, but they are peaceful at the moment, so don't worry."

"What time is it there?" I asked.

"It's 10 minutes to 8, Sunday morning," he replied. It was 11:20 p.m. Saturday night in Rockville. We talked for about 20 minutes. Matt and Chris were asleep, but Debbie talked to him about her upcoming 16th birthday party, which she had planned with a 50s theme. Bruce loved the music of the '50s so Debbie had been exposed to it all her life and grew to love it too. Debbie wanted to be a Foreign Service Officer like her dad and was impressed with University of Dallas' excellent linguistics program.

We talked and laughed, deciding that it didn't matter how much the phone call would cost because it was wonderful just to be able to talk to each other. We had been exchanging taped messages on cassettes, but those were one-sided conversations. I even sent him one of his own tapes by mistake!

He asked me if I had talked to his mother, and I told him that I had. He had not heard from her and asked me to tell her to write. He had told me that when he was in the Navy before we ever met, she very rarely wrote to him. When we were in Frankfurt, Germany on our first overseas tour and again while we were in Honduras, it was the same.

Bruce said he'd asked the Embassy Chargé d'Affaires, Bruce Laingen, if he could take his first stateside visitation early to be home for Christmas instead of waiting the six months as he was supposed to. It was approved. I went to bed well after midnight feeling happy that I had talked to him. He was counting the days until he would be home again. I was counting them, too. It was November 4, 1979 and he would be home for Christmas. Little did either of us realize what counting days would come to mean.

November 4, 1979 (Day 1). At 7:55 a.m. I was just getting the cobwebs out of my head when the phone rang. It was Sue Petro, my friend from church. She had been Debbie's Sunday school teacher some years before and we had become close friends. She asked if I had gotten in touch with Bruce and asked about the demonstrations. I repeated what Bruce had told me, that there was nothing to worry about.

She hesitantly said, "I was listening to the news on WMAL, the station that features Hardin and Weaver on weekdays. I was sure they mentioned something about the American Embassy in Iran being overtaken by militants and the American personnel being held hostage, but I must have been mistaken." She seemed apologetic. I was sure she had misunderstood which Embassy might be involved. She suggested that I listen to the 9:00 a.m. newscast for myself, adding that it was the lead story.

I turned the radio on and waited, fearing the worst. At 9:00 a.m. I heard the announcer say, "The American Embassy in Tehran, Iran, has been overtaken by militants and the Embassy personnel have been taken hostage. They are being held in the basement of the chancery where they have been tied and blindfolded."

I got a cold chill through my body. Yet, this could not be. No one from the State Department had contacted me. Surely if something this momentous had happened, someone would have called to notify the families. I tried to stay calm as I told the children, but tears streamed down my face.

My mind was racing. I tried to recall some of the people I knew from the State Department and wondered who I could call. Finally, I remembered that Bruce had left a State Department telephone directory with me and I frantically called a few numbers. No one answered. Then, I realized that it was Sunday, so of course, no one would be at the office. I called some of Bruce's former co-workers at their homes. Again, no one answered.

"There's got to be someone at the State Department," I thought aloud. Deb said, "Mom, no one is going to be there on a Sunday." I thought to myself, *there had better be someone there.*

Finally, I found a number inside the front cover of the directory for the watch officer, the person responsible for monitoring situations around the world that could affect diplomatic personnel. I anxiously dialed the number. A man answered and I identified myself and asked if he could tell me what was going on in Tehran.

"Are you with the press?" he asked.

"No, my name is Mrs. German. My husband is the budget officer in Tehran and I'm trying to find out what is going on."

"Just a moment, Ma'am, let me give you another number."

I called the other number and went through the same thing. Was I with the press? Why was I calling? My voice started to become higher pitched and I almost screamed that I was not with the press and my husband was the budget officer in Tehran. This gentleman replied, "Just a moment, Ma'am, I'll give you the number of the task force."

Task force! My heart sank. If a task force had been set up, then the news was true. This really was happening! I called the number he gave me and the man who I spoke to confirmed the news: The Embassy had been overtaken. He didn't know all the details, but the takeover had occurred somewhere between 3:00am and 3:30am our time. I numbly remembered trying to figure out the time difference. That would mean the takeover had occurred only 3.5 later after we hung up. How could this be? Bruce had said that there was nothing to worry about. It was now 9:15 a.m. Why hadn't I heard from the State Department? Six hours had passed, and no one had called me. I wasn't supposed to hear this on the radio. This wasn't how they did it in the movies. There was always an official call or visit when there was bad news.

CHAPTER 2

SHOCK AND DENIAL: MY REACTION TO THE EMBASSY TAKEOVER

The task force officer said he didn't have any other details and asked if I could call back later. I called my friend Sue and told her between sobs that the news was true. She said she had known that it was but didn't know how to tell me. I asked my other friend Katie, who I had known for years, to take the children to church while I stayed at home to wait for any possible phone call from the State Department. She suggested, "Why don't you come to church? You'll feel better."

I said, "I can't leave the house. The State Department may call and I have to be here."

Later, Katie called me from church and said that she had told Father Basil Summer, the rector of St. Mark, about the hostage situation and that Bruce was one of the hostages. When he announced it to the congregation there was a loud gasp and our fellow parishioners openly cried, especially seeing Debbie, Matt, and Chris in church. I found out later that all three children had cried all through the liturgy. The children had wanted to wait by the phone with me, but I convinced them to go and pray for their dad. Now I was feeling very guilty.

I called Pat Lee to tell her the news. Apparently, I had woken her. She seemed annoyed. When I told her of the morning's events, she screamed, "This could *never* happen!" I gave her the phone number of the Task Force and told her to call for herself. When she called back in a few minutes, she, too, was sobbing. We cried together, wondering why and how this had happened. We agreed to keep each other informed of any bit of news we heard.

I tried to call my mother-in-law, Theresa Lodeski, who lived in Edwardsville, Pennsylvania, but there was no answer. It was 9:30 a.m. and I supposed she was still asleep. I tried every 15 - 30 minutes until she answered the phone. She was crying hysterically. I explained to her that I had been calling her since 9:30 a.m. because I didn't want her to hear about the takeover on TV or radio. She said that her neighbor, Dodie, had come over and told her. When I began to explain how I found out, she interrupted me and said, "I can't talk to you now because the local television crew is downstairs in my kitchen, and they want to interview me."

I was puzzled. I asked how the media had found out about her. She said, "Dodie called them because they should know that I'm the mother of a hostage." When I asked her not to give out too much information about Bruce, she became angry.

I said, "Please don't mention that Bruce had ever worked for the CIA. If the militants find out, they will torture him."

Again, she said, "I can't talk now, I have to go."

After I hung up, I felt bewildered and anxious. Why wasn't she interested in the information I had from the State Department? I worried that she would say something about Bruce's previous career that would put him in jeopardy.

I called the State Department every two hours during the day, asking for any bit of news they might have. I was assured that the takeover would only last for a short time, just a few hours. When I asked how they could know that, I was told that it was only a sit-in. The demonstration and sit-in that had occurred in February during the Iranian revolution had lasted that long. I wanted to believe them but I knew they were wrong. I remembered that cross of clouds in the sky that I'd seen shortly after Bruce had left for Tehran. It had been too large for this to be over so quickly.

As the day went on, there were more personnel in the Task Force office, many of whom were volunteers. I stayed up most of the night, listening for the slightest bit of information I could get from the radio. I was numb with shock and kept telling myself that it was all a bad dream and that I would wake up and find everything back to normal.

I took out my Bible and began reading some passages and praying. My favorite passage comforted me: "All things work together for good for those who love God, to those who are called according to His Purpose (Romans 8:28)." I'd always believed in God and had faith that He would always handle any problems

I might have. When Jesus said to give Him our burdens, I always trusted in Him. My mother had always told me that everything happens for the best. I kept telling myself, "This must be happening for a reason. This MUST be happening for a reason!" But that felt so hollow. I couldn't see any reason for this.

I fell into an exhausted sleep around 6:45 a.m. At 7:30 a.m. Debbie woke me up to take her to school and asked if I had heard anything more. I told her I hadn't. I woke the boys, who asked the same questions. I got them their breakfast, made their lunches, and got them off to school.

The phone started to ring and continued all day. There were calls from friends I had not heard from in years, as well as my sisters and brother, Bruce's relatives and close friends from his high school days, and friends we had met during our overseas tours. Calls came from Honduras, New Zealand, Korea, and all parts of the United States. It was overwhelming, but it gave me a warm feeling to know that so many people cared enough to call.

LEARNING TO COPE WITH THE CRISIS

During those first days, Debbie called me between classes from Peary High School asking if I had heard that her father was okay. I promised I would come to the school and get her if I heard anything.

I called the State Department continuously and asked if there was anything new. Once again, I was told that the crisis would be over in a few hours, that negotiations were going on with the Bazargan government and the hostages would be released soon. I felt encouraged. When the Shah left Iran, Shapour Baktiar, his Prime minister had run the government until Ayatollah Khomeini removed him. Veteran politician Mehdi Bazargan then replaced Baktiar.

Maria Melchiorre called me and said that an Embassy employee had come in from Tehran over the weekend and had a cassette tape for me from Bruce. This guy had been lucky – he'd left Iran on Friday, November 2nd, just two days before the Embassy was overrun.

He dropped the cassette off at Maria's office and she said that she'd bring it by after work.

A few minutes later, my mother-in-law called to say that she was coming down to be with me. I told her that the children and I were fine, and it wasn't necessary. Emotionally, I wasn't up to having anyone around. She ignored my request and told me she would be arriving in the early evening by bus.

Maria Melchiorre arrived with Bruce's audiotape when my mother-in-law arrived by cab from the bus station in Silver Spring. We both listened to his tape.

"I don't want to alarm you," Bruce's message began. "But we've been told that we may have problems here because the Shah was admitted into the United States. I'm not trying to scare you; I just want you to be aware."

As my mother-in-law and I talked, tears welled up in my eyes. I worried about Bruce coping with captivity. He was a very impatient person and I feared that his actions might cause him to be beaten or tortured, but I just couldn't bring myself to say those things.

My mother-in-law was crying and said, "You don't know how I feel, Marge. I'm his mother. You'll never know how I feel!"

I didn't say anything, but thought to myself, "I'm his wife and the mother of his children, you can't know how *I* feel." It was almost as if she thought this were a contest as to who felt more emotional pain.

Just then, Chris came into the room and saw that we both had tears in our eyes and said, "Don't worry, Mom. Dad's all right and he'll be back." There is no faith like that of a child.

On Tuesday, **November 6th (Day 3)**, Father Basil stopped by to pray with me for Bruce's safe return, but also prayed for God's will to be done. If Bruce was not to come back, I had to accept that as God's will. That was not what I wanted to hear. I didn't want to think of that possibility. What would I do? How would I raise three children by myself? As Father Basil was leaving, we both had tears in our eyes and felt overwhelming pain and helplessness.

In those first days, I had done more crying than I had in the past 11 years. The last time I cried that much was when I lost our baby, Mark. He was born on Jan. 11, 1968 with a congenital heart, a hole between the left and right ventricle, and weighed just 3 pounds 14 ounces. He lived only seven hours and forty-five minutes. This situation brought back that same awful feeling of despair, anguish, and helplessness.

Later that day I got a call from the *Times Leader Evening Newspaper* from Wilkes-Barre. The woman asked me if I was in touch with the State Department and asked if they were able to tell me anything about my husband. Even though I said no, she asked two or three more questions and again I gave her "yes" and "no" answers. I did not want to give an interview and I certainly didn't want my name appearing all over the newspapers.

In the following hours, I had a vision of Bruce, wearing his white shirt with the sleeves rolled up, standing with his back to me. When he turned around, there was a big, red bloodstain over the left side of his chest. It was like a dream, yet I wasn't asleep. I prayed fervently that God would never allow that to happen. That same image would be a recurring vision for the next few days.

On Wednesday, Bruce's brother, Ben arrived. He told me he would be staying for a few days because Bruce had asked him to "give Marge a hand with the children and the house while I'm gone." I wasn't sure just how he could help me.

That day Maria called and said that Mr. Rose, Bruce's former boss, wanted to talk to me. Mr. Rose asked me if I'd like to meet with the doctors at the State Department as well as some of the other families who lived in the Washington, D.C. area. I agreed. He set up a meeting for Friday, November 9th at 10:00 a.m.

That evening my sister, Lovey, called to let me know that there was a big article in the *Times Leader Evening* newspaper with my interview. I couldn't imagine how anyone could make a story out of yes and no answers. When she read me the headline, I was furious. It read, "State Department Assures Hostage Wife That Her Husband is Alive." I vowed that I would never talk to anyone on the staff of that newspaper again.

Lovey then asked if I had heard from my mother-in-law and I replied that "Grammy" had arrived on Monday. Lovey exclaimed, "What is she doing there? Why is she down there? She should just leave you alone with the children. I remember how she is in a crisis—her hysterics make her the worst person in the world to have around."

I had to agree; my mother-in-law did get hysterical over minor things, and this wasn't minor.

FAMILY MEETING AT THE DEPARTMENT OF STATE WITH PRESIDENT CARTER (NOV. 9TH)

When Friday came, I asked my mother-in-law to go to the meeting with me, but she said, "No, I'd be too nervous." Ben agreed to go.

Driving down to the meeting was a traumatic experience since I was not used to driving in downtown Washington, D.C. I thought to myself, "Bruce should see me now!"

Parking, as usual, was almost impossible, but I did manage to get a space on C Street, right in front of the Main State building. We went to the diplomatic entrance and were directed to the right side of the lobby, where a few sofas and chairs were located, and waited until a few other families arrived. That was the day I finally met Pat Lee and her daughter, Dana. It was good to put a face with the voice I had been hearing for so many weeks.

The meeting was held in the lounge of the medical division. I met with Drs. Dustin, Haynes, and Korcak, the department social workers, and approximately 12-15 other family members. There was Pearl Golacinski and three of her children, Linda, Danielle, and Gary; Mary Holland and her daughter, Rose; Penne Laingen, wife of the Chargé Bruce Laingen, Anita Shaefer and her son, Mark, and his wife.

The doctors talked about the concerns of the families such as what the hostages were going through emotionally, as well as how to cope with nervousness and sleeplessness. Mr. Ben Read from the White House arrived and announced, "The President is on his way!" That was a big shock – I had no idea that the President was going to meet with us. Five minutes later, President Carter and Secretary of State, Cyrus Vance, entered the room with Press Secretary Jody Powell and a few others. President Carter explained why he had agreed to allow the Shah into the United States and answered our questions very straightforwardly and honestly.

"The Shah had been a friend to the United States and to return him to Iran would guarantee that he would be murdered," President Carter stated. He assured us that all that could be done at the moment was being done. After he left, the family members decided that a statement should be made to the press asking the American people to stay calm. There was a kind of frenzy in the air and we did not want Iranians in this country to be beaten or harassed, as that would give the militants an excuse to retaliate against helpless hostages.

As we gave our statement to the press, Iranians demonstrated in front of the diplomatic entrance of the State Department. To control the crowd, some District of Columbia policemen rode on horseback while others rode in police cruisers. The Iranians were chanting, "Death to America! Death to Carter!" Americans had gathered and screamed back at the Iranians to go back to Iran.

On Saturday, **November 10th (Day 7)**, I drove Ben back to the Capital Train Station in Lanham to drop him off. On the drive home, I was deep in thought, preoccupied by the crisis and what was happening to Bruce when I suddenly realized that I had no idea where I was. Nervously I turned around and found my way back to the train station and started out again. As I approached the Capital Beltway, I breathed a sigh of relief, but again my mind wandered and soon I was frantically looking for signs to see if I had passed my exit. When I finally arrived home, I was limp from the stress of the trip. In my state of mind, I should not have been driving.

Shortly after I returned, Art's wife, Rosemary, arrived. It was the weekend of the bazaar at St. Mark and I told Debbie to drive everyone to the church for some ethnic food because I didn't feel like cooking for anybody. Debbie had just gotten her driver's license and had offered to run some errands for me, so this would give her the practice with a few licensed drivers in the car. I stayed home, waiting to hear from the State Department. I still spent most of the time on the phone as it was still ringing quite frequently every day. When the family returned, I could tell that something was wrong. Debbie was mad that my mother-in-law yelled at her all the way there and back about her driving. She was very perturbed, especially since she knew my mother-in-law had never learned to drive.

Ten days into the crisis I was still reluctant to leave the house for fear that I would miss an important call from the State Department. When I heard something on the radio that the State Department had not told me, I would call State, tell them what I had heard, and ask if it was rumor or truth. Their standard answers were, "Yes, that's been confirmed," or, "No, that has not been confirmed." They asked me where I was getting my information because they had not heard it on television. I told them I listened to WMAL radio all day long.

After not leaving the house for two weeks except for necessities, I knew I had to go to church. Just about every parishioner there greeted me warmly. They hugged me and expressed their concern, not only for Bruce, but for all of us. They were my other family. Everyday Father Basil and St. Mark's parish prayed for Bruce and for all of us.

At the fellowship hour after liturgy, people gathered around us and asked if we had heard anything new, how we were coping, and what they could do to help. The only thing I could tell them was to continue to pray. Then a very strange thing happened. As six or seven people surrounded me asking questions, I felt as if I was not really there, that I was witnessing this from a far place. I could see the lips of these people moving but couldn't hear anything they were saying. My mind just couldn't grasp what was happening. I tried to bring myself back into the group by really concentrating on what was being said. Finally, I could hear them again. I answered their questions as best I could, gathered my children, and left. Nothing like this had ever happened to me before and it was a frightening experience.

Later that day I had another vision of Bruce: this time it was dark outside, and he was blindfolded, led alongside a building with his hands tied behind his back, and pushed into the back of a black van. In my heart, I just knew he had been moved. But where? And for what purpose? I was afraid for his safety. I prayed that God would continue to watch over him.

Reality was setting in at this point, and I was beginning to get a little worried about money. I didn't know what status Bruce was in as far as the State

Department was concerned: leave without pay or annual leave. I called Fran, his former carpooler, and asked if she knew how these things were handled. If Bruce was not going to be paid, I had to start taking money out of savings, which was minimal.

Fran asked, "Hasn't anyone from State Department called you to tell you what you are entitled to?" They hadn't, and Fran said she would call me back with the information.

On Veteran's Day, it was customary for the schools to invite the parents into the classrooms. The previous year, Bruce had gone to Barnsley Elementary School to Chris' classes and had stayed to have lunch with him at the cafeteria. This time I went. It was sad to hear Chris talking about "last year when Dad was here." One little boy, who was having lunch with his father, sat across from us and said, "Chris, isn't your father a *hostage?*" but what he really wanted was for Chris to confirm it for him in front of the boy's dad.

Chris said, "Yes, but he's going to be okay!"

The boy's father looked at me and said, "I am so sorry!" I thanked him and tried not to tear up. After Chris had finished his lunch, I went outside with him so he could join his friends on the playground until the bell rang to signal the end of the lunch period. I was depressed as I drove home, knowing it was hard for my children to handle this personal hurt in front of their classmates.

Later, Fran called back to tell me that Bruce would get paid his regular 80 hours per pay period. She was annoyed that no one from the State Department had called me to tell me what my benefits were and felt that I shouldn't have had to do the calling. I was just grateful that I wouldn't have to take any money out of savings.

A volunteer from the State Department called me and said, "We have the militants on the line. Can you give us a message for Bruce? They have assured us that they would give the messages to the hostages." I was delighted. I replied, "Please tell him we love him, we miss him and hope to see him very soon. And *please* tell him we do have enough money, not to worry."

The volunteer said I could start writing letters, which I did immediately. I convinced my mother-in-law, Theresa, to write too, though she said it was a waste of time; that he would not get them, and that she did not want to tell him her problems.

"Write something upbeat and pleasant," I told her. "Just so he will get a letter from you. It would mean a great deal to him." I didn't want anything she wrote to cause Bruce more stress than he was already experiencing.

Church Services at Washington National Cathedral

On the **15ᵗʰ (Day 12)**, there was a church service at the Washington Cathedral for the hostages with President Carter and many other dignitaries. I asked Father Basil if he would like to join my mother-in-law, the children, and me. He agreed to meet us at the diplomatic entrance in front of the State Department where the buses would be waiting to take us to the Cathedral.

I picked the children up at their respective schools and drove downtown. I dropped the children and my mother-in-law at the diplomatic entrance and went to park the car at Columbia Plaza. The parking garage was filled so I had to circle around, hoping and praying that I could find a parking space eventually. I drove down 22nd Street and found a metered parking space, but discovered I didn't have change for the meter. A well-dressed, bearded man was walking down the sidewalk and I rushed over to him and asked if he had change for a dollar.

He asked, "Are you the lady they're holding the bus for?"

I replied, "Probably," as I put the change he had given me into the meter. I started to run up the street. I hadn't gotten very far when he called to me that I had left my car lights on and that he had tried to turn them off but my car was locked. He asked for my keys and said he'd bring them to me on the bus. I handed him the keys and ran to the bus, hopped on, sat down, and the bus pulled out. I sat there wondering why I had given my keys to a stranger who I probably would never see again and then I wondered how we would get home after the church service. I told Father Basil what I had done and he asked who the man was. I told him that I had no idea. I felt very stupid and couldn't imagine why I would ever have done something like that.

We got to the Cathedral at 1:45 p.m. but the service wasn't scheduled until 3:00 p.m., so the families were given a tour of the building. At about 2:45 p.m. I heard a gentleman ask one of the ushers if she had seen a lady in a rust-colored coat because he had her car keys. I looked up and there was the man who had given me change for the parking meter. I thanked him for going out of his way to bring my keys to the Cathedral. He assured me that he was coming to the service anyway and he hoped I hadn't been worried about them when the bus pulled out. Later, I learned that he was the President of the American Foreign Service Association. I thought about that event and decided that God watched over those who are too distraught to watch out for themselves.

The church service included clergy from the Protestant, Roman Catholic, Jewish and Muslim religions, but there was no Orthodox Christian priest. I was glad I had brought my own.

President Carter arrived with his entourage and sat across the aisle from us and three rows forward. The media cameras were there, videotaping the service for the evening news. The solemnity of the service again caused a strong emotional reaction in me, but I tried to keep my face covered so I wouldn't be shown on the six o'clock news.

On the return trip from the Cathedral after the service, a police escort stopped traffic while our bus was guided down the wrong side of the streets. People looked curiously to see who was on the bus that had caused this rush-hour traffic jam.

We arrived back at the State Department and had coffee and cookies in the lounge on the left side of the diplomatic entrance next to the auditorium. I went inside and spoke with some of the people on the Task Force. They had wondered how I heard some of the news items before they did. Again, I told them that I listened to WMAL radio all day and when I heard something on the newscast that I hadn't heard from them, I usually called to question it. I found it disconcerting that the news media seemed to know more about what was going on with the hostages than our own government.

I asked my mother-in-law if she would like to meet some of the other hostage families. I explained that as a Foreign Service wife from the Metropolitan Washington area, I was expected to greet the families from other areas. She said she would rather just sit on the sofa. I was an introvert and very unsure of myself, but I mustered all the courage I could and tried to talk to each family there.

When we left the meeting and went to the car, I found parking ticket for overtime parking! When we finally arrived home, I was alarmed to find that I had left a candle burning on the dining room table. I had been burning blessed candles since the crisis began asking God to watch over Bruce and keep him safe. I said a silent prayer to thank Him for preserving our house. The candle was in a metal holder and had burned right down into the cup. It extinguished itself when the wax was gone and all that was left was a small piece of wick. Again, God had watched over me. I could have come home to a pile of ashes.

That evening, the news media showed clips from the church service and then announced a news bulletin. The militants said the hostages would be executed.

CHAPTER 3

THE MILITANTS THREATEN TO EXECUTE THE HOSTAGES

The next few days were particularly unnerving with the militants repeatedly accusing the American Embassy of being a nest of spies. Their evidence consisted of a passport they had found of one of the hostages containing a pseudonym. There were rumors that the hostages were being abused and that the militants had attached bombs to the walls of the Chancery and Ambassador's residence to deter any rescue attempts. The militants assured the world that the hostages would be put on trial as spies - then executed. In their warped minds, the Iranian militants felt that since the United States was an ally to the Shah, any American was guilty of the crimes committed by the Shah.

News coverage showed "Death to America" and "Death to Carter" signs hung on the walls of the Embassy grounds along with another one that said "Carter can't do anything!" The bigger humiliation was the militants carrying garbage in the American flag. My blood boiled.

THIRTEEN HOSTAGES RELEASED

On the **17th day of the crisis**, **November 20th**, 13 hostages, all black males or white females, were released. The Ayatollah Khomeini had announced that since blacks and women were discriminated against in America, he would show the "Great Satan" that Iran was compassionate by releasing all the black men and women hostages. Yet, one black man and two white women were still being held.

The released hostages flew to Denmark and then on to Frankfurt, Germany where they underwent four days of medical and psychological examinations before returning to the United States on Thanksgiving Day. I was happy for them, but at the same time, sad for the rest of us.

Nov. 20, 1979 (Day 17) Ben had arrived to spend Thanksgiving with us but it was the first Thanksgiving that Bruce was not with us and the children kept referring to previous, joyous Thanksgivings. I spent most of the meal with tears running down my face, unable to eat.

The day after Thanksgiving, **November 23rd (Day 20)**, was Debbie's birthday, a long-anticipated "sweet sixteen" celebration, but this was certainly not how she had planned to celebrate. My mother-in-law told me to cancel her party. I said that as long as Debbie did all the planning, she could go ahead with it. She and about fifteen of her friends danced to the music of the '50s, trying to enjoy the evening as much as they could under the circumstances. My mother-in-law and brother-in-law complained all during the party about the noise level of the kids. They said it wasn't "right" for Debbie to have a party when her father was being held hostage.

Bruce had discussed the party with Debbie prior to his captivity and I knew that he would not have wanted her to cancel it. After all, he was not dead, and there was no reason to act as if he were. Debbie would never be 16 years old again. I was trying to keep a sense of normalcy in the family and we didn't believe we were being disrespectful in any way.

At eleven o'clock, the late evening newscast came on. I asked Debbie's guests if they would mind if I interrupted the party to watch the latest news on the only TV we had, which was there in the rec room. However, Ben told them that it was late—and they ended up leaving.

I learned later that Deb and Ben had gotten into an argument a few days before her party; they ended up in a shouting match in her room, screaming at the top of their lungs.

"If your father was here you wouldn't act like this," Ben had shouted.

Deb yelled back, "You're right. If he were here, I wouldn't have to."

My mother-in-law was furious that Debbie would dare to stand up to Ben. I thought to myself, why don't they just go home and leave us alone? I couldn't stand this. If this was the "helping hand" that Bruce had talked about to Ben, I didn't need it.

The next day after the party, my mother-in-law and Ben said they had to get back to their homes. I drove them to the airport and felt a great sense of relief. This would be the first time the children and I would be alone since the first day of the crisis. I was glad they were gone. For the first time in three weeks, I was able to sit down and not feel that I had to entertain or take care of anybody except the children and myself. I didn't have to listen to my mother-in-law telling me repeatedly, "You don't know how I feel, Marge, I'm his mother!" She had repeated that almost daily, and it had begun to wear on my nerves. I know that she and Ben were suffering from stress, but I had to take care of my own emotions and those of my children. I couldn't handle theirs, too. I was trying very hard to keep peace in the family, but it didn't seem to be working.

I felt a need to be alone with the children, to think about the future. How in the world would I raise three children by myself if Bruce did not come back? I couldn't bear to think about it for very long.

My friend Katie called me and suggested, "How about going to B. E.'s?" We both belonged to the Barbara Ellen exercise salon, but I had not gone since the crisis began.

"No, I don't feel like it," I said.

But she coaxed me, adding, "Oh, come on, grab those barbells and slam them around to get rid of your frustration. Do you have anything to mail? We can stop at the post office before we go. I'll pick you up in 10 minutes."

I didn't really feel like it, but I had a letter to mail to Bruce, so I agreed. Katie was right. Slamming those barbells did help me to get rid of my frustrations—at least for a while. But it became a ritual to stop at the post office first to mail my care packages - letters, books, and padded envelopes of sports pages and magazines. The mail was going to the Iran Working Group (IWG), a volunteer group that had been set up at the State Department because of the crisis. From there it then went to the Swiss Embassy to be handled through their diplomatic pouch.

On **November 26th (Day 23)**, the families met with Under-Secretary of State Newsom at the State Department. He again went over the details of the takeover and what had been done to date. The biggest problem was that since the Bazargan's government had been overthrown, there was no one in Iran who could take responsibility for the hostages. The militants, many of them mere college students, seemed to be calling all the shots as the entire world watched.

Dr. Eben Dustin was at the meeting, along with some of the other doctors. He asked if the family meetings were helpful. These meetings were held at the medical unit of the Department of State. There were only a few families attending including Danielle and Linda Golasinski, Penne Laingen, Mrs. Lee Holland and her daughter Rosemary, and Anita Schaffer, but we felt that sharing any information about the crisis would be helpful. We all agreed that it was good to have a support group—people who were going through the same thing at the same time. I asked if there could be such a support group for the children because my children had begun to feel like freaks when they would notice people pointing at them at school. Other times people would badger them with questions that they couldn't answer and it made them feel uncomfortable. This type of notoriety was not something that could be avoided, but it also wasn't anything that we could have prepared for.

FIRST LETTER FROM BRUCE ARRIVES, WRITTEN BY THE MILITANTS

When I returned home from the meeting, the mail had been delivered and was on the floor by the front door. As I leafed through it, I saw a legal-sized, white envelope with foreign stamps across the top. My name and address were scrawled across the whole front of the envelope in an unfamiliar handwriting. It was from Tehran!

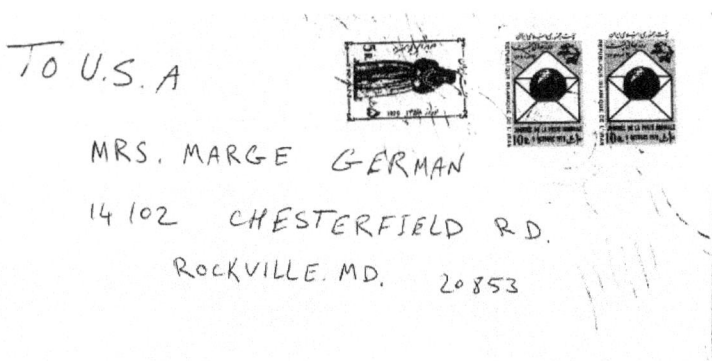

I nervously opened it and at first thought it was empty. Upon closer examination, I found a small piece of paper inside, approximately 4" x 6" and folded in half. I did not recognize the handwriting - it looked foreign.

Dear Marge,

    I feel quite well. Don't be worried about me. I am not sick here.

Ask father Basil to pray for us.

Pray that we have a safe return.

           Love,
           Bruce

Sorry, This letter is written by Moslem students

        (Excuse us)

I looked at the paper again. The closing and signature were Bruce's but nothing else. Still, I was so excited. Bruce was alive somewhere in Tehran. During the debriefing of the 13 released hostages, they had informed the State Department that they had not seen Bruce since the second day of captivity. I had been worried that he was dead.

I called the White House, identified myself to the operator who answered and told her that I had to speak to President Carter. I explained to the operator that I was the wife of one of the hostages and had some news that he'd want to know. The operator asked me to hold while she connected me with Steve Shoob, an Aide to the President's son, Chip Carter. To me, that seemed far too low on the chain of command.

When Steve Shoob came on the line, I told him about the letter and asked if he would get the message to President Carter. This was the first letter to come out of Tehran since the start of the Crisis and President Carter was going into a meeting that afternoon to discuss strategy, so I wanted him to know about it.

Then, I called the State Department and told them about the letter. They asked if I could bring it down to the Department. I had just returned from the family meeting there and just couldn't make another 34-mile round trip, but I told them I'd get the letter to them via Maria Melchiorre; however, I emphasized that I did want it returned to me.

Next, I called the office of Secretary of State Cyrus Vance and spoke with his secretary. I again told my story; I knew he would get the news through official channels eventually, but I asked her to please be sure to tell him for me anyway.

Later that day, the State Department said that another letter had come out of Iran. Dottie Morefield had heard from her husband, Dick. It was the same kind of letter, written by the "students" and signed by her husband. The State Department waited to see if any other families would get one. Days passed and no one else did. The general consensus was that Bruce and Dick must be together and had somehow talked their captors into letting them contact their families, impersonal as the letters were.

When Debbie came home from school, I showed her the letter. She pointed out that it wasn't her father's handwriting except for the signature.

"At least we know he is alive somewhere in Tehran," I assured her. I told her about calling the White House and the Secretary of State to let them know I had received the letter.

She exclaimed, "I can't believe that! You actually called the White House?" I was doing a lot of things these days that I never thought I could do.

Sometime during that week, Marian Precht called. She said an organization called No Greater Love had invited the children of the hostages to a Christmas Party, which would include the Redskins Football players. I was very skeptical. I asked Marian what she knew about the group. She had not heard of them before but said that I could call the group's chairwoman if I wanted more details. She advised me to be careful because there were entrepreneurs in this world who took advantage of the misfortunes of others.

I called the founder of No Greater Love, a woman by the name of Carmella LA Spada. I told her that I had heard of her offer through the State Department but that I needed more details before I could make a decision. She explained that the party was to be held at the Dulles Airport Marriott, that it would last about two hours, and that refreshments would be served. The Redskins players would be there to sign autographs.

"Will press be there?" I asked.

"They haven't covered the party in four years," she said. "But I couldn't be sure they wouldn't show up.

Carmella explained that the group had been formed in order to bring some cheer into the lives of some 70,000 children whose fathers had been killed in Vietnam. They had been having the Christmas party and a Memorial Day service for the past few years. I asked Debbie, Matt, and Chris if they would like to go and, of course, Debbie was delighted. She and her Dad would sit and watch the Redskins games on Sunday afternoons and yell and scream loud enough for an army. Matt, however, was a Dallas Cowboys fan, but I asked him if he would be a Redskins fan for the two hours of the party. Chris, on the other hand, wasn't even sure if he liked football.

The party was held **December 4ᵗʰ (Day 31)**, exactly one month after the takeover, and I had not slept well at all during that time. The lack of sleep took its toll; the dark circles under my eyes seemed to cover most of my face. I agreed to take the kids to the party despite my fear of people exploiting them.

We arrived without any problems. Debbie was delighted to be able to see the Redskins up close. Carmella introduced us to almost everyone and had us stand with each of the Redskins to have our pictures taken. Deb's favorite was Kim McQuilken, the back-up quarterback to Joe Theismann. Matt didn't really care who he had his picture taken with because his favorite, Roger Staubach of the Dallas Cowboys, was not there. As for Chris, he said he heard of Mark Mosley and maybe Mark could be his favorite. They collected autographs from all the players there and enjoyed themselves.

As the party went on, I noticed a black gentleman looking over at me. He seemed familiar but I couldn't remember where I had seen him before. He came over and introduced himself. It was Lloyd Rollins, one of the released hostages who I had seen on TV. I asked him if he knew Bruce and he said that he did. I wanted to know everything I could about the actual takeover of the embassy and the events immediately after. I tried to get every detail I could to visualize what had happened. Lloyd told me that he was not in the same area of the Embassy during the takeover and that he had not seen Bruce after the first day. I wanted to know if the hostages were given food to eat (and if so, what kind), what the sanitary conditions were, if they were allowed to take showers, and if there were any restrictions on bathroom privileges. Lloyd told me that the hostages had their hands tied most of the day and only had them untied or loosened to eat food prepared by the Chargé's cook. The hostages had to ask permission to use the bathroom, and showers were very infrequent. I asked Lloyd about his own capture and was totally absorbed in his every word.

While I spoke to Lloyd, the children were engrossed in the talents of two cartoonists at the party, Bill Rechin and Don Wilder, creators of the syndicated comic strip *CROCK*. They drew personal cartoons for the children, incorporating each child's name into the cartoon. Dave Butz, a defensive tackle of the Redskins, played Santa Claus and distributed little gifts for each child. Even I got to sit on his lap and have my picture taken. We left with some very fond memories, and I was glad that I'd made the decision to attend.

On **December 7, 1979 (Day 34),** there was a big meeting held in the Secretary of State's conference area on the 7th floor of State Department. Hostage family members were brought in from all over the United States. When I'd been called about the meeting two weeks earlier, I had been told that only one member per family could attend. Since I had been at the last meeting, I suggested they ask my mother-in-law if she would like to attend this one, but I was told that she was *not* immediate family because she did not live with us, and that if I didn't attend, no one from our family would be allowed.

When I arrived for the meeting, I was asked how many were in my party. I felt a bit confused and said, "What do you mean? There's only one. I was told that only one family member could attend." The woman picked up my nametag and said that the State Department had decided against that rule halfway through the planning.

"They decided that they would pay the transportation of one family member, but if others wanted to come, they would have to pay their own way," she explained.

"Why did no one call me and tell me of the change of plans?" I asked. She said that she didn't know and was sorry but there was nothing she could do.

We met with Peter Constable, Henry Precht, Sheldon Krys, and Jim Eggers - all involved with the hostage crisis. They discussed the futility of trying to communicate with the Iranians and couldn't give us any timetable on the release of the hostages. Some of the family members asked if anything at all had come out of Tehran from the hostages. Dottie Morefield and I shared our letters with them. Although the other families had not received anything, everyone was relieved that someone had heard from a hostage.

It was an all-day meeting with a break for lunch. Afterwards, we went back to the meeting and at approximately 4:30 p.m. President Carter, Secretary of State, Cyrus Vance, and Assistant Secretary of State for Public Affairs Hodding Carter came and talked with us. They stated that they would not take military action against the Iranians and that the lives of the hostages came first. We asked what we should say to the press since each family was being inundated with calls for interviews. They replied that we could talk to whomever we wanted and could say whatever we wanted as long as we did not claim to speak for everyone. That would turn out to be another mistake.

At the end of the meeting, each family had their picture taken with President Carter and Secretary of State Vance.

On my way home that evening, I heard Dottie's letter being read on the radio. Apparently, some family member or members had taped the whole family meeting and given it to the press. I learned later from Penne Laingen that it was the daughters of one of the hostages. I felt personally betrayed - I had freely shared my letter from Bruce with these people and couldn't believe that someone would do that. Luckily my letter was not read on the air. Because of that incident from that time forward, the State Department stopped telling the families what was going on, claiming that they couldn't be trusted. That infuriated me because I was being punished for someone else's stupidity. How was that any different from the militants holding my husband responsible for things that the Shah had done?

When I got home and called my mother-in-law to give her the details of the meeting, she was furious with me. She said that she should have been at the meeting because she saw how many people were there. Again, she said, "I'm his mother, I should have been there! Don't tell me it was only one family member!" I explained to her that I had just found out about the change in plans that morning, but she implied that it was all my doing. She again said, "You don't know how I feel, I'm his mother! Everyone is asking me why I wasn't at the meeting. I'm his mother and I should have been there. That's not right! You shouldn't have done that." I didn't have anything to say anymore. There was no use trying to explain. She wasn't going to believe me.

Christmas was approaching, and I began receiving Christmas cards from people all over the world, just like the phone calls I had received at the beginning of the crisis. I had not even thought of sending cards, but with all the cards coming in with such heartfelt wishes for Bruce's safe return, I knew I had to make myself write the cards and include personal notes with each. Some of the department stores started a Christmas card campaign, donating cards to anyone who wished to write to the hostages. The only expense was a stamp.

Matt's classmates at Parkland Junior High School sent 766 Christmas cards to Bruce as a gesture of support for Matt. Most cards were delivered by the truckload to the Iranian Embassy on Massachusetts Avenue in Washington, D.C. with the request that they be forwarded to the hostages. Others were sent by international mail directly to the American Embassy in Tehran. We had no idea how many actually got through.

While I sat writing cards, I listened to the radio. That had become a routine—no matter what I was doing, I had to have the radio on. The announcer, Tom Gauger, was asking people to send cards to the men on the USS Kitty Hawk, which was delayed from returning to the United States for Christmas due to the Iran Crisis. He said there were many disappointed families and sailors who would not be together at Christmas. I wrote a card to those sailors, thanking the men for being "at the ready" if they were needed to bring the hostages home and for the sacrifices they were making during the Christmas season, which was a time for families. I felt it was the least I could do after all the kindness the hostages and their families were receiving.

On **December 15th** (**Day 42**), Chris invited a few of his friends over to celebrate his 9th birthday. Although his birthday wasn't until Monday the 17th, I decided that celebrating on Saturday would devote the whole day to him. We were in the middle of his party games when the mail was delivered. Again, there was a long, white envelope with Iranian stamps on it. I was so excited that I tore it open. Inside I found a bigger sheet of paper than the last time and a longer message. The format was the same, written by militants and signed by Bruce, but this time there was a paragraph that said the hostages would be held until the Shah was returned.

Dear Marge,

Try not to be worried. We are quite well. We are fed fairly well. Ask the children to be good in the period of my absence, I love them.

They have told us that they only want the SHAH, and if CARTER prefers us to SHAH, we will be released. Do what you can to make that happen.

I hope you have enough money. I would like to meet you very soon. Pray that we have a safe return soon. all my love,
Bruce

Sorry, this letter is written by moslem students.   (excuse us.)

The broken English and odd capitalization made me wonder if Bruce had dictated part of the letter or if the militants had composed it themselves. Debbie and Matt continued with the party games while I called State Department and read the second letter. I asked if they had heard from any other family that had received any mail, which they hadn't. They seemed to think that Bruce had somehow persuaded one of his guards to let him write letters. Again, they asked me to bring it down to them so they could look it over.

The next day, Sunday, **December 16th**, there was a Wreath Laying Ceremony at the Lincoln Memorial. Members of the families laid a Christmas Wreath with a large yellow ribbon to honor the hostages, along with a plaque containing a quote from Abe Lincoln. It said, "*Those who deny freedom to others deserve it not for themselves, and, under a just God, cannot long retain it*"

Penne Laingen remembered the song *Tie a Yellow Ribbon Around the Old Oak Tree* by Tony Orlando and Dawn, which had to do with a prisoner coming home. If he saw the yellow ribbon, he'd know he was still loved and welcome. The yellow ribbon would soon become an enduring symbol of the hostage crisis.

Duncan Kennedy, son of Morehead and Louisa Kennedy, and Chip Laingen, son of Penne and Chargé Bruce Laingen, were chosen to place the wreath at Lincoln's feet. Dana Lee, daughter of Pat and Gary E. Lee; Rose Holland, daughter of Col. Lee and Mary Holland; and my Christopher were picked to put the plaque next to the wreath. The Marine Guards marched in full dress uniforms and posted a guard to stand watch over the wreath until after Christmas. When the brief ceremony was over, the families went back inside and sang Christmas carols. It was emotionally draining and extremely heartbreaking to see the children's faces. Christmas was coming and it seemed less and less likely that the hostages would be released in time.

We left the Memorial and went to the Iranian Embassy on Massachusetts Avenue for a candlelight vigil. We hoped the Iranian Embassy personnel would see us as the private citizens we were and that our presence would somehow encourage them to relay that message to the militants holding our people. The D.C. police wouldn't let us stand on the same side of the street as the Embassy, so we gathered across the street where we held our candles and sang songs. Penne Laingen and Mary Jane Enquist, sister of Catherine Koob, took a Christmas Wreath of flowers into the Iranian Embassy as a gesture of peace.

We stayed for an hour in freezing temperatures. I wasn't sure how to get home from there at night, but I managed to find my way. Those trips downtown were extremely emotionally draining, but I just kept telling myself that I had to do these things for Bruce.

The children and I had a small celebration on Chris's actual birthday, just to let him know we hadn't forgotten it. He was growing up so quickly due to the crisis. He always managed to say, "Don't worry, Mom. Dad is okay and he'll be coming home soon." At other times, I could see his frustration when he would say, "Mom, why won't they let my Daddy come home?" How could I explain it to him when I didn't have the answer myself?

CHAPTER 4

VERY DISAPPOINTING MEETING WITH THE CLERGY

I found out that some ministers from the United Methodist Church had received permission to go to Tehran to conduct Christmas services for the hostages. I was able to send a short message through one of the ministers, Rev. William Sloane-Coffin. The message said that the children and I were fine and that we did have enough money. I knew it would lift an enormous burden from Bruce's shoulders if he had some word from home, especially since he was so worried that we didn't have money.

The secretary of the United Methodist Church in New York called to tell me that Rev. Sloane-Coffin had seen Bruce. The hostages had been split up into three groups so each of the ministers would see one-third of them. The ministers were returning to the United States on the **28**[th] **(Day 55)** and would meet with the families to give any messages they had from the hostages. I asked the children to go with me. They were reluctant, but I persuaded them, telling them that there might be a message for us from Bruce.

On that day, we drove to the United Methodist building for the meeting. When we arrived, the press was already there with their cameras and microphones in full force. I wondered who had leaked word of the meeting. As we tried to enter, reporters shouted questions at the children and me, sticking microphones in our faces. I guided my children past them and walked by without saying a word.

After an hour and a half of waiting, the ministers arrived. As they came into the room and down the aisle, they shook hands and introduced themselves. The children and I were sitting with Pat Lee & Pearl Golacinski. Rev. Sloane-Coffin shook my hand and when I introduced myself, he said, "You're Bruce German's wife! He was in my group. I have a message for you and I'll tell you later." I was in a state of euphoria.

The ministers described in detail how they had arrived in Tehran and been taken by car to the Embassy grounds. The windows of the car had been covered with newspapers so they could not see out. They had to negotiate with the militants on the logistics of how each of them would see the hostages. The militants agreed to have the hostages come in small groups for the church services.

After more than an hour, we divided into small groups. Each family went with the minister who had seen that particular hostage. My group consisted of Louisa Kennedy, Penne Laingen, and a few others. Rev. Sloane-Coffin talked to Penne Laingen and then to Louisa Kennedy. Then he got up to leave.

I asked, "What about my husband? What is the message you have for me?" He looked at me rather blankly and said, "What is your name again?"

"Marge German, my husband is Bruce." I replied. Then he asked, "What religion are you?" That surprised me. Why was he asking that and how did that have anything to do with the message he had?

I answered, "I'm Russian Orthodox."

"Is your husband Orthodox, too?"

"No, but he has attended church with us regularly for the past five to seven years." As I wondered what relevance any of this had, he looked at me and said, "To tell you the truth, I don't remember your husband. He just seemed to blend in with all the rest."

I sat there dumbfounded and unable to move, thinking that I had misunderstood him. I asked, "Did you give him the message I had for him?"

He said, "What message?"

I said, "The message I called into your office in New York before you went to Tehran?" "I never got a message," he replied. I began to feel frantic.

I blurted, "The priest from my church, Father Basil Summer, who is a friend of Father Kiskovsky, called your office and left a very short message for you to take to my husband."

He flippantly replied, "Well, we got so many messages, we just couldn't take them all."

"But he said it was from me to my husband," I insisted.

"I'm sorry, but I never got it," he said flatly.

I wanted to scream. As we left the building, Debbie was livid. The frustration she felt came to the surface and she shouted, "This was the biggest waste of time. Why did you make us come with you? I never want to come to these meetings again." Matt was visibly upset but just looked very disgusted by the whole thing and said, "Why did he say he had a message if he didn't even remember Dad?" I could not answer him. As for Chris, he looked bewildered, but said nothing. My heart ached for my children.

The next day I called Pat Lee. Before I could say anything, she asked, "What message did the minister bring back for you? I've been anxious to hear every word."

I replied, "Did Rev. Sloane-Coffin really say he had a message for me?"

"Yes, that's what he said when he talked with us. Why?" I told her what happened. She was shocked. She exclaimed, "Why would he tell you he had a message and then say he didn't remember Bruce?"

"I don't know. I just know that I was so happy to hear there was a message and crushed when I found out that he didn't even remember Bruce." Pat had better luck with the minister who saw Gary - he did bring back a short message for her. I was happy for her and Dana.

December 31st New Year's Eve (Day 58) I received a call from someone at a local TV station who said that some film had been released from Iran about the hostages and that it would be broadcast later that night. She couldn't tell me if Bruce was in the film but did say that 30 hostages appeared in it. I appreciated her letting me know. I went down to the rec room and set up the video recorder. I was glad that Bruce had wanted a VCR the previous year. Now I'd be able to tape the broadcast and if he was on the film, I'd be able to replay the tape whenever I wanted.

TELEVISION BROADCAST OF THE CHRISTMAS SERVICES

I waited impatiently for the film to air. Finally, after the 11:00 p.m. news, a special report came on. Since the start of the crisis, ABC Television had been running a nightly special: "The Iran Crisis - America Held Hostage." It would eventually become *Nightline*. Frank Reynolds was the program's newscaster and it usually started out with the number of days into the crisis. The announcer would boom, "The Iran Crisis - America Held Hostage. Day 58!" It amazed everyone that the crisis had lasted this long.

Frank Reynolds announced that the film of the hostages had been released from Iran and would be shown in its entirety. The tape started with about 50 minutes of propaganda in which a woman militant read a long list of complaints against the Shah in perfect English. Those complaints were leveled against the United States by association.

Finally, the Christmas services were shown. The hostages were brought through a black-curtained doorway. On the back wall, prominently displayed, was a menacing picture of the Ayatollah Khomeini; in one corner was a decorated Christmas tree; and in the middle of the room was a sofa with a coffee table in front of it. As each hostage entered the room in single file, they seemed to be blinded by the bright lights greeting them, making them squint until their eyes adjusted to the brightness.

I looked in vain for Bruce. He was not in the first group, nor the second, nor the third. When the fourth group came in and he was not among them, my heart sank, and I felt he wouldn't be in the film. I braced myself for disappointment.

Then the fifth group started in. Four hostages filed in and introduced themselves to the minister. And then there was Bruce. Chris and Matt had stayed up to see this and when Chris spotted Bruce, he started to laugh and cry and jump up and down. "There's my Daddy, there's my Daddy!" he squealed. He was so excited. I was happy to see Bruce, but I was happier for the boys because it made them so happy.

The quality of the film was very poor, but the fact that we saw that Bruce was alive sent adrenaline pumping through my body. What a wonderful, belated Christmas gift!

When the broadcast was over, I rewound the tape to play it back only to find out that it was blank. Nothing had been recorded. I was aghast! What had I done wrong? I checked all the wires and was sure I had set the video recorder properly. Why hadn't this worked? It was exasperating.

When the clock struck midnight to announce the New Year, I hugged the boys and made a toast to 1980 being a better year. They both hoped so, too. Just then Debbie, who was at a friend's house' for a party, called to wish us a Happy New Year. I told her about the Hostage Crisis special TV broadcast but that I hadn't gotten it on tape. She was disappointed that she hadn't seen the broadcast herself.

The phone rang again, and it was my mother-in-law calling to wish us a Happy New Year. I had never been away from Bruce on Christmas or New Year's since the day we met, July 17, 1958, and it made me very sad. Ben also called from New York and I controlled my emotions long enough to wish him a good year.

After I hung up the phone and the boys were in bed, I sat staring at the TV set but not really seeing what was on. I was thinking back to when Bruce and I had first met at The Lakeway bar in Pennsylvania. My friend Bernadine introduced me to Bruce, and we were attracted to each other right away – dancing the night away and already making plans to see each other again the next week.

The playing of the *Star-Spangled Banner* blared from the TV, bringing me back to the present as the television station concluded their broadcasting for the evening. Still, those memories had made me feel that I'd somehow reached across the ocean to wherever Bruce was and touched him through a kind of telepathy.

January 1st (Day 59) At the start of 1980, there was still no break in the hostage crisis. Everyone had thought that the hostages would be released for Christmas because the first thirteen had been released before Thanksgiving.

On **January 2nd (Day 60)**, I had a call from the Iran Working Group (IWG) letting me know that the film from Iran containing the Christmas services was at the Task Force Center. They asked if it would be possible to come down that day to see it again. I dropped everything and went. When I got there, I watched the film and pointed Bruce out to one of the Task Force officers. They were still trying to identify each of the hostages because up until now, they only had names and weren't sure which ones had appeared on the film.

I watched as Bruce squinted as he entered the room into the bright lights and looked at someone behind the camera with a quizzical look, as if to ask, "What's this all about?" He walked over to Rev. Sloane-Coffin and introduced himself. The only thing I heard him say was "Bruce German." I tried to absorb as much of the film as possible, so it would be burned into my memory. I wanted to remember every detail.

UNEXPECTED MAIL FROM THE MEN OF THE USS KITTY HAWK

On **January 6th (Day 64)**, I was in the bedroom when our dog Mindy started to bark. I looked out the window and saw the mailman coming. As I walked down the hall to the living room, I heard a thump, thump, thump, thump, thump. When I got to the stairs, I looked down at the landing and saw a pile of letters and cards scattered over the floor. As I picked them up, I noticed the return addresses read "USS Kitty Hawk." There were letters included with Christmas cards, each of them with a word of encouragement. The Captain of the ship had read my Christmas card to them over the ship's TV system. His message read, "Mrs. German is a very brave and compassionate person who, in spite of the stress she is under, made the effort of wishing the men of the Kitty Hawk good wishes for a nice Christmas. The sailors should not gripe that they wouldn't be home for Christmas when her Christmas would be so much worse."

The letters spoke of each sailor's hometown and family, future plans and words of encouragement. Some sent the ship's newspaper and pictures of the Kitty Hawk, along with a description of their jobs. I discovered that, in addition to many planes that made up the carrier's main cargo, the Kitty Hawk had approximately 5,000 people on board.

It was an emotional experience to receive these cards. I had not expected an answer to my card, since I had just addressed it "To the Men of the USS Kitty Hawk." Truly, people are compassionate and caring. My faith in humanity was raised greatly.

January 8th (Day 66) I received a call from the IWG to inform me that three more clergymen were going to Iran. The spokesman said that if I wanted to come down and meet with them that morning, I was welcome to do so. They were meeting with Sheldon Krys, the Task Force officers and the IWG. I was also told that if I had any mail, I could bring it to them. I quickly wrote a letter and drove to the State Department. The ministers, Rev. Moore, Rev. Miller, and Rev. Everett asked for a picture of Bruce to help them recognize him if they got a chance to see him. They said they would also tell him that they had spoken to me.

I gave them the picture I carried in my wallet and asked them to please tell him that his family was fine and that we had enough money. I was still trying to get that message to him because he seemed concerned about it. I left there feeling good. Their purpose in going to Iran was to see if they could get the hostages released.

On **January 8th (Day 66)**, the Christmas present I ordered for Bruce, a bar and three bar stools for the rec room, was delivered. I put a large red ribbon on top and arranged the rest of his gifts around the bow. Christmas had passed, but I wanted to have everything ready for his return. Then it would be Christmas for me.

Deena Flowers, one of the social workers, called to tell me that arrangements had been made for the children of the hostages to meet at the office of Dr. Plotsky, a psychiatrist, on **Saturday, Jan 12th (Day 70)**. I was stunned and wondered why. I understood Dr. Dustin, the head of the Medical Office, wanted the children to meet as a support group, just as the wives and mothers were meeting to discuss their feelings. I knew it would help for Debbie, Matt, and Chris to know that other children were going through the same emotions. I was not pleased with this arrangement at all because instead of getting the children into a support group with other hostage children, they arranged for them to see a psychiatrist.

Reluctantly I took the children to Dr. Plotsky's office over their most verbal objections. I sat in the waiting room while all the children disappeared into the next room. After an hour, the children emerged and we left. On the way home, I asked my children how the session had gone. They said that I must think they were crazy to make them go to see a psychiatrist; that they hadn't talked at all except to answer one question that the Dr. asked each of them: "Who do you like better, your father or your mother?"

I was appalled! Why would he ask such a thing? The question put them in a "no-win" situation. How could they answer it and not feel guilty? If they said they liked their mother more, it would make them feel they were abandoning their father who was being held hostage. If they chose their father, they'd feel they were betraying their mother whom they now depended on for their every need. I called Deena Flowers and let my dissatisfaction and anger come through about Dr. Plotsky's tactics. She defended him, stating that it was a very normal question to ask. When I consulted a few other psychiatrists later in the crisis, I found that it was not so.

Letters finally started to arrive from the hostages in the middle of **January through February 1980**. State Department wanted copies of the letter for the psychiatrists to read, to determine how the hostages were coping. I asked who else would see these letters and was told "no one," only the doctors would see them. Since I knew Dr. Dustin, the Head of the Medical Department, I decided to give my letters directly to him. I asked Maria Melchiorre if she would take my letters to him but asked that she not leave them with him. She agreed. Somehow, it bothered me that they wanted copies. I didn't want any copies to be made. When Maria returned them to me, she assured me that she had waited inside Dr. Dustin's office while he read the letters and that she'd taken them back as soon as he was finished. He called me to say that, other than the normal stress experienced by someone being held captive, Bruce was doing okay.

Though I was hounded by the IWG to make copies of my letters to send to them, I refused. Many times during the crisis, I would get a call asking where my copies of Bruce's letters were. I always told them I wasn't sending any. This always caused friction, but I stood firm. I did not trust the volunteers and what Bruce wrote to me was none of their business. These volunteers seemed to be impressed with their own importance.

January 16, 1980 (Day 74) I was somewhat depressed. I had been writing to Bruce continually and whenever the State Department called to tell me that the militants were on the phone, I'd give them a message for him. So far nothing seemed to be getting through. The Iranians were using us—playing with our minds. This was cruel mental and emotional torture.

That evening at about 8:00 p.m. the doorbell rang. It was a woman from the neighborhood holding some mail. "Mrs. German, I live around the corner on Parkland Drive and the mailman delivered these letters to my house by mistake."

I looked down and saw two letters with Iranian stamps, but this time a wonderful, familiar printing was scrawled across the envelopes. They were from Bruce!

I exclaimed, "They're from my husband!"

I called to the children that we had received two letters from Dad. They exclaimed, "At this time of night?" When I told them that the post office had delivered them to the wrong address, they wondered how they could make such a mistake.

The letters were dated **December 13 and 26, 1979**. Both were printed in block letters and in red ink. I assumed that Bruce had been told to print and that the letters were being censored. He had a very distinct, clear handwriting and I was sure he would have written the letter rather than print it. Part of the first letter read:

"KNOWING THAT YOU AND THE CHILDREN ARE ALL RIGHT AND THAT YOU ARE WAITING FOR ME IS ALL THAT KEEPS ME GOING. I GET VERY DEPRESSED SOMETIMES, BUT THEN I THINK ABOUT HOW HARD IT MUST BE FOR YOU. EVERYTHING IS ON YOUR SHOULDERS. I HOPE THAT MONEY IS STILL BEING PUT INTO THE BANK. I WORRY ABOUT YOU HAVING ENOUGH MONEY.

It was signed, "All my love, Bruce."

Anger began to well up within me because he mentioned how he not received any of my letters, despite having written to him every day. The second letter was much of the same.

I called the Task Force and told them about the letters. Again, I was the first to report a mail delivery. I told them the letters were delivered to the wrong address, but all that mattered to me was that I received them.

On the 17th (Day 75), two more letters dated **14 Dec. and 25 Dec. 1979** arrived for me and one for the children dated **26 Dec**. The children always enjoyed reading my letters, but they were delighted because this letter was just for them.

The next day I called Marian Precht at IWG and told her how upset I was that Bruce had not received any of the mail I had sent and threatened to call Tehran and give those militants a piece of my mind. I had been writing continuously since November 12, sending letters and cards almost every day. By now he should have received at least 20 to 30 pieces of mail.

I told Marian, "I don't know why Bruce hasn't gotten any mail. I'd like to give the militants a piece of my mind."

Marian was the wife of Henry Precht, the head of the Task Force that had been set up because of the Hostage Crisis. She said, "Let me check with Henry and I'll call you back." A few minutes later she called back and said, "Why don't you call?" She told me how to place the call, gave me the number of the U.S. Embassy in Tehran and wished me luck

THE PHONE CALL: MY FIRST CONVERSATION WITH AN IRANIAN MILITANT

Jan 18, 1980 (Day 76) I had thought about calling on the 17th but couldn't muster enough courage to do so until the 18th. I had just been venting and never thought they would even think of having me call. Now I was committed, but how would I do this? How would I communicate with someone who literally had my husband's life in his hands? I waited until about 11:30 pm to place the call. I put my little tape-recorder near the phone along with a pad of paper and pencil so I could record the conversation. I knew I would only be able to tape my side of the call, but I thought I could write down whatever the militant said so I'd have it to review later. I gathered all my courage. My heart pounded in my chest as I phoned the operator to place a call to Tehran.

After about five rings I heard:

"Hallo?" said the militant in a thick Iranian accent.

I began speaking very slowly as I would to a small child, enunciating each word carefully to be sure there would be no misunderstanding. Are you an Iranian student?"

"Yes."

"My name is Mrs. German. My husband is a hostage there. I received some letters from him. Thank you for letting him send them to me. Could you tell me why he has not received any letters from me?"

He replied with something unintelligible.

"I have sent many letters. Do you understand?" I asked.

"No."

"Is there someone who speaks English?"

"Moment!"

Then he was gone. I was feeling I had failed in my attempt to communicate. After a long pause, another militant answered, and I began again.

"My name is Mrs. German. I am calling from the United States. My husband is a hostage there. I received some letters from him. Thank you for letting him send them to me. Could you tell me why he has not received any letters from me?"

"All letters...we give to hostages. You send, we give."

"I would like to give a message to my husband."

"You can leave message...if you want."

"Please tell him his wife and children are fine," I said slowly. "Please, tell him that we have enough money. Could he come to the phone?"

"No," the militant said.

"Could <u>he</u> call <u>me</u>?" I asked.

"No. Hostages release when Shah returned," he told me.

I did not want to get into a conversation about the Shah, so I continued. "I don't know anything about the Shah. Would I be able to send some books...for my husband to read?"

"Books—okay to send books."

"Will you tell him that I called you?" I asked.

"Yes, I give the message."

"What is your name?"

"I'm a student, I am a student!" the militant exclaimed.

None of the militants wanted to be identified, just in case there would be repercussions when the crisis ended, so I could understand why he was so determined not to tell me his name.

At this point I felt that there was nothing more to say. By the time I hung up the phone I was emotionally drained. My heart was still pounding wildly, but at least I felt that I may have communicated enough to get Bruce some mail. Being a Foreign Service wife, I was aware of the language barrier, but this was much more of a challenge. My husband's life depended on me being able to communicate with these people and getting my point across. It was the difference between Bruce getting mail from the children and me, or feeling that we had abandoned him

I called my mother-in-law to tell her we had received the letters. She said, "Read them to me." I read the letters and she started to cry that he was so depressed. Then she said, "You know, Marge, I should be getting a letter from him soon." I told her I was sure he had written and that it was just a matter of the militants letting the mail out of Iran.

I was so happy to get those letters that were in his handwriting or printing and were longer than a few sentences. I felt he would be okay. He always had faith in God, but his renewed faith was giving him strength.

Jan. 19, 1980 (Day 77) A volunteer called from the State Department to let me know a minister from the United Methodist Church, Rev. Adams, had met with John Thomas, an American Indian who had gone to Tehran to talk to the militants. John Thomas had brought some mail back for the families and there was some for me. I was told to come to the United Methodist Church on Maryland Avenue to pick it up since the mail wouldn't be going to the State Department. It had to be delivered by someone either from John Thomas' Indian tribe or the United Methodist Church per the militants demands.

The children agreed to come with me to pick up the mail. We finally arrived at the United Methodist Church and were shown into a little chapel where other families were waiting for John Thomas to arrive. While we waited, I told the families that I had called Tehran and related the conversation. They were very surprised that I had made the call and even more surprised that I had gotten through to someone willing to speak to me. It seemed to give them a lift.

When Rev. Adams and John Thomas entered the chapel, we listened intently as John gave us the details of his trip to Tehran. He had not seen any of the hostages but was given mail for us. He gave me two letters and a Christmas card with a short note on an 8 ½ by 11 sheet of paper that had been torn in half horizontally.

It was dated **December 24, 1979.**

"Dearest Marge,

On this very special night I wish that I could be with my loved ones to celebrate Christmas. If our Government would only do something maybe we could come home. Until they do it looks like I will stay here. Please keep praying for my early release so that I can see you again.

I miss you all very much. Please write to me, because I need to know how you are doing. Take care of yourself.

All my love,

Bruce"

I glanced around the room and saw some of the families crying. I asked one mother if she had bad news and she said her son's letter read like a Last Will and Testament. I felt sad for her and tried to assure her and her daughters that since the letters had been written more than three weeks earlier, some of the depressed feelings were gone. I read part of Bruce's letter to them to show that his particular letter did not contain anything really depressing.

Later I called my sister, Lovey, and told her about the letters and card. She was very happy for me. Then, like someone flipped a switch, I just felt so overcome with despair that I started to cry. "What will I do if he doesn't come home? What am I going to do? I can't live without him, I just can't. Life has no meaning if he isn't here with me. How am I going to raise three children by myself?"

She tried to comfort me, saying God would watch out for us just as he was watching out for Bruce. After I hung up, I wondered why I felt so depressed. I had two new letters and a card, and should be feeling wonderful, but somehow, I didn't.

CHAPTER 5

A SURPRISE VIDEO TAPE ARRIVES

January 20, 1980 (Day 78) A small package arrived in the mail from ABC-TV. Inside was a videotape labeled "Hostage Special," the Christmas program that I had not been able to tape record. The technician at ABC had thoughtfully rearranged the groups and placed Bruce's group at the beginning and then included the entire program as it had appeared in the broadcast. Steve Bell, the news reporter from ABC national news, who was very active with No Greater Love, had arranged to have the videotape made for me after Carmella had told him what happened when I tried to tape it.

PACKAGES FOR THE HOSTAGES

January 27, 1980 (Day 85) Rev. Adams said he would be going to Tehran and that he would take a shoebox-sized package to each of the hostages if the families could get the packages to him within the next two days. I found a sturdy shoebox from size 10 men's shoes and purchased underwear, socks, a book by John D. MacDonald (Bruce's favorite author), and as many little things as I could stuff into the spaces in between. I managed to pack small sizes of deodorant, shampoo, a toothbrush, toothpaste, disposable razors, and vitamins into that little box. I was sure Bruce was not getting any fruit, so I found dried apple slices to include as well. I wanted to do what I could to give Bruce the strength to get through this terrible ordeal. I sometimes wished I was the hostage.

I had written a few letters to Bruce and waited to see if I should mail them through international mail or if Rev. Adams would take them with him. When I got word that Rev. Adams would take them, I grabbed the 11 letters I had written and blessed each one with holy water. I put all my faith in God, knowing He would get these letters to Bruce.

After much publicity, Rev. Adams and his group left for Tehran and returned a few days later with mail for the families and the postcards that the hostages had filled out. Bruce said he had received 11 letters and the package and described the contents. This was concrete proof that God was watching over us. Along with Bruce's postcard were 13 letters for the children and me. What a glorious day!

I put the letters in chronological order so that I could read each one as it had been written. I anxiously opened the envelopes, wondering why they felt so heavy and stiff, as if they were cards instead of letters. What I saw shocked me. Enclosed with Bruce's letters was some propaganda, written in poor English. *"Come let's unite and abolish the hands of the right wing and left-wing criminals on top of them (sic)America,"* exclaimed one with a picture of Khomeini. Another showed two pictures, one with President Carter kissing a little girl with Rosalyn Carter eating something in the background, and the other one picturing a very emaciated child surrounded by rubble. The third one was a card, tri-folded with green Persian designs on a deep blue background that read *"Merry Christmas and a happy new year."* Inside was a long message from Khomeini, again calling for Christians to demand that President Carter hand the Shah of Iran over to the Khomeini government for punishment. I decided I'd read enough of that. I concentrated on Bruce's letters.

February 3, 1980 (Day 92) The State Department decided to have another family meeting, bringing families from all over the United States to the Washington, D.C. area to discuss the latest events in the hostage crisis. It was scheduled for **February 4th (Day 93)** at 9:15 a.m. My mother-in-law was invited to attend this time, so we went down together. The State Department had given her an airline ticket from Wilkes-Barre/Scranton/Avoca airport to Washington National airport and paid her per diem. Once again, the people who lived in the Washington area were not entitled to money for mileage unless they lived more than 20 miles from the building.

We sat through meetings discussing the Presidential elections in Iran and the fact that Bani Sadr had just been elected President that morning. He would need time to get his administration into position, which could take weeks because the election of the Majlis (the Iranian equivalent of our Congress) would not take place until May 9th. We would have another wait.

We were also cautioned about entrepreneurs who might pressure members of the families to endorse products that would benefit them, not us. No one should get rich by cashing in on our problems. We were further cautioned about telling the press what went on at the meetings. It seemed the media always knew when and where a meeting was taking place.

We also spoke to the doctors about the mental health of the hostages and discussed the problems that some members of the families were having, such as trouble sleeping, anxiety, depression and anger. These are all very normal reactions to such a traumatic experience; however, the one thing we were told not to do was to self-medicate with tranquilizers.

We were then ushered into the conference room and told that someone would be with us in a few moments. We waited about 20 - 30 minutes and discovered that Rosalyn Carter would be meeting with us. It was now almost 4:00 p.m. and I had wanted to be on my way home by this time to miss the rush hour traffic. We each met with Mrs. Carter and shook her hand while photographers took pictures of a few of the families as they walked by. Then we went on our way, finally arriving home at 5:15 p.m. It had been a long day.

A TOTALLY UNEXPECTED PHONE CALL FROM DAD

"You'll never guess who called," exclaimed the children excitedly.

"Who?" I asked.

In unison they replied, "**DAD**!" I felt numb!

"When?" I asked.

The children showed me the calendar where they had written, "Dad called - 4:53 p.m." I had missed him by 20 minutes!! If I had not waited to meet Mrs. Carter, I would have been home to talk to him. I went into my room to change my clothes and just sat there - I couldn't cry, I couldn't scream, I couldn't show anger. I just sat there on the edge of the bed.

I came back into the living room and asked all the details of the telephone conversation. Bruce told Debbie to write down everything he said, that it was very important for her to do that. He read a statement stating that the hostages would not be released until the Shah was returned to Iran.

I asked, "Did you tell Dad that the Shah is not in the United States any longer, that he is in Panama?"

"No, because I was afraid that the militants might hang up on me," she answered. She said Bruce repeated the statement twice and then chatted with each of the children. He was very upset when he learned that I was not at home. Deb said, "Mom, I thought he was going to cry! He was so upset. All he kept saying was that he wanted to talk to you." She told him about school and her plans for going to college and that she wanted be a Foreign Service Officer, just like him.

Bruce then told Debbie the "students" had said it was alright for me to send him some cookies and to tell me not to send any more crossword puzzle books - he had enough. I had been sending him sports pages from the *Washington Post* and *The Evening Star* newspapers, small crossword puzzle books, and some paint-by-number sets along with a few small toiletry items, but he had not received any of the sports pages. I wondered why. I sent each in a strong padded envelope large enough to hold a magazine without rolling or folding it. Why were some items getting through and others not? I felt that if Bruce could remain busy, he would endure the captivity better. I did all I could to keep his mind busy.

Bruce also told Debbie that he had written a letter to me and one to the *Washington Post* newspaper in the hopes that someone would do something to get the hostages released. When he spoke to the boys, Matt spoke timidly and said just a few words about school and bowling because he was concerned that the militants might hurt Bruce if he said the wrong thing; Chris also talked about school and bowling.

I called Hal Saunders' office at State Department and told his secretary about the phone call and that I was angry that I was made to stay and wait for Mrs. Carter. Why had they made me stay there? Later, Hal Saunders called me back and said he understood how upset I was, but this was the militants' way of mentally torturing Bruce, the children, and me. To allow Bruce to call home made them seem to be decent people, but because of all the media attention given to the meetings, they knew all the families were in Washington, D.C. and that no one would be home. This was a tactic the militants used because they knew that kind of disappointment might break some of the hostages. Hal said that I could have missed the call if I had gone to the store or just been out of the house for other reasons and to try not to blame anyone but the Iranians for this. I respected Mr. Saunders opinions and was grateful that he had called me back. Later, I learned that about five other hostages had indeed made calls to their families that day.

The next day I hurried to bake cookies and bought some pretzels and a few other snacks, made up a package, and took it to the post office. The postal clerk, a woman named Lilli, wouldn't take it because she said there was no mail delivered to Iran because of the hostage crisis. I told her that I had checked with the State Department about mailing the package through International mail and they okayed it because there was no longer mail delivery through the diplomatic pouch. I said that my husband was there. After a few other questions, she realized that Bruce was one of the hostages. The postal employees at that post office branch - Lilli, Nick, and Joel - got to know me very well during those next 12 months and helped make my daily ritual as painless as possible. I later wrote a letter to the Postmaster General to praise the three for their kindness and helpfulness that went beyond their job requirement.

I told the State Department of the militants offer to tape a message for Bruce if I called back. They told me to come to the Task Force office and they would place the call for me. I had prepared an outline of topics I wanted to tell Bruce, but wasn't sure how long the militants would let me talk. When the connection was completed, I identified myself to the person who answered and explained that I was told to call back. I also took the chance and asked if I would be able talk to Bruce. The militant said "No" but that he would record my message. My heart was pounding. I began talking as fast as I could for the recording, constantly fearing that I would be cut off in mid-sentence. I tried to sound happy, not wanting Bruce to hear the shakiness in my voice.

I talked about the children's activities along with the improvements I had begun to make in the house. He was an avid sports fan, so I gave him the latest news of the Los Angeles Dodgers, the Washington Redskins, and the University of Maryland sports programs.

Before hanging up, I thanked the militant for making the recording for Bruce. I wondered if Bruce would really get to hear it. I had no way of knowing he would.

CHAPTER 6

THE NIGHTLINE INTERVIEW, DAY 100

February 10, 1980 (Day 99) **The** State Department called me to ask if I was interested in doing an interview on ABC-TV's *Nightline*. The volunteer said that since the crisis was lasting so long this would be shown on February 11, the 100th day of captivity for the hostages. I didn't tell her, but that was my birthday. She said it would be good if I did the interview to let the Iranians and the American people see that Bruce was a husband and father whose family loved and missed him. I grudgingly agreed.

The ABC-TV crew came on February 10th, taking pictures of the yellow ribbons on the trees in front of the house, the unopened Christmas packages on the bar waiting for Bruce, and the American flag hanging in our front picture window. There were questions about how I felt when I first found out Bruce was a hostage, questions for the children and also for my mother-in-law.

February 11, 1980 (Day 100) When *Nightline* aired that night, it was a special broadcast that was extended from a half-hour to a full hour. I watched as Ted Koppel, who had replaced Frank Reynolds, interviewed Iranians and experts in Persian history. I wondered at which point in the broadcast we would appear. At 12:20 a.m. our segment was televised. It lasted between four and five minutes—after three hours of taping! It was chopped into smaller segments with narration and film clips of Bruce interspersed between those of us. I was disappointed by it because I didn't think it showed the American people just how much of a family man Bruce was.

Feb. 13, 1980 (Day 102) Bruce's letter appeared in the *Washington Post* newspaper. Marian Precht called to tell me to expect calls from the press. Matt had an appointment with the orthodontist, so I wasn't too concerned about them reaching me.

While Matt was with the doctor, a nurse came out and said I had a phone call and that I should take it in Dr. Levy's office. When I answered the phone, I found it was a reporter asking me if my husband had told me that he was writing a letter to the *Post.*

I didn't mention Bruce's phone call but did say I was aware of the letter. The reporter assumed I had received a letter from him. He asked me why my husband would write a letter to the newspaper and what he hoped to accomplish by it. His tone made me angry. I could tell that this guy was hoping to print something to sensationalize it. I politely told him that I was not with my husband when he wrote the letter, and therefore, I could not guess his reasons. The reporter pursued it. I told him I was sorry but that I really could not comment on it. After I hung up, I apologized to the Doctor for having his office routine disrupted. The reporter had called Debbie at home, gotten the doctor's name and phone number, and then called me there. This was why I had become more and more distrustful of the media.

Jeri, from Rev. Adam's office, called telling me she had six letters from Bruce to give to me. I left immediately to pick them up, trying to forget that unpleasant episode and the reporter. In one of the letters, Bruce explained how a journalist had called pretending to be his brother Ben. My blood pressure must have risen 30 points after reading that letter. What a terrible thing for a journalist to do to a captive. My opinion of the media was very low already, but this brought out a real hatred for them.

Another letter was written on **11 Feb**. He had written in the upper right-hand corner under the date "**100 Days**."

"Looking at the calendar I suddenly realized that not only is it your birthday, but we have been held for 100 days. And not a single thing has changed. People continue to pray but our status remains the same. It's so totally unfair & unjust. This must be one of my "down" days, so you'll have to forgive me"

Again, I called my mother-in-law and told her about the letters, and again she said, "Read them to me." Since she always said she should have had a letter from Bruce, I began making up a paragraph in my letters to make her feel better. Usually I would say something to the effect of: "Please tell my mother I think of her every day and that I love her. I have written to her a few times and hope she has received them. Tell her to take care of herself and not to work too hard."

February 20, 1980 (Day 109) Father Basil called and said NBC Channel 4 was interested in coming to St. Mark Church to get pictures of the children and I attending services, but he wouldn't make any commitment unless I agreed. The tape would be used as background when Bruce was released. Barbara Allen and Nancy Campbell from Channel 4 taped the Divine Liturgy on February 24th while George Leleck, the warden of the church, explained to the liturgy and pointed out Matt and Chris as they carried their candles out of the altar. Later, at the coffee hour that followed the liturgy, the reporters waited until George introduced us. They were not pushy, nor did they ask stupid questions. I was impressed.

Mar 4, 1980 (Day 121) There was another meeting at the State Department, this time with Deena Flowers, one of the social workers. I felt driven to attend everything. Deena discussed the frustrations the families were feeling from this long ordeal and asked how I was coping. I told her I had my "down" days, but I couldn't allow myself to lose control of my life. I had to be mother and father to my children, and I had to keep the family together for Bruce. In my heart, I felt that this crisis must be happening for a reason and I had to survive it with a whole mind and body. I couldn't let myself get sick or go to pieces in self-pity.

She asked why I felt that way and I replied, "All things work together for good for those who love God and are called according to His purpose. They happen for a reason." Although I didn't know right then what that reason was, if it was God's will that Bruce, the children, and I should go through this, then I had to accept that. I didn't know why we had been chosen, but I knew that God's plan was better than any I might come up with. Deena replied, "That's a good way to look at it."

CHAPTER 7

INTRUSION BY THE MEDIA CONTINUES: A PHONE CALL AT 4:00AM

I t had been more than four months since Bruce had been taken hostage and I was still having trouble sleeping. There were days when I would fall into bed, exhausted and then, just as I was about to drift off, suddenly I would be wide-awake, unable to sleep at all. I grew to welcome the feeling of sheer exhaustion in the hope that I would sleep for at least one or two hours. It seemed that on these nights the phone would ring between 1 a.m. and 4 a.m., jolting me out of a dead sleep. My heart would pound as I breathlessly said, "Hello?" waiting for the news that Bruce had either been released and was free, or that he was dead. Instead of someone from the State Department Task Force, it would be a reporter asking what I thought of the latest turn of events in Iran or the latest statements of garbage from the militants or the Ayatollah Khomeini. Usually I would tell them I had no comment. One night, I fell into an exhausted sleep at approximately 3 a.m. The phone startled me at 4 a.m. With my heart pounding I answered, expecting to hear from someone on the task force. It was yet another reporter. At that moment, the bottled-up anger inside me exploded. I screeched into the phone, "Do you know what time it is? Do you think that just because you are awake that I should be awake, too?" With that I slammed the receiver down into the cradle, livid to think that anyone could be so insensitive. I was shaking uncontrollably, and my heart was pounding so hard I had difficulty breathing.

The next morning, I called Pat Lee and told her about the call and what I had done. By this time, I was feeling very guilty about screaming at the reporter because an outburst like that was not me. Bruce used to tease me that I wouldn't say "crap" if I had a mouthful! I'm usually soft-spoken, but the stress of the crisis was changing my personality; however, Pat felt he deserved it.

FILM CLIP OF BRUCE

On **March 12, 1980 (Day 129)** I saw a film clip of Bruce being examined by Iranian doctors. He was holding his T-shirt up while the doctor listened to his chest. I wondered if Bruce had been sick; why else would he be examined? I decided to call Tehran again. I bought a little gadget from Radio Shack that I could put on the earpiece of the telephone and plug into the tape-recorder, allowing me to record both sides of the conversation. I decided to try it on the next phone call.

On **March 17, 1980 (Day 134)** I made the call to Tehran and was able to record a message for Bruce. I asked about his health, gave him suggestions for things to pass the time, and updated him on the children and his favorite sports teams. I wrote,

Whenever you get home, whether it's next week or next month, we will have so much to look forward to and be thankful for. I feel we have become better people through this and that God is watching over us—both of us. We have one fantastic marriage and it can only get better when you return. I love you very much and I will be here, no matter what—waiting for you. You've always said you're a one-woman man; well, you are the only man I'll ever love. I want to leave you with that thought. It was fate that brought us together that day in July 1958."

BEN'S PHONE CALL TO ME

On Monday, the repairman informed me that I would have to pay him $30 to come to the house for the broken refrigerator and that the repair would be in addition to that. I was in no position to argue, so I agreed to his terms. It was a no-win situation. While the repairman worked on the refrigerator, the phone rang. It was Ben. He began yelling and screaming, "You're keeping my mom and I out of the crisis! Remember, we've known Bruce longer than you – blood is thicker than water. *You* are only his wife; *we're* family."

He went on to say that when Bruce married me, they were happy about it, but now he was fed up with me. I wasn't telling them all I knew about the crisis; that although I "claimed" my phone bill was high, he didn't know who I was calling because I certainly wasn't calling them, including his Aunt Mildred.

I couldn't believe what I was hearing. With all the calmness I could muster, I replied, "There's a dial on your end of the phone too. The State Department tells me very little. I get my information from the radio; then I call State Department and tell them what **I've** heard. Usually they give me the same answers; it has been confirmed or it has not been confirmed".

Ben's tone changed then, and he asked me if I was going to Pennsylvania for Easter and I told him "No!" very emphatically. I was not about to take this kind of abuse in person. Then he said, "Well, Honey, I just wanted to get that off my chest," and hung up.

By that time the refrigerator repairman was almost finished. I paid him, removed all the spoiled food, and scrubbed the inside. As I thought about the phone conversation repeatedly in my mind, my stomach began constricting and I felt very sick. I called my friends Katie and Sue. I needed to unload some of the anger before I had a stroke. Whenever I was upset or stressed out, I would call on Katie or Sue to cry on their shoulders or rant and rave about the way things were going. Katie and Sue were my best friends from church and I could depend on them to keep our conversations private. They didn't even discuss my conversations with each other. As usual, they let me cry on their shoulders.

My mother-in-law called to see when I was coming. I told her I had changed my mind and wouldn't be coming. She brought up Ben's phone call, apologized for telling him "things" that made him angry and begged me to come. I told her I'd have to think about it because I would not put up with any more accusations. She was noted for telling "her boys" things so they would "tell people off" for her. Then she would brag about it. Well, let her brag about this to her neighbors. She'd be the one who looked stupid.

The next day a meeting was arranged at the Deanery of the Washington Cathedral with two former Prisoners-of-War from Vietnam and their wives, a Senator, a psychiatrist, and an expert on Iranian affairs. I really hated to leave the boys by themselves at this time, but I needed to get to this meeting. When I arrived with the Golacinski family, the press was all over the area. I wondered how they had found out about it and who was giving them this information after all of us had been told not to inform the press of these meetings. As we walked by, microphones were stuck into our faces with questions about the meeting. We just kept walking.

Commander Paul Galante with his wife Phyllis and Captain Dick Stratton with his wife Alice, shared their experiences as POWs and POW wives. Dick and Paul had been POWs for more than seven years each. They spoke of their emotions, reactions, and feelings while they went through captivity. When they returned home, they were surprised to find that their wives had experienced the same emotions while waiting for them as they had during their captivity.

Dr. Piecznek explained some of the problems the hostages and we would face when they returned. He described flashbacks, irritability, sleeplessness, and other symptoms. I was more than willing to face whatever lay ahead, just as long as Bruce came home.

Mr. Hannah described the Iranian culture and how punishment usually consisted of amputation of a hand or foot. The plans for the Shah were not to give him a fair trial, but to execute him. But first there would be torture. They were people who seemed to relish dismembering their enemies. His vivid description sent chills up my spine.

I returned home with a better understanding of the emotional turmoil I had been feeling, but worried about Bruce's safety.

March 29, 1980 (Day 147) Ministers again were going to Tehran for church services, this time for Easter, but there wasn't enough time to write a letter and take it down to the State Department, so I dictated a message over the phone.

March 31, 1980 (Day 149) Although I did not want to spend Easter in Pennsylvania, we went up anyway on March 31, Bruce's 44th birthday. My children and I had discussed the fact that Dad would not have any birthday cake, let alone his favorite German Chocolate triple layer cake with coconut pecan frosting.

Just as we put our suitcases upstairs in my mother-in-law's house, she placed a call to Tehran to leave a birthday message for Bruce. After much frustration and waiting, the connection was made at 3:30 p.m.

My mother-in-law spoke first and started to cry, then handed the phone to me. I had asked her to sound as upbeat as she could so Bruce wouldn't be upset by the message. He would have a hard-enough time hearing it. Knowing she was crying would not help him in the least.

I took the phone and forced myself to sound happy and upbeat. I didn't want him to hear my voice quiver or sense the heartbreak I was feeling. I wished him a Happy 44th Birthday and promised a big celebration when he got home, then turned the phone over to Debbie, Matt, Chris, and Al. Each said a few words, wished him a Happy Birthday, and told him they loved him, missed him, and wished he could have been with us for his birthday and Easter.

I took the phone again and said a few more words and expressed my love for him. I was about to hang up when the militant came on the line. He began questioning me about the Shah again. Frantically, I tried to think of answers that wouldn't infuriate him, but would get my point across. I had nothing to do with the Shah, nor his admittance into this country. These calls always took a toll on me when I had to spar mentally with Iranians who could rationalize anything they did.

I called the State Department and told them about the latest call to Tehran and mentioned that the militant had said 50 hostages were being punished for the crimes of the Shah. Marion Precht asked me to repeat what I had just said. She said, "I'll tell Henry. That's an important piece of information. The militants admitted to holding 49 hostages and denied that Michael Metrinko was among them. This is proof that he's there."

I remember reading in the newspaper that the Iranians had been claiming that there were only 49 hostages, and Michael Metrinko had not been seen nor heard from since early in the crisis. With this information, they could now push the militants to admit he was there.

April 1-8 (Days 150-157) While the ministers were in Iran, I had a call from ABC Network Television asking me to come to their studios to see the taped message for me that had just come out of Tehran from Bruce. I declined, telling her I would wait to see it on TV. She was appalled that I would rather see it on TV than come to the studio. I was tired of making that long trip downtown and knew the TV stations would show the film in its entirety as they had done for every other bit of news about the Hostage Crisis.

As usual, the regularly scheduled programs had been interrupted. The film showed some of the hostages receiving communion and some talking to the ministers. They were seated at a table, three or four at a time. I watched intently, waiting for Bruce to appear. At last, there he was!

He began: "To my dear wife, Marge, my children, my daughter, Debbie and my sons, Matt and Chris..."

He had tears in his eyes and was biting his lip to gain control but was all choked up and couldn't speak. At that moment the scene was cut, and another group of hostages were shown. I waited for the message that the woman from the TV stations had said would be forthcoming, but it never came. That was the extent of my message. Whatever Bruce had to say to us had been cutoff. I couldn't stand it. I prayed, "Please, God, help him!" This was tearing me apart.

The ministers came back from Tehran on **April 8th (Day 157),** and I had an opportunity to meet with Rev. Bremer at the United Methodist Church. He was the minister who had seen Bruce and brought a short verbal message from him as well as four letters. He told me that Bruce was in good spirits, or as good as he could expect him to be under the circumstances. He said that Bruce wanted me to know that he loved me, missed me and the children, and hoped this ordeal would be over soon. He asked about our Easter and wanted me to keep writing and sending him sports magazines.

I thanked Rev. Bremer and hurried home to read the letters. I wondered where he was that he had access to a typewriter. It made for a longer letter and I was delighted.

*"You have no idea how much I need your expressions of love and the confidence you feel. It was reassuring, Honey, when you tell me that God is watching over me, and that he will bring me back to you. I honestly believe it, too, even more so after I get mail from you. You are the rock I lean on and you give me the courage I need to see this thing through. I **will** make it, and **we will** be reunited. Our faith in Almighty God and our love for each other will see us through. And as you said, every day brings us one day closer."*

The next two letters were pretty much the same, with him agreeing with me that God was not on our timetable, as I had told him many times before he went to Iran. Bruce was a very impatient person and wanted everything yesterday. I would tease him that God would teach him patience one day, just to prove to him that He was not on our schedule. This was certainly not how I thought He'd do it.

CHAPTER 8

PHONE MESSAGE FROM THE INTERNATIONAL RED CROSS

April 14, 1980 (Day 163) The International Red Cross representatives had been allowed to see the hostages at Easter and began calling the families with messages after they returned to New York. I waited by the phone for the call though I wasn't sure just when it would come.

When the phone rang, I answered it excitedly, ready with my tape recorder to tape whatever the message was. However, this call was from a TV station asking if I had gotten my call from the Red Cross. I told him I hadn't. The reporter asked if I would call him back when I did receive the call. I said, "No, I'm sorry." I had received about eight calls from the media and the last person got the brunt of my anger, frustration, and exasperation. I yelled into the phone, "If you'd stay off the phone, I might just be able to get my call!" I hung up. My heart was pounding, and I was very angry. The media had just intruded in my life too much and I was sick of it.

Finally, the call came. I turned the tape recorder on. The gentleman on the other end spoke with a very heavy French accent and spoke very slowly.

"I have a message from Bruce German in Tehran," he began. As you know we were able to visit him on Monday and to record the message. The letter is dated **14 April 1980 (164 days)**

My Dearest Marge,

Wanted to take advantage of this to let you know that I am fine. I have written you on the average of every other day, for example in April so far, I have written 7 letters. I do hope you received most, if not all, of them. Be assured, Honey, I write as often as possible, as I know you do, too.

*I also hope you heard the tape I made; it was supposed to be given to you by phone. The last letter I got from you was dated **3/24**, and I have received one box of cookies, and a tin of pretzels. Have not received any other boxes, however.*

Your special hour (2-3 p.m.) has become mine as well. I do nothing except think of our reunion. I agree that it's only a matter of time, but how much longer? If only I had something to base my faith and hope on. In any case, I love you with all my heart, and long for the day I see you again. Stay well, try not to overexert yourself, and may God watch over you, for me.

All My Love,

Your Bruce

I thanked him, hung up, then replayed the tape for myself and when the children came home, I played it for them. They were glad to hear the message but were disappointed that it wasn't their father's voice.

DISCUSSING BRUCE'S CONCERNS WITH SHELDON KRYS

April 15, 1980 (Day 164) I called Sheldon Krys, the State Department Administrative Officer handling the Crisis, and made an appointment to see him after my stop at the United Methodist Church where I'd drop off more letters for Bruce. I wanted to get some answers to the many questions Bruce had in his letters. Sheldon said he would be available to meet with me at 3:30 p.m. In January, when plans for the hostages' homecoming were being made, Sheldon and I did not agree on many points. I didn't want Bruce to be used for political purposes; I just wanted my husband home so we could resume our normal life. Although at this point in time, what was normal?

I delivered my letters to Jeri at United Methodist and picked up the three that had been brought from Tehran. Then I arrived in Sheldon's office when I was told he was in a meeting and would be with me in a few minutes. Approximately 15 minutes later the door opened, and Sheldon squeezed between it and the doorframe—as if trying to hide whomever was in his office. He greeted me, saying we'd have to use someone else's office because his was occupied. We went into another office and asked me what I had on my mind. I explained that Bruce wondered how he could be evaluated for his work performance if he was a hostage and not working on the job. Sheldon stated that Bruce would not be penalized in any way for being a hostage, but he wouldn't automatically get a promotion just *because* he was a hostage.

Again, there was a knock on the door and again materials were needed from the desk. After the second interruption, I again asked how Bruce would be evaluated and was told that the promotion panel would use his last evaluation, which had occurred before he'd left for Iran. I replied that this was not a realistic way to evaluate anyone. Times change, responsibilities change, personalities in his former office were different from those at the American Embassy in Tehran, and the duties themselves in each of the jobs would make a difference.

I asked the difference between a Foreign Service Officer (FSO) and a Foreign Service Reserve (FSR) and was told that there was no difference. I was confused because Bruce had always told me that there was. FSOs seemed to be held in higher regard. Bruce was an FSR. I asked about overtime and Sheldon became agitated. "Foreign Service Officers are not eligible for overtime pay," he stated.

I answered, "Bruce is Foreign Service Reserve and I would like to know the difference."

He countered, "In some instances there is overtime, but no one gets paid for 24 hours a day. They have to sleep sometime." His tone was arrogant.

I explained that I wasn't talking about 24 hours a day. He then asked, "Well, how would it look if Bruce asked for overtime?"

I could feel myself getting angry, and I looked him in the eye and asked, "And how would it look if the State Department refused?"

Again, there was a knock on the door and another interruption. By this time, I was becoming irritated; I had made an appointment 24 hours in advance, Sheldon had chosen the time that was "convenient" for him, and in 15 minutes I had been interrupted three times. I had come there for answers and felt I should have been shown the courtesy of his undivided attention for this short time. It was pointless asking any other questions. The visit was a total waste of my time. I thanked Sheldon and left.

I still had not fully adjusted to Bruce being gone, but I found that I wasn't crying all the time now. Was I getting used to the stress? Didn't I care anymore? Was it because the news and the press played havoc with my emotions? They'd announce, "The hostages could be freed in two or three days if such and such happens;" or "The hostages will be tried as spies." Over the past months there had been terror, then hope, then fear, then hope again. My emotions were becoming dulled. The only thing I was feeling now was anger.

When anyone asked me if I was hopeful that Bruce would be released soon, I couldn't really say "Yes." This crisis would not be over quickly. There was that ever-present memory of that huge cross of clouds in the sky on the day he left the United States. Somehow, despite all we'd already experienced, I knew that there was more to come.

April 20, 1980 (Day 169) I called Tehran to hear the message that Bruce had recorded for me. When the militant answered, I told him who I was and that I wanted to hear the message. He asked, "Who told you there was a message?" I explained that Bruce had told me in his Red Cross message. He told me to "hold the line" and returned a few minutes later. At long last, I was able to hear the message from Bruce – in his own voice. In part of his message, he said,

"I am in pretty good health. When you saw me being examined, it was only as a precautionary measure. The doctor took my blood pressure and checked my heart. Physically, I haven't changed too much, except I think there is a little grayer hair. The daily exercises I do consist of sit-ups and push-ups and so forth. For a while, I tried jogging in place, but I haven't done that lately. I'm going to resume jogging because I think it helps the circulation. My daily schedule consists of reading, playing cards, and chess. The food is pretty good, thanks mainly to the Chargé's cook. We generally get an American-style meal for lunch every day…

I'm glad to hear that the kids are doing so well at school, especially Matthew and Chris. Perhaps Debbie is taking this harder than we thought, but even so, she should be doing better. I have written to her and explained how I feel about her schoolwork and social life, but I haven't received an answer yet…

I want to tell you how great you looked in that picture you sent. It made me realize how lucky I am and how much I truly miss you. I hope you'll send more photos because I think I have this one worn out from looking at it. Also, Honey, I want you to know how much…how very proud I am of you, with all the problems you have to contend with—keeping the house, taking care of the kids—you are doing one fantastic job."

The message was cut off and the militant came back on the line. I pleaded to listen to the rest of the message but the militant was adamant. I figured there was no use arguing with him—he had the upper hand, and if I said something he didn't like, he'd hang up on me and I probably would never be able to get another message through to Bruce again. I just resigned myself to the fact that the militants liked playing these mind games. They did just enough to make you believe they were kind, but then zap you when you were most vulnerable.

At least the children and I were able to record our own message for Bruce. We took turns updating him on our personal lives. Debbie spoke first, filling him in on her grades, her tryouts for a play at school, her progress in bowling and the fact that Mindy, our dog, needed to lose weight after growing to enormous proportions. Matt was next and talked about much the same—school, bowling, and Mindy. Chris started off by telling Bruce he hoped he'd come home soon because we all missed him. Then he, too, told him about bowling and two movies he had seen I finished the tape with a few words of encouragement and a message of love. Then the militant came on the line, paranoid about the call being tracked by the U.S. Government. I assured the militant that Bruce just worked for the State Department and that we had no ties to the government.

After I hung up, I was drained emotionally again. That was one of the longest conversations I had with the militants and I was nervous when he asked questions about taping the phone calls. Later I learned that Henry Precht had called Tehran from the State Department and told them to expect my call later on that day. He almost blew it for me.

April 23, 1980 (Day 172) One of the IWG volunteers called to tell me that a meeting of the families would take place at the State Department on Wednesday, April 23rd at 6:00 p.m. All other meetings were held early in the morning at 9:00 a.m. I didn't like driving downtown at night, but since I was the Secretary of FLAG, I had to attend. I took my tape recorder to keep complete minutes for the families who lived outside the Washington, D.C. area. More family members were attending the meetings now and recording the proceedings made it easier to keep track of who asked questions and made comments. Danielle and Linda Golacinski and I drove down to the meeting together. We met in the conference room on an upper floor in State Department

Newsom, the Under-Secretary of State, told us that the United States had broken diplomatic relations with Iran and discussed the effect that everyone hoped it would have. Perhaps now the Iranians would buckle under the pressure of the world and free the hostages. The families asked about a rescue attempt and Mr. Newsom responded that if the previously mentioned calendar of events didn't bring about the release of the hostages, sanctions would be used, then an attempt might be made - but only if there was no other recourse.

As I was taking notes and adjusting the microphones on the tape recorder while all the discussion was going on, I felt a strange undercurrent in the room. The feeling didn't have any specific description, but it was like a sixth sense. The more I listened to the discussion, the stronger the feeling became.

When the meeting was over, I went over to Danielle and Linda and remarked, "They're going to try a rescue attempt." I don't know why I said it; it just popped out.

They both said, "No, they're not! Didn't you hear the timetable of events before they will even consider it?"

I couldn't shake that strange feeling and replied, "They're going to try a rescue attempt and it's going to be soon. I can feel it. There is such an undercurrent in this room. I know they're going to try it."

They both disagreed with me and then I really felt foolish for having made the comment. Maybe it was just my over-active imagination at work. I dropped the subject and didn't mention it again. Maybe I was becoming paranoid.

A few of the families went out to dinner to a Thai restaurant in Virginia, enjoying a hot, spicy meal while rehashing the events of the meeting. There were minor irritations between State families versus military families, but despite our differences, we had to present a united front. The biggest difference was the sharing of information. For the Military families, they seemed to get almost daily briefings while we at the State Department very rarely were told anything. This made it extremely stressful between the two groups and made it difficult to feel we were all equal because one group knew what was going on and the other had no idea.

CHAPTER 9

April 25, 1980 (Day 174) At 1:15 a.m. the phone rang. It was Mark Johnson from the State Department. He told me there had been a rescue attempt, which had to be aborted, and that eight were killed.

I exclaimed, "Eight hostages?"

He replied, "No, eight commandos have lost their lives."

He explained that the plan was daring, and if it had worked, the hostages would have been free at that moment. He said eight helicopters and three C-130 Transport planes were to meet at an area named Desert One in Iran. The plan called for no less than six helicopters to ensure a successful mission. On the flight from the *USS Nimitz*, one helicopter was lost in a sand storm and had to return to the carrier, and one helicopter malfunctioned when it got to the rendezvous point. At this point, the mission was aborted because there was also a problem with the third helicopter. In the process of pulling out, one helicopter collided with a C-130 Transport and they both burst into flames. That was how the eight servicemen died. Five were Air Force and three were Marines.

I asked, "What happened to the hostages?"

Mark said, "We have no knowledge about them at this time. We just don't know. President Carter has made an announcement that the militants are responsible for the safety of the hostages and hoped they would not be harmed."

"Who would keep them from killing the hostages?"

He replied, "We will let you know of any information as it becomes available."

President Carter took all the blame for aborting the rescue attempt, but that didn't make me feel any better. The whole situation had gotten worse. Right now, I was concerned that the militants would retaliate against the helpless hostages. I prayed and prayed that Bruce would not be beaten or tortured and that he was still alive.

As I talked to Mark I was shaking violently. By now Bruce could be dead. I thanked Mark for calling and hung up. I didn't realize it then, but my phone went out of order. I learned later that the news media began calling the families at 2:00 a.m. and continued all night. As for me, news crews from Channel 9 rang my doorbell before 7:00 a.m. and asked if they could come in and talk to me. I bent down to pick up the *Washington Post* and scanned the headlines about the aborted rescue attempt. Jim Clark, the television reporter at the door said, "Oh, that's all obsolete. A lot has happened since then. Let us come in and bring you up to date."

My mind raced. That could only mean that some of the hostages had been killed. All that I could think of was that the terrorists had taken out their revenge on the hostages. I told Jim Clark that I had to call the State Department to find out what happened. It was at that time that I realized the phone was not working. I whacked the bottom of the phone, and right then, I got a dial tone and called the State Department.

I asked what had happened during the night and the Task Force member asked, "Didn't you get your phone call at about 1:00 a.m.?"

I said, "Yes, I did, but what has happened since then?" I was told the reports coming in didn't say much, but that President Carter was going to be on TV in about two minutes and I should watch.

I asked, "Do you know anything about the hostages, or if any of them have been harmed or killed?"

He replied, "No, we have no information on the hostages."

I was angry with Jim Clark for causing me such moments of agony. I got dressed, had some coffee, and then went to the door and said, "I'm sorry, I have no comment at this time. President Carter is coming on TV and I want to hear his explanation." I closed the door and went down to the rec room to watch. After about ten minutes, Debbie and Matt said that the press was still waiting outside and asked how they would get to school. I told them not to worry, I would handle it. Fortunately, the press left after about another minute or two without me having to confront them.

MEMORIAL SERVICES AND FEELINGS OF GUILT

For the next two weeks, the Iranians displayed the charred bodies of the dead commandos for the entire world to see, taunting the United States that Iran had the hostages and the U.S. couldn't do anything about it. The gruesome pictures were televised all over the world. It was hard for me to imagine what the families of the commandos were feeling, to see such heartlessness. My heart went out to them.

May 7, 1980 (Day 186) A memorial service was held at Henderson Hall in Arlington for the eight commandos. Pearl, Pat, and I went together. Many hostage families attended the service. As the chaplain read the names of the dead and the names and ages of the children who were left fatherless, the tears streamed down my face and I began to sob openly. My insides were in knots again. The guilt was too much to bear. Three men were U.S. Marines who died trying to escape their RH-53 Sea Stallion helicopter: Sgt. John D. Harvey, 21; Cpl. George N. Holmes, 22; and SSgt Dewey L Johnson, 31.

The five members of the United States Air Force who died in the cockpit of their C-130 Hercules transport were: Maj. Richard F. Bakke, 33; Maj. Harold L. Lewis, 35; TSgt. Joel C. Mayo, 34; Capt. Lyn D. McIntosh, 33; and Capt. Charles T. McMillan 28.

May 9, 1980 (Day 188) A memorial service was held at Arlington Cemetery in the amphitheater. I drove to the gate and was guided to a Marine escort who accompanied me to a parking area and walked with me to my seat. As we walked, he remarked that I must be very strong to endure the hostage crisis that had been going on for such a long time. When I answered that these families were much worse off than I, he said he wasn't so sure. My life was in limbo and would continue to be so until my husband was released. These families knew that death was final and the pain would be intense, but then they would go on with their lives; I would not be able to do that. I understood what he was trying to say but I felt very guilty that someone had died for my husband. He reminded me that these men had all volunteered for this mission.

President Carter and many dignitaries and friends attended the service along with the hostage families. The service was solemn, and again, I felt my insides churning. As the Air Force planes flew overhead in the "missing man" formation, I began to sob again.

FLAG MEETING

May 10, 1980 (Day 189) I went to the State Department for the official incorporating of FLAG (Family Liaison Action Group) to sign my initials, as secretary, in a circle that would be used as a seal to make us official. The other officers were Katherine Keough, President; Gisela Ahern, Vice-President; Bonnie Graves, Treasurer; Louisa Kennedy, Media Representative; and Penne Laingen, Editor of the Bulletin.

By this time, I was getting bogged down in typing the minutes from the meetings and other secretarial duties. Katherine called me and told me to type an agenda for the meeting and to have the minutes from the last meeting ready. This was not what I had agreed to do, but I tried to get both ready in time. I told Katherine at the last meeting I was getting overwhelmed typing not only one but two sets of minutes. After each meeting, I'd spend three hours going over the tapes, just to get them down on paper. She said she'd get me some help. At this meeting, she informed me that the minutes were already done and I just had to sign them. I objected because it would not be a true account of the meeting. Katherine told me the minutes I had been providing were too detailed and the people outside the Washington, D.C. area did not need to know everything that was discussed. I disagreed. They should know everything since they were involved. Katherine suggested I keep two sets of minutes. I refused. I didn't have that kind of time. She also told me not to name the person who made comments or suggestions. I felt very uncomfortable about the whole process and decided to step down as secretary. I directed my energies into mail delivery.

Ideas were given on how we could get mail in or out of Iran, and suggestions were made to contact Embassies of friendly nations to see if they could help in any way. Another was to contact the Algerian Embassy because they were taking care of Iranian interests since the breakdown of diplomatic relations. It was agreed. I would contact the Algerians.

INTERNATIONAL RED CROSS MEETING IN NEW YORK

May 14, 1980 (Day 193) I met with Jeanne Queen, mother of Richard Queen, to discuss the mail situation. No mail had come out of Iran since the rescue attempt. We decided to contact the International Red Cross (IRC) to see if they would intervene on our behalf. She said she would meet me at the Red Cross office in New York on **May 19th**. I boarded the shuttle flight for New York at National Airport and settled into my seat. It was then I realized that this was the first time I had traveled alone in years. It was very unnerving not to have Bruce beside me.

I was trembling and the man sitting next to me noticed my white knuckles and tried to console me, saying he had taken these flights very often and never had a problem. My trembling was not a fear of flying, but a combination of the fear of traveling alone, anxiety about the meeting, and the expectations I had about a positive response.

I arrived in New York without incident and took a cab to the IRC. The taxi driver zipped in and out of traffic at speeds reserved for the highway, and I was amazed we weren't in an accident. When we pulled up to the IRC building, I barely had the strength to climb out of the cab; my knees were shaking as I paid the driver and went inside.

The office was on the second floor and Jeanne and the Red Cross representative were waiting for me. We discussed the lack of mail since the rescue attempt and were told the Iranians were blaming the Red Cross for the rescue attempt because they had been allowed to see all 50 hostages. They'd do what they could to help but they weren't optimistic.

I returned home that night and hoped something good would come out of my efforts. But nothing happened. The news media had put the hostage crisis on the back burner. Days went by with a slowness that anxiety brings. The children and I occupied ourselves with the usual daily events, the church picnic, and other outings arranged by No Greater Love.

May 30, 1980 (Day 209) A letter arrived from Bruce in a brown envelope with US postage and a Prince Georges, Maryland postage meter cancellation on the stamp. Inside I found a typed written letter to me from Bruce and two inserts that I knew Bruce did not include. The shorter message from the militants accused the American government of preventing the hostage letters to be delivered to the families. The second message was titled "A MESSAGE FROM THE IRANIAN PEOPLE"

Dear people of America:

"Dear Fellow Citizens of a Just World:
"Have you ever seen your son's body roast sizzling on a hot iron bed? Have you ever heard the horrifying screams of your best schoolmate as his leg is being sawed off? Have you ever witnessed the heads of thousands of your fellow citizens explode with bullets? Have you ever received the news of your wife or sister's death under the torture of a broken coke bottle? No, surely not! Because even the sickest movie director has not produced such horrifying scenes in his thrillers. Yet the Iranian people witnessed all these and thousands of other merciless atrocities during the 37 dark years of the Shah's reign in Iran."

It went on for six more paragraphs, but I didn't read it. What did they hope to gain by putting this propaganda in my letter? Did they think I'd be swayed to their way of thinking? They were taking their revenge out on innocent people.

Father's Day

June 15, 1980 (Day 225) No Greater Love had arranged another outing for the families, represented by Kalps, Aherns, Lees, and us. First, we enjoyed brunch at The View restaurant at the Key Bridge Marriott. Next, we were treated to the National Theater production of *Showboat*. Before going inside the theater, the press surrounded us and did interviews. Debbie talked freely about her dream of becoming a Foreign Service officer like her father. The reporter was truly amazed that after the heartache, fear, frustration, and anger of this crisis, Debbie still wanted to be in that field. I was impressed with Debbie's calmness and maturity as she spoke. I marveled at how my children were growing up before my eyes and Bruce was missing it.

After *Showboat*, we were off to Tom Saris' Orleans House for more delicious food. Carmella didn't want the mothers to have to worry about doing any cooking today. It had been a most enjoyable day for the children who missed their fathers, and for the mothers who appreciated the activities that kept them too busy to dwell on their depression.

June 22, 1980 (Day 232) I still had not had any mail from Bruce since the rescue attempt and I felt myself going into a depression, but having children to take care of made it impossible for me to sink too low. I still sent Bruce sports papers, paint-by-number sets, little bottles of shampoo and deodorant, dried apple snacks, lifesavers or other goodies, but I had no way of knowing if he was getting any of it. Something just had to get through.

The continued stress was causing me to have some physical problems. I began having pains in my back and legs and found it difficult to sleep. I tried taking aspirin before I went to bed but four hours later, I would wake in terrible pain again. I knew I was restless while I slept, but I couldn't understand why there was such pain. I tried to ignore it, but then I began having pains in my jaw and cheek on my right side. I tried to take aspirin for relief. Nothing seemed to help. After an appointment with Dr. Bresler, he prescribed a muscle relaxant for me that relieved some of the pain. Someone had told me that continued stress could cause all kinds of ailments and I was beginning to believe them.

A DAY AT KINGS DOMINION

July 9, 1980 (Day 249) Another activity arranged by No Greater Love was a trip to Kings Dominion in Virginia. Carmella called to tell me that two employees from the Vets Administration offered to come with us. She said they felt they wanted to "do something." Carmella explained that both were Vietnam Vets who had been wounded in the war. Jim Mayer would come with me, and Corbin Cherry would go with Pat Lee. We'd meet at the Marriott in Roslyn and go from there.

I pulled into the parking lot and Debbie said, "There's the car!" Matt asked, quizzically, "Why are we meeting him?" I just explained that Jim wanted to come along. I got out of the car to introduce myself. He apologized that his car wasn't big enough to fit all of us, so he rode with us.

As he climbed into the car, he looked into the back seat and said, "You must be Debbie, you must be Matt, and you must be Chris," as he looked at each one. They were astounded! Jim went on to say he had something for Matt from someone in Texas. Matt took the package and inside was a plaque that said, "DALLAS COWBOY SPOKEN HERE." His eyes lit up!

As we drove, Jim told us a little about himself. He had stepped on a land mine in Vietnam and lost both his legs below the knee. He asked what the State Department was doing to help us.

I asked him what he meant, and he asked, "Is there someone to do your shopping for you and to answer your phone? Things like that."

I told him the State Department didn't see things that way. Foreign Service wives were supposed to be self-sufficient. He replied that in a crisis, no one is self-sufficient. The emotional stress sometimes hindered a very rational person's thinking.

When we arrived at Kings Dominion, we gathered at the entrance and Jim asked if anyone was hungry. The kids were all hungry, and he offered to place the order. With that, he walked over to a trashcan and spoke into the lid, "I'd like to place an order." The look on the kids' faces was priceless. They thought he was sick! Jim continued his ordering and when he saw he had their full attention, he gave them a confused look and asked, "Oh! This isn't where I order?" The kids giggled. They were beginning to see he had a great sense of humor. The rest of the day was pleasant. Pat and I took a short vacation from the children, letting them have some of the much-needed camaraderie of being "hostage children."

July 16, 1980 (Day 256) Three letters arrived from Bruce. This was the first mail I had received since before the rescue attempt. When I looked at the return address, my heart began to beat faster. All that was printed was:

Bruce W. German
Hostage - Iran

I knew then that Bruce was no longer in Tehran. I read the letters eagerly. He now realized he had not been getting all the mail that I sent and he was angry for still being there after almost 8 months and took action by writing a letter of appeal to Senator Ted Kennedy.

As I began the third letter, he seemed to be in deep despair. The second paragraph frightened me:

"When I think of the letters of appeal that I have written, and statements made which have all gone unheeded or ignored, I get so discouraged and very weary of it all. Especially since none of it makes any sense or is not accomplishing a single thing. So far, they have deprived me of being with you and the children, taken away my human rights and dignity, and stolen 8 months of my life. And at my age, time is something we have little enough of. If I sound bitter and unhappy, I am sorry, but under these circumstances it's hard not to. What our government has allowed to happen, and what's worse, to continue, is unforgivable and inexcusable. For the past 8 weeks I have felt as if I were enjoying the facilities of Lorton. You know, that vacation spot."

I called the State Department and talked to one of the task force members, relating Bruce's clue to where he was. The gentleman tried to console me that maybe that was not such a bad place to be because he was safe from the mobs that constantly gathered outside the Embassy. I was not buying it. I was worried sick.

Aug 5, 1980 (Day 276) I had an appointment with the Algerian Ambassador Malek's aide, Mr. Slim de Bagha, to request assistance in getting mail out of Iran. Very few letters were coming out of there and we hoped the Algerians could help. Mr. de Bagha suggested that I collect two letters for each hostage and he would send them to Iran through their diplomatic pouch and then wait a few days and request answers. I was delighted to make those arrangements.

THE FAMILY MEETING IN SAN FRANCISCO

Later that day, my mother-in-law arrived to stay with the children while I flew to the meeting in San Francisco. This would be the first meeting I would attend outside of the Washington, D.C. area. Ever since the aborted rescue attempt, very little mail or news had come out of Iran and phone calls were non-existent. I had to know the latest plans for getting Bruce and the others home.

Pat, Pearl, and I sat together on the flight from Washington National to San Francisco and although it was pleasant, we were apprehensive about the content of the meeting. What could they tell us? When the flight attendant asked if we would like a cocktail, we each ordered one. I did not drink very often, but I ordered a Bloody Mary and gave the attendant the money. Later, as she passed by on one of her many trips up and down the aisle, she dropped the money I had given her into my lap. I was confused. Later I found out that all the hostage family members on that flight were served a free drink.

Every minute of our stay in San Francisco was planned. We were escorted from the airport to our hotel, with heavy security around us. While our meals were served, the State Department notables spoke of the latest happenings, but I soon realized there were no latest happenings. Some family members began to show the effects of this long ordeal and tempers flared. They were angry and depressed and demanded to know why more wasn't being done. It became apparent that the military families were much better informed than the civilian families, which caused resentment and hostility. There were many times during the past months that the military families were told to get ready to move out to meet their hostage while nothing was ever told to the civilian families. Nerves were frayed, and many heated discussions ensued.

Finally, one of the State Department officials asked if anyone had any suggestions. He was dead serious. It struck me that my Government didn't know what to do. What a shock and disappointment.

There was one session on posttraumatic stress disorder presented by Commander Richard Rahe, a Navy psychiatrist that was more helpful to me than any other topic. CDR Rahe had worked with many POWs from the Vietnam War and shared his experience with us. He mentioned problems we may face in the months ahead after the hostages were released. He told the wives to watch diligently for signs of depression and post-traumatic stress disorder, describing some of the obvious symptoms including not being able to sleep, being jumpy at any noises that one was not expecting, feeling guilty for being helpless against their Iranian captors, and general irritability.

What helped me most was the emotional reaction timetable that he described of some psychological feelings that the hostages might experience, from gratefulness to being alive to becoming self-centered and feeling the world owed him for his suffering.

Then the emotional pendulum would begin to swing back toward the other side and the hostage would finally adjust to freedom and begin to lead a normal life. That stage could take up to ten years to complete. CDR Rahe said not all the hostages would go through those stages, but this was a very common behavior for someone who had been held captive. And if the hostage (or POW) had somehow collaborated with the "enemy" he would feel tremendous guilt after his return to freedom.

I felt enlightened. This was the first time that someone had given a timetable. I realized this didn't mean that a certain thing would happen at a specific time, but it gave me an idea of what I was facing and how long it might take.

CHAPTER 10

COMMUNICATING WITH THE MILITANTS

Aug. 20, 1980 (Day 291) I had received a letter from Bruce saying he had taped a message for me. I tried again to contact the Embassy to see if I could get through to hear it. Perhaps I could leave a message for him as well. The conversation didn't go as well as I thought it would because the militants kept dropping my call and they still couldn't tell me why I wasn't able to listen to a message that Bruce had supposedly made for me. I repeatedly called over the next couple of days but was greeted with excuses about the tape recorder not working.

I called the State Department to let them know that I had no luck getting through the way I used to. I felt I wasn't doing too well "for my country." It seemed the militants were pulling our chains.

FREE THE HOSTAGES-UNITE THE FAMILIES

For the past few weeks there had been a lot of talk about yellow ribbons since Penne Laingen had tied one on the Georgia maple tree on the White House grounds. Carmella LaSpada had contacted various people trying to find a symbol that would make the American people more aware that the Hostage Crisis was still going on. After coming up with a "Free the Hostages" pin, she asked me if I would give a speech at the ceremony dedicated to the hostages that would be held at the Georgetown University Quad under the sponsorship of No Greater

Love and the student government. I told her I didn't like to make speeches in front of people, but she coaxed me into accepting and finally I agreed. I drove to Georgetown University with Pat and Pearl. The program consisted of the ABC news correspondent Steve Bell, who was Master of Ceremonies, Judge John Sirica of Watergate notoriety and a member of the No Greater Love National Advisory Council, President of the Georgetown University Student Government David Goldwyn, Carmella La Spada, and myself. The ceremony was to emphasize the effect the crisis was having on not only the families but the American people, as well as prioritizing reuniting the families. It was called "Free the Hostages – Unite the Families."

When Steve Bell introduced me, I carefully made my way to the podium with very shaky knees. As I started my speech, a plane flew overhead, and I had to wait until the noise of the engine got quiet enough so that I could be heard. During the speech my knees were shaking so badly that they were knocking together, and I wondered to myself if anyone could hear them. The hardest part was to turn around and walk back to my seat. I didn't think I could make it without falling flat on my face.

Steve Bell came to me later and asked how many speeches I had done. I answered, "This was the first and it will be the last!" He was impressed and teased me that he'd have to be careful that I didn't take his job. No worries there.

Set. 23, 1980 (Day 325) The "Free the Hostages" pins were a big success. Hundreds of people requested them. A new shipment arrived, and I went down to the No Greater Love office to help package them. It made me feel good that so many people supported the hostages.

The next day I met with Bonnie Graves, wife of John Graves, and went to Capitol Hill to speak to congressmen and senators about the Hostage Relief bill that had been proposed. The Hostage Relief Bill proposal was created so the hostages would have certain benefits when they came home including restitution, Iranian accountability, and full health evaluations and treatment if necessary. We pinned Free the Hostages pins on each one as we spoke with them. I stopped by the office of Senator Ted Kennedy, whom Bruce had written to pleading for some congressional action to free him. Senator Kennedy sent me a copy of Bruce's letter dated 17 June 1980 in which he asks Senator Kennedy for "help and assistance" in expediting his immediate release. Today, the Senator was not in his office, but I left a pin for him with his secretary. Later that week I received a thank you note.

PSYCHIATRIST DR. HAUBEN TO SEE BRUCE

Sept. 25, 1980 (Day 327) I met with Dr. Hauben, the psychiatrist who would be seeing Bruce in Wiesbaden upon his release. Dr. Hauben wanted to know our family background, what kind of marriage we had, what the children were feeling, how this was affecting them, and other pertinent information. He asked how I would rate my marriage: as a good one, a bad one, or in-between. I responded that it was an excellent one.

"Why do you think that?" he asked.

"Bruce and I were best friends besides being husband and wife, lovers, and parents," I responded.

"Any disagreements? Arguments? How do you handle them?

"We didn't agree on some things, but we never argued about them. We just talked about our different views until we came to an agreement. I don't remember ever having an argument."

Later I thought about Dr. Hauben's perspective of my comments and was sure he thought I was under the emotions of the crisis—that we must have fought many times, but because of the crisis, I blotted that out of my memory and could only remember the good times.

Oct. 16, 1980 (Day 348) My car had been giving me problems and was expensive to run. It used premium gas and gas prices had skyrocketed to $1.50 per gallon. When Bruce left for Tehran, gas sold for $.85 per gallon. Gas shortages were making life miserable as gas lines formed at any station that had any to sell. Many stations turned customers away even though they had gas.

I began looking for another car that was more economical, but I was skeptical about going to a dealer without Bruce. Even though he knew as much about buying a car as I did, he was a man and there was still a stigma against women when they had to deal with salesmen.

After getting some guidance from parishioners at St. Mark parish, I settled on a Ford Fairmont station wagon demonstrator. I went to the State Department credit union for a loan only to be told that I could not get a loan on our joint account. I would have to open my own account since Bruce was a hostage and could not co-sign the loan. I showed the loan office the power of attorney that Bruce had given me, but she still said I had to open my own account. I paid the $5.00 required to open my account, the loan was approved, and I brought the car home that night.

Oct. 27, 1980 (Day 359) The first anniversary of the hostage crisis was approaching and there didn't seem to be any changes in policy by Iran. I settled into as normal a routine as possible. I sent more packages to Bruce—sports papers and magazines, playing cards, books, and snacks. It was life as I had come to know it. I longed for my normal life of so long ago.

I collected more mail from the other families and delivered it to the Algerian Embassy where I spoke with Mr. Slim de Bagha, picking up tidbits of information from him that the State Department had not relayed to any of us. Sometimes it was about the latest information coming out of Iran and other times it was just comments about Iran's politics.

I had not called the Iran Working Group for some time. I was upset with the controlled information the families were getting based on decisions of the volunteers. They decided what they would or would not tell the families. In my opinion, they had no right to know the information before the families, let alone keep it from us. Whenever I met with Mr. De Bagha, I learned more about the latest events of the crisis in 15 minutes then I did from the State Department in two weeks. I always shared what I learned with the other wives and mothers in the Washington, D.C. area. The State Department was not pleased, but that was their problem. I was not pleased with them either.

CHAPTER 11

IRANIAN MAKE THEIR DEMANDS KNOWN

Nov. 2, 1980 (Day 365) The Iranians came up with some terms for the release of the hostages and word out of Tehran was that the Majlis would release the hostages in groups as each of the terms of the agreement was met. They wanted the Iranian assets released, and they wanted an apology from the United States for meddling in their affairs. This was not acceptable to the United States Government or to the families of the hostages. We wanted all of the hostages released together. Who knows what would happen to those that were left behind?

Nov. 4, 1980 (Day 367 - One Year Since the Crisis Began) Well, here we were a year later, and nothing had been resolved. Bruce was still a hostage and my children and I were still living life in limbo. Not only was it the one-year anniversary of the Embassy takeover, but it was also Election Day. Many people were upset with the way President Carter had handled the crisis and his opponent, Ronald Reagan - with his movie star celebrity status - had a large following. As the days went on, it became apparent that the people wanted a change. Ronald Reagan was elected.

Father Basil had a prayer service for Bruce at St. Mark at noon. He had an especially beautiful sermon and I was so grateful that he was so supportive. He laughed with us and cried with us through the last year and I appreciated it more than I could ever express to him.

Nov. 17, 1980 (Day 380) The United States accepted Iran's terms "in principle" for the hostages' release. Secretary of State Muskie said the details had yet to be worked out.

I tried to decide whether I would go to Frankfurt, Germany when the hostages were released. But I wasn't planning on any particular day or time because there could still be a monkey-wrench thrown into the plans. It had been happening for all these months, so there was no guarantee that it wouldn't happen again. The State Department was really getting me ticked off. They did nothing but aggravate me with their plans such as having a lot of dignitaries greet the hostages at Andrews Air Force Base while the families were kept out of the way, and then the families would greet them. That was not going to happen if I had anything to do with it.

Nov. 22, 1980 (Day 385) Warren Christopher briefed the families at the FLAG meeting, giving details about the latest negotiations. Iran was still making unacceptable demands. The one-year anniversary of the takeover had come and gone, and Bruce was still a hostage. In one of his first letters, he said there was enough food in the Embassy commissary for about a year. If the commissary was running out of food, maybe that would end the crisis.

Nov. 23, 1980 (Day 386) - Deb's Birthday. Well, not only did Bruce miss Debbie's 16th birthday, he missed her 17th as well. She was becoming a young woman and he wasn't even here to witness it. Somehow it was harder to bear the second birthday without her father. Who would have ever believed this would last so long? We marked the day with the four of us going out to dinner. Thanksgiving came and went, and Bruce was still a hostage.

FLAG held a wine and cheese party on Nov. 30th **(Day 393)** to show the new offices they would occupy at 888 16th St. in Northwest Washington, D.C. The law firm of Covington and Burling represented FLAG and I assumed they somehow managed to get this space for us. Though I was not privy to how it came about or who was paying for it. I was glad that I no longer was secretary. I had no intention of spending my days downtown, and I didn't approve of the way FLAG was turning out. It seemed to me that some people wanted the crisis to go on for a long time so they could act like CEOs of a large company. That wasn't for me.

MEETING WITH DR. EWALT OF THE VETERANS ADMINISTRATION OFFICE

Dec. 7, 1980 (Day 400) At several of the family meetings at the State Department, we were told that the hostages might have adjustment problems when they returned. Jim Mayer said that Dr. Ewalt at the Veterans Administration would be a good person to talk to. He had treated many of the

Vietnam Veterans who returned from the war and had a lot of experience. I wanted to talk to someone who was an expert in the field. I made an appointment with Dr. Ewalt because I was not convinced that I would know what to do in any given situation of Bruce's readjustment to home life.

Dr. Ewalt was wonderful. I told him about some of the problems I was having with Bruce's family: being accused of trying to keep them out of the crisis and that I was only his wife, they were his family. It was taking its toll and I wanted to know how to handle it. I told him that besides being husband and wife, we were also best friends, and that we relied on each other for everything. I also told him we didn't have fights, even though we didn't agree on everything. As for my mother-in-law, Dr. Ewalt said that I had to face the fact that Bruce's mother was hurting also, and he thought she felt threatened by the relationship Bruce and I had. I knew she was hurting, but some of her comments were very hurtful to me and although I didn't say anything to her, it was eating away at me.

After hearing some of the examples Dr. Ewalt had of returning POWs, I felt much better about being able to handle any crisis that might occur. Our meeting lasted about an hour and a half and I left feeling much better than when I first sat down with him.

Dec. 8, 1980 (Day 401) In spite of the hostage crisis, life still went on. Debbie would soon be off to college! Since I never had the opportunity to go to college, I was at a loss as to what I had to do. The Family Liaison Office at the State Department had some counselors that could help me with the basics, so I made an appointment and talked with them. They gave me some information on colleges and scholarships. Still, I didn't feel comfortable about helping Debbie make a decision. Bruce should have been here to help her.

Dec. 9, 1980 (Day 402) Another meeting of the hostage families was held, this time in Alexandria, VA. It was another meeting of not being able to tell us anything specific. I was in charge of the Free the Hostages pins that No Greater Love had produced. They were being sold for $1.00 each to anyone who wanted them, but each family was to get 50 pins free to distribute as they wished. Luckily, I left them locked in my room, otherwise, they would have disappeared. Katherine Keough came to me and said she wanted a bag of them to give to someone, practically demanding that I give them to her. I told her no. I had promised to be sure each hostage family received one bag and I had only enough for each family. After much discussion, I agreed to give her one bag with the understanding that she was responsible for them. Katherine always tried to intimidate me and looked down on me because I was "only" a housewife and didn't have a job outside the home. I tried to ignore her patronizing behavior.

I came away from the meeting feeling very depressed. I didn't realize how some people would act. We were in this together and everyone should have respected everyone else, but we were a very diversified group, and I shouldn't have been surprised.

Dec. 16, 1980 (Day 409) Debbie had an interview at American University in Washington, D.C. We spoke to the counselors and then were given a tour of the campus. It was a very small school but had an excellent reputation. Since Debbie wanted to follow in her father's footsteps and go into the Foreign Service, American University had the best program for international studies. She loved the campus, but when I saw the cost of the tuition, I had my doubts as to whether we could afford to send her there. We would have to check out a few other schools.

Debbie and I went to visit the Georgetown University campus. It was further away than American University in D.C. but sat majestically on the banks of the Potomac River. The old buildings gave the appearance of medieval times, which was an impressive sight. Again, we spoke to counselors and had a tour of the campus. This was where I had given my very first speech - in the Quad - and it brought back memories of the anxiety I felt. I can still remember my knees actually knocking together!

Dec. 17, 1980 (Day 410) Here it was—Chris' birthday again. No one ever thought that his father would miss his 9th and 10th birthdays. This child had experienced more in his ten years than most. Through it all, he remained hopeful and reassuring to everyone that his Dad would come home, but I knew he was hurt that his father was not here. My heart broke for him. He asked if I thought his father would miss any other birthdays or holidays. I pulled Chris close and hugged him, saying, "God is watching out for your dad, just like he is watching out for us. He will bring daddy home when the time is right."

Dec. 21, 1980 (Day 414) It was Jim Mayer's birthday, so No Greater Love arranged for us to celebrate at Blackie's restaurant in Georgetown. Thank God for No Greater Love and all the activities they arranged. The children enjoyed their little support group and had a chance to forget the constant despair and frustration. The children also enjoyed celebrating Jim's birthday because he had been a Big Brother to them, taking them on outings to the arcades in Rockville and Springfield, VA and to various movies and events during these last few months. They especially enjoyed his out-of-control sense of humor.

Dec. 28, 1980 (Day 421) A meeting was arranged for the families to meet at Ambassador Malek's residence in Washington, D.C. When we arrived at the residence, there were hordes of camera crews outside, blocking the way into the parking area. I drove into the driveway, not slowing down any more than I normally would to get into a driveway, and then parked in back of the residence. As we left the car, the media came running toward us and I ran as fast as I could up the steps and into the residence.

At the meeting, Mr. Slim de Bagha handed out mail to a few of us that had come through their diplomatic pouch. I was fortunate to get one from Bruce. During the discussion, the Algerians seemed to think the crisis would be over soon. I had heard that before, starting in September 1979. Why should I believe it now?

Later that evening, I was invited to a Christmas gathering at the house of Katie Mikuluk's sister, Ann Groner. Her house was so beautifully decorated, and everyone was so kind to me knowing that this was the second Christmas that my children and I were without Bruce. I stayed for about two hours and then left, glad to have spent a pleasant evening. I went home with mixed feelings. Everyone at the party was very happy and talking about Christmas and all I could think about was my lack of plans. It was hard to imagine a happy Christmas without Bruce being here. I enjoyed the evening, but the reality of the crisis came rushing back. Bruce was still a hostage.

Dec. 31, 1980 (Day 424) Another New Year's Eve and Bruce was still a hostage. Little did I know last year at this time that the crisis would last this long. There were times when I thought about Bruce and couldn't remember what he looked like. I'd search for the picture that was taken for our church directory before he left for Tehran and be relieved that I could renew my memory. Why was this happening? Didn't I care what happened to him? Didn't I love him anymore? Why couldn't I remember his face—the face I loved so much?

Jan 5, 1981 (Day 429) Oh, happy day! Today the children received a Christmas card from Bruce. They were so excited. Although his letters to me were also directed at them, they were thrilled to get mail addressed to them. I knew Bruce was writing to them more often—they just weren't getting the mail, just as Bruce wasn't getting all the mail I sent. I was sure that only a small fraction made it to him.

Jan. 9, 1981 (Day 433) I made another trip to the Algerian Embassy to drop off mail. I just left it with the person at the front desk instead of meeting with Mr. De Bagha. It was becoming a long-hated drive down Connecticut Avenue to deliver the mail, but I knew I had to keep doing it. The hostages, and especially Bruce, needed as much mail as I could collect and deliver.

FRANK SINATRA'S INVITATION TO THE INAUGURATION REHEARSAL

Jan. 19, 1981 (Day 443) Frank Sinatra invited the hostage families to the gala rehearsal of Ronald Reagan's inauguration at the Capital Centre. I always liked his singing but never swooned over him as some teenagers did when he was young. However, I was really impressed with his hospitality and kindness toward all of us.

There were so many celebrities at this event; we were in awe of everyone. Most of them came down to our seating area and took time to talk with us, have their pictures taken with us, and sign autographs. The most notable were: Ben Vereen, Rich Little, Charley Pride, and Donny and Marie Osmond. Dean Martin, Ethel Merman, and Five-Star General Omar Bradley, who was confined to a wheelchair, also attended, but they did not come over to talk to us. I wanted to speak with General Bradley but was unable to get over to him before he left.

The news media announced that the hostages were going to be released and that two Algerian jets were standing by to take them to freedom. Later they said it was too late for them to take off. Again, it was a disappointment. When would this end?

CHAPTER 12

NEGOTIATIONS STILL GOING ON

JAN. 20, 1981 – INAUGURATION DAY – DAY 444

Day 444 and negotiations were still going on. The Americans decided to free up 8 billion dollars in frozen Iranian assets as part of the negotiations. Although the Iranians wanted an apology for allowing the Shah into America (and being a friend to the Shah for years prior), that did not happen. Another part of the negotiations included Iran not being held accountable as well as ensuring the families of the hostages could never sue Iran. Everyone waited for word that the hostages were freed, but there were more delays because the Iranians said it was too dark for the plane to take off. The Iranians stubbornly waited until Carter was no longer president before allowing the plane to take off. Then Ronald Reagan took the oath of office as President of the United States. About a half hour later, he made the announcement that the plane carrying the hostages had just taken off. The crowd at the inauguration shouted their approval and happiness. After 444 days, it would finally be over. The Iranians made sure that Jimmy Carter was out of office when they allowed the plane to take off. I still couldn't believe it was happening! After so many disappointments, I was expecting the media to come back and say it was a mistake. If it was true, my fear now was that the Iranians would shoot the plane down while it was in their air space.

Time seemed to stand still as we waited for word that the plane had cleared Iranian air space and would head for Athens, Greece where the hostages would be formally transferred to the custody of the United States.

People everywhere were glued to their TV sets waiting for any bit of information. Then. the plane was on the ground and the hostages were led off the plane and into a room at the airport where the papers were signed that formally transferred the custody of the hostages to the United States. To those of us waiting for word, this seemed to be an eternity. There were protocols to be followed, etc. The freed Americans then boarded *Freedom One* and headed for Germany. The news coverage continued all night, and as soon as the plane landed at Rhine Main AFB, coverage continued. Frank Reynolds interviewed me that night. The ABC crew had been at my house since early morning and I was really tired of the whole mess. They were camped out in my house for hours. I was frazzled because all I wanted was to see that Bruce was okay and they completely disrupted the household. They were supposed to do a short interview for *Good Morning, America*, but they had their connections to the studio through my phone lines making it impossible for anyone to call me, and that was an infringement on my time and hospitality. I should have given them a time limit to do their story.

Frank Reynolds asked me to identify Bruce when he came down the stairs of the plane. I pointed him out and Frank asked how he looked to me. I told him he looked great, but I didn't recognize the sweater he was wearing under his suit jacket. At that moment, the children and I celebrated with a sip of champagne that was provided by George Strait of the ABC crew.

We watched as the former hostages deplaned and boarded buses to continue their journey to Wiesbaden Air Force Hospital. Bruce sat in the front seat on the second bus and I strained to see him until the bus was out of camera range. Despite the freezing weather, there were hundreds of people standing alongside the road waiting to greet them with signs of welcome, flowers, and hugs and kisses. We waited anxiously for the returnees to arrive at the hospital and wondered how long it would be before Bruce would be allowed to call home.

At 2:24am, January 21st, Bruce called. What a moment! Debbie answered the phone and just squealed and chattered almost uncontrollably. Finally, I was on the phone with him and it was wonderful. We talked and talked and tried to catch up on everything that happened in the past 444 days. At 5:25am, we finally said our "Goodnights" and hung up which we did very apprehensively. We feared that once the connection was broken, we would not be able to contact each other again.

The next day, Ed Hotaling from Channel 4 asked me how I felt that Bruce was free. I responded that the crisis was not over for me. It wouldn't be over until I could put my arms around him and hold him. At that moment, I'd know that it was really over.

I went about preparing for our reunion. The plan was for the former hostages to have complete physicals and be examined by psychiatrists and have a decompression time. They would stay in Wiesbaden for four days. The families were finally able to make the preparations that they had been planning these long months. Hair appointments and shopping for clothes were paramount. The State Department arranged for the immediate families to stay at the Crystal City Marriott to prepare for the big reunion.

Bruce called to say his mother was upset that she was not included in the homecoming plans.

"The trip to the Military Academy was for immediate families only," I told him, "and if she lived with us, she would have been included."

"Why don't you demand she come?"

"No." I could tell he was stunned by my answer. "If I did that, then other families would be mad that their other members weren't included."

For those hostages who were married, the wives and children were immediate family. For those who were single, the parents were immediate family. I told him that we would meet her when we returned to the D.C. area. This was a very sore point and I found out later that when my mother-in-law was interviewed by one of the newspapers from Wilkes-Barre, she told them that I didn't want her there and that I shouldn't have done that to her. For her to publicly make that statement was very hurtful. Her comment to the newspaper was uncalled for. I refused to let her intimidate me anymore.

The children and I traveled to the Crystal City Marriott and stayed overnight on **January 24th**. On the **25th,** we were bussed to the White House to meet President and First Lady Reagan and Vice-President George H. and Mrs. Barbara Bush. After about an hour, we were bussed to Andrews AFB where we boarded planes that took us to Stewart AFB in New York. *Freedom One* was due to land at 3:00pm. We had about a two-hour wait, and as the time got closer and closer, the anxiety level got higher and higher. Some of the children did magic tricks and started a sing-along. One wife began throwing up; others showed signs of hyper-activity, pacing the floor. Tensions were mounting. It was almost more than one could stand.

When the plane finally landed, the families rushed toward the terminal doors, but they had been locked to keep us inside until the plane had come to a full stop. One of the military wives yelled out in salty language that she would break the door down if it weren't opened immediately. As the door was opened, I grabbed my children and hung on to them, telling them again to be sure they didn't fall or they would be trampled as we exited the terminal to the tarmac.

The door of the plane opened amid cheers and screams of joy. As each former hostage appeared in the doorway, the crowd became louder and louder. Finally, Bruce appeared, and Debbie let out one thundering scream, "Dad!" and he was able to pinpoint exactly where we were. He made his way down the stairs and over to us and hugged and kissed the children.

And then he was in my arms.

Now the crisis was over for me. I broke down and sobbed, but this time it was tears of joy. It was finally over.

We went inside the hangar and a chaplain said a prayer of thanksgiving. A few dignitaries made comments, but no one really wanted to listen to them; we wanted our reunions to begin.

Debbie, Matt and Chris talked a million miles a minute over top of each other trying to fill their dad in on every detail of the past 444 days. Bruce wanted to know everything. He asked about the kids schooling, bowling, and any other detail he could glean from them to make up for all his missed time.

Our Stay at West Point Military Academy

We went by bus to the West Point Military Academy, where we spent two nights. The buses traveled about 5 – 10 miles per hour and gave everyone a chance to wave at the hostages, some of whom were hanging out the windows shaking hands. The atmosphere was wonderful. America had come together in this ordeal and the spoils were hers.

While we were at the Academy, buffet tables were filled with food at all hours of the day and night. Food was plentiful. While Bruce and I were at various functions, the children were taken care of at the dorms. There was a game room where all the children could play video games for as long as they wanted.

We had dinner with the whole class of cadets at the Academy. There were the usual speeches welcoming the hostages home and a prayer of thanks for this reunion.

On **January 27**[th] we flew to Andrews AFB. There were hundreds of people there to greet us. As we left the plane, there was a line of dignitaries to greet us and shake our hands. The media area was roped off and it was a wonderful feeling that they couldn't get to us. Some called to Bruce to come over and talk to them, but he didn't go. We were told to board the buses that would take us to the White House to attend a reception to honor the "Freed Americans." As Bruce shook hands with the crowd, he was getting further and further from the bus and I got off to call him back because we were told the buses were ready to leave. I ran down the line and caught up with him just as a woman in her twenties put her hand out to shake his and then pulled him toward her and French-kissed him. I was not pleased, and I was at a loss as to whether I should ignore it or let her have a right cross to the chin. I decided to ignore it, but I didn't forget it. The thought of it still annoys me.

WHITE HOUSE RECEPTION

Finally, the buses were on the move and we inched our way down the streets of Washington, D.C. with the hostages hanging out the windows and waving to the crowds. It was a wonderful feeling to know so many people cared. The reception at the White House was a memorable one and some of the children got autographs from President and First Lady Reagan and Vice-President and Mrs. Bush.

After the reception, the buses made their way to the State Department where the colleagues of the hostages welcomed them with a thunderous roar. Bruce got off the bus and found his sports buddy, Will Robinson, who greeted him with a bear hug. They were so delighted to see each other.

The fireworks lit up the night sky at the Mall. The celebration and excitement continued well into the night as everyone chattered away, trying to make up for the 444 days without any real contact.

PARADE IN NEW YORK

Jan 29, 1981 One of the former hostages, Barry Rosen, invited us and the other hostage families to New York City to be part of the ticker tape celebration welcoming them home. We flew to New York and were warmly welcomed by thousands of New Yorkers. Our accommodations were at the Waldorf Astoria where we were made to feel like celebrities. The word elegant comes to mind. Each room had large flower arrangements, baskets of fruit, and a Waldorf Astoria cookbook.

The Mayor of New York, Ed Koch, had assigned a plain-clothes detective to each family for their protection. During the parade, Bruce and I rode in a convertible car with our detective Lou Polantis; Debbie, Matt, and Chris were in a second car with a sunroof, and my mother-in-law and Bruce's stepfather, Al, were in another convertible. At one point in the parade, a woman ran up to our limo and handed an envelope to Bruce. Before he could do anything with it, Lou Polantis examined it thoroughly before he let Bruce open it. The thought had never crossed my mind that there would be any danger from anyone. It turned out to be a welcome note.

It was freezing riding in open cars, so blankets were provided to cover us. It was brutally cold, and I wondered how the thousands of people standing along the parade route could stand being there. Being part of the parade was an incredible experience and something we will never forget. Since ticker tape is no longer used. people were throwing IBM sheets and IBM punch-cards out the windows. The parade route was knee deep in debris by the time the parade was over.

We were treated to two Broadway plays, *Sugar Babies* and *A Chorus Line.* we arrived late for the *Sugar Babies* show. The start of the show was held up until we arrived, but the audience didn't seem to mind and greeted us with a standing ovation. Many celebrities were in the audience and we had the thrill of being invited onstage after the performance to meet Mickey Rooney, Ann Miller, and the rest of the cast.

Each day of the weekend was filled with activities and meeting celebrities. Another first for us was having lunch at the Windows on the World restaurant in the World Trade Center. That evening we watched the fireworks from the 102nd floor. How amazing to look *down* to see the fireworks since we were up so high.

After the New York scene, we returned home to relax and get our life back to normal. Life had become so hectic. On **Feb 2, 1981** we were invited back to GEICO, so Bruce could remove the yellow ribbons that I had tied there during the hostage crisis. They wanted Bruce to cut them down once he returned, safe and sound. We had lunch with the employees and management and again enjoyed the very special reception we received.

SPEAKING AT THE CHILDREN'S SCHOOLS

Bruce made a commitment to speak at each of the children's schools as a gesture of thanks for the support they gave our children during the crisis. On **Feb. 4, 1981** we attended the assembly at Parkland Junior High as the first part of that commitment.

Bruce told the students about his experience and then answered some questions. The kids lined up to ask questions about normal things such as "Were you allowed to take a shower? Did you get food to eat? Were you beaten or tortured?" As Bruce answered each question, the students became more and more interested in every detail of his incarceration.

A big surprise for us was that Matthew got an award for academic excellence, given by all his teachers and the principal for his maintaining an "A" average while coping with the hostage crisis. We were so very proud of him. We were more surprised when Matt actually made a "Thank You" speech. He was very thrilled and proud of his award, and we were just as thrilled and proud of him.

Feb. 7, 1981 When Bruce first called me from Frankfurt, Germany the day he arrived after being released, he told me he had a surprise for me and he'd tell me about it when he saw me at home. I hated when he did that because many times, he'd forget what it was he wanted to tell me. But this time he remembered. He told me he wanted to become Orthodox. I asked if he was sure. We had been married almost 20 years and I would never ask him to become Orthodox - it had to be his own decision. I remembered the Easter service that was shown on television while he was a hostage, where he made the sign of the cross as an Orthodox Christian would: forehead, chest, right shoulder and then left shoulder. He explained that he never would have made it through the ordeal if it weren't for me and the strong faith I had. That was the one thing that kept him going, even when he was at his lowest point. After asking John Mikuluk to be his sponsor, Bruce was chrismated into the Orthodox Church. He was happy that at last we were a truly united family.

Feb. 11, 1981 My Birthday—a far cry from the last year's where it was announced the 100th day of captivity for Bruce. We celebrated as we usually did with a special meal for the honored birthday person and a home-made German Chocolate cake. Bruce surprised me with a beautiful amethyst pendant on a gold chain, but my best gift was him being home.

On **Feb 12, 1981** Bruce and I went to Peary High School for their assembly. Debbie, Bruce, Dr. Dumais the principal, and I sat on the stage of the auditorium with Bruce making a few opening remarks and then opened it to questions.

The gist of Bruce's speech began with the day's events: "Most people ask us what happened that day - Nov. 4th, 1979 - and I usually start with that morning. It was a Sunday morning, dreary, drizzling and already the demonstrations had begun. There was chanting, screaming, and praying, but that had been going on for the previous two weeks and we at the Embassy didn't think it was anything by which to be alarmed. At about 10:30am the demonstrators started coming over the walls, throwing rocks at the windows in my office. The glass shattered as the rocks smashed into them. I hurriedly gathered my office personnel together and guided them up to the second floor, supplied them with gas masks, and waited. The militants began pounding on the doors and after a while the Security Officer went out to speak to them to try and calm the crowd, at which time they said that if we didn't open the doors, they would kill him. At that point we opened the doors and that was the beginning of 444 days of captivity."

Home Coming in Wilkes-Barre, Pennsylvania

Feb 13, 1981 A massive homecoming was planned in Wilkes-Barre, PA for Bruce. On Public Square in Wilkes-Barre, a stage had been set up with many politicians speaking and one of Bruce's old high school friends, Tom Feeney, giving a short speech to welcome him home. I recognized many of my old friends and neighbors and tried to acknowledge each one. We went off to Edwardsville and Larksville with more of the same. Every politician within 50 miles was represented. By the time we got to Bruce's mother's house, it was after 2:00pm and we were tired, hungry, and needed a pit stop very badly.

At his mother's house, relatives, friends, neighbors and high school classmates greeted us with the festivities lasting well into the night. We were invited next door to the Catholic War Veteran's building where a band was playing and we danced to the "Green, Green Grass of Home." It was good to be back in Bruce's arms, dancing as we used to when we dated.

On Sunday, we attended the church service at St. Hedwig's Roman Catholic Church and Bruce's mother expected Bruce to take communion. Since he had just been chrismated into the Orthodox Church, he could not. His mother was very upset because she said she was embarrassed. Later, the priest told Bruce as we were leaving the church that if he wanted to talk to him about coming to communion, he'd be glad to speak with him. Bruce didn't go into any details about being Orthodox, but I'm sure he felt a bit uneasy about it.

Feb 21, 1981 We were invited to the final home game of the University of Maryland basketball season. As guests of the University of Maryland faculty, we were introduced and as usual we were warmly welcomed with the crowd thunderously cheering, "USA, USA. USA." Just to be there as the guests of the University was an honor, and when the Terps won, it was the perfect ending to a perfect day.

Later that evening we were invited to a party at Maria Melchiorre's house. She had delivered my mail to the diplomatic pouch when that was the only way to get the mail through and I couldn't thank her enough. I felt I owed her much gratitude for all she did for us. The only thing I remember from that evening is that one woman sat next to me and just asked question after question until I felt that my brain was fried from all the answering.

On Feb 22, 1981 It was our turn to show our appreciation to our neighbors and we held an Open House. They had collected money as a gift to Bruce and we wanted to thank them for their support during the crisis. It was nice to have neighbors meeting neighbors for the very first time. Some had lived in this neighborhood for many years but never met each other, and others were newcomers who appreciated the get together.

Since Bruce's release, our lives had been a whirlwind of activity, so we decided that as of **March 2ⁿᵈ** we would curtail our personal appearances and all the commitments and just go off by ourselves for a while. My mother-in-law came down and stayed with the kids while we took advantage of invitations we received from the St. Mortiz Hotel owner, Mr. Mechanic, in Miami Beach on **March 8ᵗʰ·** We were also invited to spend a week in Orlando. In Miami Beach, we ate at the very best restaurants, saw a few shows, and had a car provided for us. At one hotel, we met Tony Bennett and got his autograph for the kids. While we were in Miami Beach, Bruce got a call from his Aunt Betty who he had not heard from for many years. Bruce was extremely excited to hear from her. She invited us to her home and out to dinner the next day, and Bruce was thrilled to be with one of his favorite aunts.

From Miami Beach, we flew up to Orlando. We were provided with a car — this time it was a brand new 1981 Cadillac. That was first class! We were able to go to the Kennedy Space Center and even drove to see one of Bruce's relatives who lived in western Florida.

MARCH 15, 1981, FREEDOM DAY AT PEARY HIGH SCHOOL

A large, patriotic celebration was planned for Peary High School with a few politicians, neighbors, and local businesses honoring us. We met very informally with most of them and again received many kind words and wonderful gifts. I was very pleased with the genuine patriotism shown and wished that this celebration could be an annual event—not for honoring us but to honor America. I didn't want the patriotism to fade as it usually does after a few months.

Our Congressman, Mike Barnes, attended and told Bruce that if there was anything he needed help with or anything he could possibly provide for him, to please let him know. I thought that he was just being a politician, but when he gave us his home telephone number, I felt he was genuine. As it turned out, Bruce did need his help a few weeks later when the State Department refused to give him the home leave that he earned while in Tehran. Because he had not been overseas for 18 consecutive months, he was not entitled to home leave. So, Bruce spoke with Mike Barnes and he said he would do whatever he could. He promised Bruce that he would get his home leave even if it took Mike to literally introduce legislation in Congress.

The State Department decided to give Bruce administrative leave rather than home leave or as Bruce called it, "basket leave." His home leave would sit on the books until he finished his next tour. The fact that Bruce was only in Tehran sixteen months seemed to indicate that he should have been held hostage for two more months to qualify for home leave.

On **April 6**[th] Kenny Rogers invited us to the Capital Centre as guests of his show. He sent us tickets for a box of seats so we could invite 12 of our friends. We invited the Petros and Mikuluks. It was amazing to me when waiters came to take our drink orders and serve us in our seats. This is how the rich and famous lived. We were living in a dream and I knew that it couldn't last forever, but I was enjoying it as long as it lasted.

We were getting invitations from so many people in the area and we tried to accommodate each one: the comedian, Gallagher, who was very funny with his antics of smashing food, a Baltimore Orioles baseball game where each of the hostages were introduced before the game, and a gymnastics tournament starring the Marvateens group from Rockville.

There was a ceremony at the State Department on **Apr 13, 1981** where the hostages were to receive awards. I took Debbie, Matt, and Chris out of school and arrived early so that we could be in the front seats to see Bruce get his award, but Bruce Laingen receive his award on behalf of all the hostages. State Department employees who were on the Task Force got their awards and I waited for the hostages to be recognized, but they were not acknowledged. It was very disappointing. They were told to pick their awards up "at their convenience." I was very upset and my kids were very disappointed.

The State Department had made arrangements for the hostages to get together at Coolfont Resort in West Virginia as a way for them to see how everyone was coping. We realized that Debbie's senior class trip to Germany was that same week, so we declined the invitation. I was pretty uptight about her going overseas by herself anyway, even though her teacher, Mr. Clark, assured me that Debbie would be fine. But after just going through the hostage crisis, I was still very nervous about the trip.

As it turned out, she had a wonderful time and arrived back home excited about the sights and sounds of Germany and Austria. She was very impressed with seeing the grounds of the Van Trapp family from the movie *The Sound of Music* and being able to visit the garden where the movie was shot.

CHAPTER 13

WHAT IS "GETTING BACK TO NORMAL?"

A package about the size of a shoebox with Iranian stamps was delivered in April. It was all of the mail Bruce had received in Tehran. He had mentioned to me that while he was in Iran, he had written me a very long letter over the months as he moved from place to place. The militants wouldn't let him bring it home when he was released but promised to send it to him. The fact that they actually did keep their promise was a pleasant surprise. He scanned the letters and cards and found the envelope containing the long letter—all 22 pages of it. Inside the envelope were some dried Palms that I had sent him after Palm Sunday. He asked me to read the letter and to comment on all the thoughts he expressed throughout.

To say I was overwhelmed after reading the letter was an understatement. To have a 22-page letter written to me, that he carried with him on his many moves to various locations during the hostage crisis, said volumes to me as to how much he loved me.

I tried to go page-by-page, making comments as I went about his childhood, his disappointments, his hurts. I told him I could not imagine losing my father at the age of 11—it would have been so painful, and my heart hurt for Bruce. Everyone who had known his father, Arthur German, described him as a wonderful husband, father, and friend. Most of their comments were, "You couldn't find a better man or human being." He was a big strapping man of 6'2" and weighing about 200 lbs and was as strong as an "ox," as Bruce's mother had described him to me. He died at the age of 39 from a bleeding ulcer in a hospital in New York. What a terrible tragedy. At that time (in 1947) hospital rules did not allow any children under the age of fourteen into the hospital, so Bruce never had a chance to say goodbye to his Dad. What heartbreak he must have felt. I can't imagine anything so cruel.

As for his expressions of love, I told Bruce that just reading those last pages made me blush, even after so many years of marriage, but I was happy that he felt so strongly about writing them down. I told him I'd never have any doubts about his love for me. His comment about not being jealous of any woman ever made me laugh because during the crisis when he was being examined by the Algerian doctors, I told him some hussy would want his body because his bare chest was published in Time magazine for the world to see. He felt lucky to be alive, back home, and back with us. It was a wonderful feeling to be so loved.

May 18, 1981 Matt's 15th birthday—happier than his 14th. Our usual birthday celebrations gave the honored person his/her choice of dinner and dessert. Matt's favorite dinner was pork chops, rice, <u>Hanover</u> brand frozen Shoepeg corn, and blueberry pie for dessert. His best present was having his Dad home to help him celebrate.

June 1, 1981 Bruce went to Germany on temporary duty and missed Matt's award ceremony that was held on **June 3.** Matt received awards for English, Math, Social Studies, and Science. The award for overall excellence was announced and Matt's name was called yet again. What a thrilling moment for him and us. Of course, he was disappointed that his dad missed it but at least this time he knew Bruce would be home after his trip.

JUNE 11, 1981 DEBBIE'S CONVOCATION AND GRADUATION

Peary High School held its Convocation ceremony, which is something they did that other high schools did not. Since most of the students don't get to attend the graduation ceremonies, Convocation is a preliminary graduation where the undergraduates can be part of the celebration. Debbie was ecstatic to be graduating and going on to college. Her course of study was Spanish Translation. She loved learning languages and she had a head start in Spanish when we were stationed in Honduras.

She moved into the dorm at the University of Maryland on **August 21**[st] amid all the usual excitement and chaos. She was happy to be on her own and away from home. I supposed it made her feel grown up and was looking forward to freedom from parental rules and regulations. I looked forward to Bruce helping her with some of the decisions she would have to make, thus relieving me of that burden. At the same time, Matt had orientation for Peary High on the 31st and entered another phase of his life. Time was marching on and I wasn't really ready.

CHAPTER 14

THE FALL OUT – TRYING TO GO BACK TO THE WAY THINGS WERE

On Oct 22nd Bruce had a speaking engagement in Beverly, Massachusetts and later commented that because everyone there was very political and asked all kinds of questions on his political views, it made him uncomfortable. He never had been interested in politics and many times didn't bother to vote. Despite that fact, the one thing I did notice was that he really enjoyed the notoriety that the crisis afforded him as a "Hostage Hero."

Bruce had made arrangements to speak at a school in Pennsylvania on **November 11th.** I was extremely upset with him. How could he do that without checking with me first? Every Veteran's Day, Montgomery County Schools had a Parent's Day when parent and child spent the day together. Chris wanted to show his friends and classmates that his dad was home. It would have meant so much to Chris to have his father eat lunch at the school and be there with him. Bruce said he didn't realize Chris was upset, but he had already made the commitment. I told Bruce he should have cancelled because this was so important for Chris.

When he arrived home from his speaking engagement, he seemed different. He stood by the door at the bottom of the steps and had a very guilty look on his face. I asked if something was wrong but he said that it had been a long trip and traffic was lousy. He brought his suitcase up the steps and took it into the bedroom to unpack. When we sat down to dinner he seemed to be preoccupied.

The kids asked how his speech went and wanted all the details of his trip, but he said very little. For the next three days, he hardly spoke to us. The kids asked me what was wrong with him but I had no answer for them.

BRUCE'S BEHAVIOR BECOMES NASTY AND DEVIOUS

On **Nov. 20, 1981** at about 11:00am, Bruce was on the phone and I heard only "uh huh, I understand, uh huh, I understand." When Bruce hung up, I asked what that was all about and he said, "I have to go up to Pennsylvania to be a witness for my mother."

"When?" I asked.

"Next Friday," he said. The day after Thanksgiving. Evidently his mother had been cited for selling liquor after hours again and was possibly going to lose her liquor license because she had had so many citations in recent months and the fines would be extremely high.

I said to Bruce, "You can't be a witness for your mother, you're a relative." He replied flatly, "That's all I was told—to be there." He said his mother needed moral support.

Nov 27, 1981. Bruce announced he was going to Pennsylvania by himself. He didn't want me to go because "I had my nose out of joint for no reason." His behavior this past month made me feel our marriage was in trouble and I told him that. He replied angrily, "I'm worried about my sanity and you're talking about something that has no basis! Besides we can't leave the kids alone." We had left them alone before, so I was mystified why all of a sudden, he said this.

His plan to go up to PA on Friday and come back on Saturday changed once again. He called to let me know that Ben couldn't come from New York until Saturday and they were going to the lawyer's at 1:00pm that afternoon. Usually when we went to Pennsylvania, I always took things up to my sisters, so this time I had a box of things for my sister Elaine. I called Elaine the next day and told her that Bruce had some things to drop off for her.

She asked, "Where was he yesterday, did he say?"

"No," I answered.

"Well, his mother called here looking for him. I called Lovey to see if he was there, but she said she hadn't heard from him. Nobody could find him."

Something was definitely wrong, but I couldn't imagine what it was. He came home on the **29**th and said he met a friend but wouldn't elaborate.

MORE DISAPPOINTMENTS FOR THE CHILDREN

Dec. 10, 1981. Ben called Bruce and they chatted as usual, but then Bruce moved out into the family room and started whispering. I heard him say, "I'll go up on Tuesday and come home on Wednesday. I think Mother will like that." He never said anything to me about it. The following week I told him I'd like to go to Pennsylvania to visit my sisters after Christmas since I hadn't seen them since August. He said he'd go with me and I said he didn't have to because he had been there so often. He insisted. About two days later, he announced that we'd be going to Pennsylvania on Tuesday before Christmas and coming back on Wednesday. I told him we couldn't because the boys had school. He answered, "We'll take them out of school."

I said, "We can't—Matt has exams."

Bruce replied, "We'll take Chris out of school and leave Debbie and Matt home. I haven't seen my Mother at Christmas in a long time.

Dec. 22, 1981. Bruce, Chris, and I went to Pennsylvania. We took the suitcases and gifts upstairs, but Bruce and his mother stayed downstairs. Bruce still had his jacket on and said he was going over to the school that had sent him many nice letters from the day he had visited Voc-Tech. He left before 1:00pm, and Theresa left to go shopping. Usually she would ask us if we wanted to come with her, but this time she didn't. So there Chris and I were - alone in the house.

Four and a half hours later, the phone rang. It was Bruce saying he had met some friend. I was *angry*! I wanted to meet Elaine so he said he'd be right home. He came in at 6:00pm just as his mother was coming in with the groceries. It seemed odd that they were both coming in at the same time.

Dec. 27, 1981. His mother called to say she'd be down on Sunday to drop off presents. Why did I feel that this visit was preplanned without me having any part in the decision? We went to church in the morning and at coffee hour, Bruce came over to me and said that John Petro couldn't take my car to fix today because he had two others to do first. That struck me as odd because John had called me on Friday to tell me he'd take the car on Sunday. So, although I thought that it was strange because John never went back on his word, I accepted it as something that might be an emergency.

When we got home, Theresa called to say she was on her way and would arrive about 6:30pm. Bruce, Debbie, and Chris went to the bus station in Silver Spring to get her. She came in and talked to Debbie and Matt for about 5 minutes and then fell asleep on the couch. I came upstairs and Debbie said, "I don't want you to get mad, Mom, but Dad told Grammy he'd take her home on Tuesday." I went back downstairs, and his mother woke up. I asked her how long she could stay and she said, "Not too long." She said that when she came to Honduras and stayed three months.

At about 7:00am the next day Monday, Bruce woke me up and said, very apologetically, "I'm going to take my mother home. I don't want her to take the bus."

I asked, "When?"

"Now," he replied.

"Today?"

He responded, "Yes."

"Bruce, when did you decide this?"

He went into the bathroom and said, "Just now."

I retorted, "Bruce, you did not just decide this. You planned this long before this morning." He got very excited and said, "That's not true! That's not true!"

I replied, "Your mother came down here specifically for you to take her home." He became agitated and said, "Believe what you want."

I asked, "What about the kids? We can all go up to Pennsylvania with you."

He snapped, "They don't like to go to Pennsylvania and besides I want to talk to my mother about some things." When I asked what things, he said some things that were on his mind. As usual, it was like getting no response at all. I told him the kids expected him to spend the week with them because they were off from school all week for Christmas break.

When he told the kids, he was taking Grammy home, Chris said, "You mean to the bus station?"

Bruce said, "No, to Pennsylvania."

Chris had such a hurt look on his face, I could have smashed Bruce in the mouth. Bruce went out to the car with Grammy's bags and she gave the kids hugs and then came to me and said, "What can I do? He wants to take me home." I was furious; however, I thanked her for coming and tried extra hard to be pleasant. I did not want the children to see how upset I was. She went out to the car and then Bruce came back to the door and kissed me and said, "Don't think bad thoughts, okay?"

I asked, "Bruce, What the hell is going on in Pennsylvania?"

He replied, "Nothing's going on! Nothing's going on!"

"Something *is* going on."

He said rather apologetically, "Don't think bad thoughts, okay? I just want to get away by myself."

I countered, "Bruce, what am I supposed to think? Getting away by yourself shouldn't include your mother! We need to talk things through and if you are having problems, we should be communicating with each other."

He left, and I was really upset. I felt something was very wrong. The kids were very hurt by all of this and asked why he went to Pennsylvania without us. I couldn't give them an answer.

On Tuesday, **Dec. 29th,** I called Sue Petro and asked her if she wanted to go to the new Susan Kay Cosmetics that opened in Greenbelt with Katie and me. She said she had a lot of work to do so she couldn't.

I told her, "I should be doing a lot, too, but Bruce took his mother home and I thought this would be a good time to go."

She replied, "Yes, I know. John said Bruce told him on Sunday at the coffee hour that he was taking his mother home, so John couldn't take your car." That hit me! I asked, "Bruce told John that?"

She said, "Yes, why?"

I told her the story of Bruce lying to me and she said, "Oh, I hope I didn't cause any problem. I shouldn't have said anything."

"Well, did John say he couldn't take the car?"

Sue responded, "No, you know if he says he'll take your car, he does it." I was hurt and very angry and told Sue, "Well, Bruce lied and his mother and brother are involved in this."

When I picked Katie up, I was crying almost hysterically. She asked me if I wanted her to drive since I was so upset, she didn't think I could see where I was going. I said I was okay. I said, "That bastard! That son-of-a bitch! He lied to me and his mother and brother are part of it. They are bastards!" As I drove, I continued with a tirade of language I didn't know I could ever utter, but the hurt and anger were so deep; I couldn't help myself. Finally, Katie, said, "Hey, come on—try to get a hold of yourself. You're not doing yourself any good right now. Try to calm down."

I tried to pull myself together, but the tears came and went all the while we were out. I don't even remember much about the Cosmetic Center but was glad that Katie was with me. I certainly didn't want my kids to see me like this. How do you tell your children that their father, grandmother, and uncle are liars and are doing something so hurtful on purpose? How spiteful can they be? I had to accept the fact that Bruce was a pathological liar and his mother and brother were going along with it.

I called Jim Mayer and told him that things were not going well with Bruce and I and wondered what he knew about post-traumatic stress. He suggested I talk to Dr. Ewalt at the VA who would have had experience with these types of situations.

APPOINTMENT WITH DR. EWALT

When I went to his office, Dr. Ewalt again asked a lot of questions about our marriage, how we got along previously, how I got along with his family, how I would rate our marriage. I answered as honestly as I could. We had decided early in our marriage that we didn't want a marriage where we screamed at each other or threw things at each other. We both had experienced that while we were single. My father had a very bad temper, and although my parents didn't argue a lot, when it happened, it was scary. My dad would pound the table and swear at my mother, which upset me terribly. My mom told me that he had hit her across the ear once and she had a hearing loss from it. Bruce's mother and stepfather had many fights that turned into physical abuse; Al had once kicked her.

I told Dr. Ewalt that I was trying to cope with Bruce's mother and some of the things that had happened. He suggested dealing with our own problems before coping with my mother-in-law. He spoke about post-traumatic stress and that flashbacks that could sometimes occur. He gave me an example of some of the cases he had. He also told me that I should be aware of Bruce's behavior and that there might come a time while we are in bed when he may become violent in reliving some of his experiences during his sleep. I was to sleep with one ear open, as I did when I listened for my babies when they were first born.

I thanked him for taking the time to talk with me, and I did feel a bit better. I thought that if Bruce had PTSD, I would help him in any way that I could. I still, however, didn't know what to do about his mother.

FIRST ANNIVERSARY - FREEDOM PARTY

Jan 16, 1982 In honor of Bruce's release from Tehran, we had a party to celebrate the first anniversary. I worked for two days getting everything ready, cooking and cleaning to be sure the house and food were perfect. I made Chicken Kiev as the main course along with pierogies (some filled with potato and cheese and some with sauerkraut—Bruce's favorite), halupkis (stuffed cabbage), poppyseed rolls, nutrolls, and homemade bread. Katie and John, Sue and John, Pat and Gary Lee, Will Robinson and his girlfriend, Marge and Glenn Johnson, and a few of the neighbors were there to help us celebrate. It was a lot of work, but everything went well. Bruce, however, seemed to criticize everything I did. Why didn't I spend more time with the guests? Why did I have to have so much food? I didn't understand what his problem was. Later when we were getting ready for bed, I asked him if he thought the party went well. He answered nonchalantly, "What's not to like?" I was very hurt.

My birthday, Feb. 11, 1982 I made a cake for myself and the kids sang "Happy Birthday" and brought out their gifts to me. Bruce went down the hall and came back with a bag from Montgomery Ward. It contained a brown coat with a zip-in lining. I tried it on and it fit except the lining didn't fit the coat. I told him I'd have to return it for one that did. I thanked him and the kids, but it wasn't a special day. Last year he bought me a beautiful heart-shaped amethyst pendant on a gold chain. Somehow, I felt he just wanted to have something in a bag to show the kids he didn't forget.

Then on **March 1, 1982,** Bruce made arrangements to have a surprise party for his mother (or so he said), but the kids and I weren't invited. A few times I've suggested we all go someplace together, and he refused. The kids didn't know what was going on with him and had asked me several times what was wrong with Dad and why he didn't talk to us anymore. I told them that I didn't know, but as soon as I found out, I'd be sure to tell them.

PHONE CALL FROM BRUCE'S BOSS

Mar 15, 1982 The phone rang at about 2:00pm and when I answered, a male voice said, "Hello, may I speak to Bruce, please."

I said, "I'm sorry, he's at work. May I take a message?"

He said, "This is Bill Kelley from Eur/Ex. Bruce is not in today. I'm calling to ask him a few things."

I was shocked and repeated, "He's not in?"

"No."

I stammered, "Well, he left for work at the regular time. Maybe you should call Medical? He might be there."

Bill replied, "I'll call around and see what I could find out."

I was frantic! I got in the car and drove to where he usually parked for his carpool. His car wasn't there. I called Will Robinson, but he was at a meeting. I left a message for him to call me. I called one of his co-workers, Ray Scroggs, but couldn't find the right office number. I called Sue and told her what happened and I was very worried that maybe he had been in an accident. I didn't know where to look. Of course, his car wouldn't be at his carpooling site on Independence Street if it was his turn to drive. If he didn't, then where was he and could he possibly be in a hospital somewhere and no one knew who he was?

Sue asked if I thought Bruce might be so distraught that he would do something to harm himself. I told her I didn't think so, but I was very worried.

She said, "Well, it's raining out and maybe he will be home a little late due to traffic. If he's not home by 6:15pm, I'll come up and we'll start calling the hospitals." Just then, I heard the door open and said to Sue, "He's here" before hanging up the phone.

As Bruce hung up his coat, he looked over his left shoulder toward me and asked, "Did you call the office today?

I said, "No, why?"

He said, "Those girls don't always give all the messages."

I answered, "Oh, really? Well, Bill Kelley called."

Bruce looked shocked and guilty and replied very excitedly, "What did he want? What did he want?"

I responded, "It was 2:00pm when the phone rang. When I answered, he said, 'Hello, may I speak to Bruce, please? This is Bill Kelly from EUR/EX. Bruce isn't *in* work today. I needed to ask him a few things.'"

I repeated the rest of the conversation and what I had done and how worried I was that something had happened to him. I asked, "Where were you?"

"I went to that shrink," he replied.

"What shrink?"

"The one whose name I got."

"Who did you get the name from?" I asked.

He said, "Dr. Hauben."

"When?"

"Last week," Bruce said. "It was only the rough meeting – only the rough meeting."

I asked where the shrink was located, and he answered, "In Washington."

I asked, "So what did you do the rest of the day?" He said he drove around.

"All day?"

"Yes."

"Around where?"

"Around the beltway," he said.

Getting any information was like pulling teeth. I didn't believe for a moment that he drove around the beltway all day, and I felt he was lying, but I had no idea where he was. The next day I called Sue to let her know what had transpired and she was at a loss as to what he was up to. She was afraid he would harm himself if he were depressed.

On the evening of **March 26, 1982**, when I came upstairs from watching TV, I saw a suitcase at the top of the stairs. I asked Bruce, "Are you going someplace?"

He announced, "I'm going to Pennsylvania."

"When?" I asked.

"Tomorrow."

"Tomorrow?" I repeated. "The boys have their karate tournament tomorrow. You're not going to be there?"

He answered almost defiantly, "Nope."

Why was he acting this way—I felt that he was punishing me for some reason, but I had no idea what I had done to him. I was furious. I went downstairs and said, as loudly as I could so Bruce would hear me, "Matt and Chris, Dad won't be at your tournament tomorrow. He's going to Pennsylvania. We'll have to call someone and give them the ticket we had for him."

Chris looked so disappointed. Matt just kept his feelings to himself, as usual. Later the boys said Bruce told them he'd come to the tournament for a while and then go to Pennsylvania. He told me some guys were having a birthday party for him and that he had told me about it but I chose not to listen. That I did not believe. I said, "Isn't it nice that your children and your wife are not invited?"

He responded, "This is all guys—there's not going to be anyone else." I knew his friends in Pennsylvania—they didn't give parties like that. They just went to bars. Again, I felt he was lying. I said, "Don't tell me your mother isn't going to have something for you."

"She's not," Bruce retorted.

I didn't really want to believe that he was lying, but what else could it be? He went to the boy's karate tournament and stayed until noon, then left.

After Bruce came back from Pennsylvania and his birthday party, I found birthday cards in his sock drawer when I was putting the laundry away. There were cards from his Aunt Vic, his cousin Jean Stroyny, someone named Theresa Hahn, and one from his mother. I read hers and got angry. It said, "Bruce, you made me the happiest mother in the world because you're spending your birthday here with me."

March 31, 1982 was Bruce's birthday. Although he had acted so rotten, I made a nice dinner and his favorite German Chocolate cake for dessert. After we ate and cleared the dishes from the table, I brought out the cake with candles.

He got really nasty and said, "I don't want any singing. I don't want any singing."

I said, "Did you tell your mother not to sing for you when you were in Pennsylvania? I'm sure you didn't dare say that to her."

Why was he acting this way? He didn't even try to be sociable. The kids just looked pitiful as we sat and ate the cake in almost complete silence. Why did we wait for him to come back from Tehran only to have him do this?

PALM SUNDAY LETTER

April 4, 1982 - Palm Sunday. I came home from church with the children and went into the bedroom to change my clothes. I found an envelope on my cosmetic tray addressed "Marge" in Bruce's handwriting. Inside was a typewritten paper with no "Dear Marge" - just the body of a letter telling me he didn't love me anymore and that he wanted a separation. It wasn't signed. After I read the letter, my heart was pounding, but at the same time I had mixed emotions—a relief to finally know why he had been acting so strangely since November. On the other hand, I was totally unprepared for this.

I went down into the rec room where he was watching TV and told him it was kind of a relief to know what the problem was, but I needed time to think about his letter, to which he answered arrogantly, "It's not going to make any difference."

"But evidently you've thought about this for some time and I should also have time to think about it." I was in a state of disbelief. I began examining my actions to see if I had done something to offend him, but I couldn't come up with anything that would get this kind of reaction.

Family Relations Institute

The next day the tears came again. I called Lori Eisenberg at the Family Relations Institute (FRI) and told her of Bruce's letter and that he wanted a separation. She asked if I had cried in front of him, and I told her "No."

"Why not?" she asked.

"I don't like to cry in front of people," I said.

"I think you should call him right now to come home because you're in such a terrible emotional state." She added, "He can't just pick up and leave – there's much to be done before that." She suggested we both come in to see her four days later.

I called him to come home, but he said he had work to do and couldn't leave. When he came home, I tried to discuss his letter but all he said was he wanted out. He didn't want any responsibility, that I had to take care of the children, and he wanted to be able to come and go as he pleased. He went to the kitchen to eat dinner with the boys and called to me to come eat, but my stomach was in knots and I just couldn't.

On Friday, when we arrived at FRI, Lori introduced herself to Bruce and showed us into her office. She asked him if he knew why he was there. He answered curtly, "She asked me to come so here I am." Lori asked him many questions about himself and what he wanted to do.

"To go off by myself somewhere," he said.

"How about taking a month off?" Lori suggested.

"I'm at a new job. I can't take time off."

She asked a lot of questions about his childhood and what happened that he put such a wall up around himself. He spoke of his father's death and people telling him that <u>he</u> was the man of the house now, even though he was not quite 11 years old. She suggested he not make any major decisions until he had a chance to change some of the things that bothered him. After we got home, I asked him if anything she said made sense. He answered "Yes—but I didn't expect to be there that long." That told me that he was not really interested in anything she said. I just felt he was not the least bit interested in the children or me—he was just so self-centered, everything was "me, me, me." That was the phase that Dr. Rahe had warned us about.

ANOTHER WEIRD PHONE CALL

May 25, 1982 The phone rang in the early afternoon and a male voice again asked for Bruce. When Bruce came home, he sat down, ate, and never mentioned anything. Finally, after dinner, he went into the living room and stood looking out the window. I went over to him and said, "So why weren't you in work today?"

He looked very surprised and snapped, "I just took the day off."

"Where were you?"

He got annoyed and said, "I just took the day off, okay?"

At that point, I just couldn't contain myself. I said, "If you're going to leave then you get in there and tell your children," as I pointed in the direction of the kitchen where the kids were doing dishes. He got a bit uptight and said, "What brought this on?"

I replied, "I can't live like this. If you're leaving, you tell the kids—now!"

"What brought this on? What brought this on?"

"I can't take this anymore. You're like a shadow here."

"Why did you call the office anyway?"

"Because I got another weird phone call!"

When he asked who it was, I told him I didn't know. He asked, "He didn't identify himself?"

I said, "No."

He went down the hall into the bedroom and I followed him. I asked him if he did anything to change his hospitalization plan since it was open season. Because it was open season, we had the opportunity to change our health insurance coverage to any of the other plans being offered. If he didn't do it now, he would have to keep what we had and wait until next year's open season to change it.

He said, "No, you didn't tell me what you wanted."

"It doesn't make any difference what I want," I said, "because when you leave, I won't have any hospitalization.

At that point, Sue Petro stopped by to pick me up for a microwave cooking class that a few of the ladies from St. Mark Church had arranged. I came home an hour later and didn't bother going downstairs to talk to him. Later Deb came home from her friend's and asked what the big discussion was all about. I told her some of what was said, and she asked, "What did the word 'leaving' mean? - I heard the word leaving."

I told her that her father had written me a letter saying he didn't want the responsibility of a wife and three children anymore and he wanted to leave. She burst into tears and cried as uncontrollably as I had the day I got his letter.

Deb said, "I've always done everything, so he'd be proud of me, I've always respected him. Why does he want to leave?" She continued, "Mom, we waited so long for him to come home and I was so happy when he finally did come home and now, he wants to leave—why?"

I answered, "Deb, I don't know."

By this time, I was crying again myself. She asked me what had happened to us. I had no answer. She asked if I had tried to talk with him. I said I had and asked him to try to work things out, but there was nothing to work out.

Our Meeting to Talk

Tuesday, June 8, 1982 I had called Bruce at his office on Friday, June 4th and asked him if we could talk the next day. He said, "Oh, we haven't seen each other much and I've been meaning to tell you that I'm going to NY tomorrow." When I asked when he decided this, he said, "A few days ago."

"When will you be back?"

"Sunday. I can't take any days off." We agreed to meet on Tuesday for dinner.

When he walked in the house on Tuesday, he had a very pained expression on his face and said, "I feel lousy. I have a terrible headache." So, I told him to take something for it and then asked if he was ready to go. I knew his "Poor me, I'm sick" act was just that—an act!

We drove to Oscar's on Old Georgetown Road and Rockville Pike and made small talk until we got seated inside. We ordered a drink and our dinner, and I looked at him and said, "Well?"

He looked at me and said, "You know."

"You still want to leave?"

"Yes," he said.

"It's hard for me to understand why you are being so defiant. You haven't even thought about the possibility of our problems being worked out."

"There's nothing to work out."

At that point, tears began streaming down my face. We had already had our salads and a waitress came to take the dishes. Bruce said, "God, I hate to see you cry!"

When the waitress picked up the salad plates, she took a good look at me. Bruce whispered, "This isn't the place to talk about this. Wait until you eat because you'll only get yourself upset." I think he didn't want to be embarrassed—he didn't really care if I was upset or not.

We finished with coffee and left, driving around for about an hour with me doing most of the talking. I asked him questions about his feelings and his concerns about his job, his boss, and the fact that he did not get promoted. I asked him if he was still seeing his shrink and he said, "Occasionally." When I asked what he thought, he answered that the shrink thought he had a mental problem. Bruce would tell his psychiatrist his plans and supposedly the doctor would just shake his head.

"When you take these days off, do you call in sick?" I asked.

"Yes."

"And then your boss calls up and finds you're not home?"

"That's right," Bruce replied. "Bill Kelly really raked me over the coals because of that on my personnel rating. He only put 'Satisfactory' and when I asked him about it, he said he wouldn't change it. And I didn't sign it either."

I asked, "When you take time off where do you go?"

"I ride around the Beltway."

I felt I had to ask, "Bruce, is there someone else? Have you found someone else?"

"No, it would be a lot simpler if I had."

"Had I done something to you?"

"No."

"What has happened to us?" I pleaded. "We were best friends. You always said I was your sounding board."

"Those days are gone forever."

"Did your Mother know I was in Pennsylvania last week?" I asked him through my pain somehow. He said she did but didn't know much of what was happening.

"I told her we're having our problems," Bruce replied, "She said to work it out the best we could." Why didn't I believe that?

Dear Marge,

Try not to be worried. We are quite well. We are fed fairly well. Ask the children to be good in the period of my absence, I love them.

They have told us that they only want the SHAH, and if CARTER prefers us to SHAH, we will be released. Do what you can to make that happen.

I hope you have enough money. I would like to meet you very soon. Pray that we have a safe return soon.

All my love,
Bruce

Sorry, this letter is written by moslem students.   (excuse us.)

One of Bruce's first letters written by the militants that he was only allowed to sign.

Marge with President Carter and Secretary of State Vance at State Department for a meeting with the families.

Some families gather at the Wye Oak Tree (the largest White Oak Tree in the United States located in Talbot County, Maryland) to tie a yellow ribbon around the tree trunk with Governor and Mrs. Hughes.

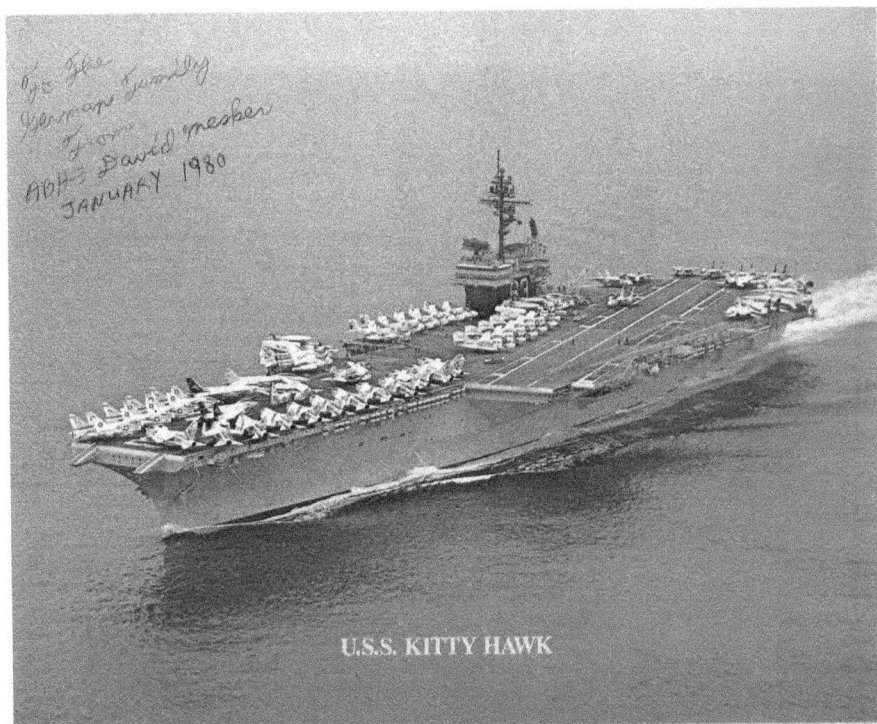

To The
German Family
From
ADH-3 David mesken
JANUARY 1980

U.S.S. KITTY HAWK

The sailors on the USS Kitty Hawk sent hundreds of letters to the German family.

Tie a Yellow Ribbon

Marge German (left), wife of Iranian hostage Bruce German, thanked those surrounding her for their support last Friday at a ceremony at GEICO Plaza in Chevy Chase.

During the festivities employees and residents tied yellow ribbons and yellow flowers around the trees on the company's grounds below. The employees themselves came up with the idea because of the lack of any such activities in the area lately.

The prisoners have remained in captivity almost 400 days since the takeover of the American Embassy by student militants.

Staff Photos by Linda White

My second speech - given

Marge was invited to a yellow ribbon tying ceremony at Geico Plaza in Chevy Chase, Maryland with the understanding that Bruce would untie her ribbon when he returned.

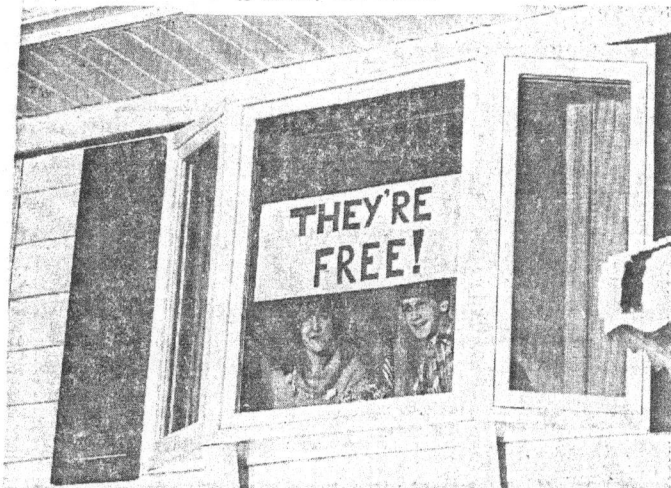

Debbie displays sign she made
as soon as she heard that
Bruce was on the plane enroute
to Greece, from Tehran, Iran.

Two of Bruce German's children, Debbie, 17, and Matthew, 14, proclaim their happiness at their home in Kensington.

Sandra Rosen for The Washington Star

Wife May Travel to Meet Husband

By Joan Lowy
Washington Star Staff Writer

Hostage wife Margarite German finally came to believe yesterday what she has refused to allow herself to accept for the past year — that her husband is on his way home to her at last.

All through the last week's reports of agreement and rumors of departure, German has maintained she wouldn't believe any of it until her husband, government budget officer Bruce German, was "out of Iranian air space and actually free."

Even as late as yesterday morning, reporters calling German at her Kensington home received a taped message that said she still didn't consider her husband released, despite the American-Iranian agreement.

And as television crews hauled cameras in and out of her home all afternoon and reporters sat on her doorstoop, German maintained her cautious restraint in case there might be one more "last minute hitch."

"You never know," she said later, "with things how they are over

there. I kept thinking someone might set off a bomb at the airport, try to shoot them down or slash the plane's tires."

But shortly before 2 p.m. yesterday came that long-awaited call — the State Department phoning to say an Algerian plane carrying her husband had taken off from Tehran airport and cleared Iranian airspace.

"This is the day we've been waiting 14½ months for," German said after learning of the release. "It is a day of thanksgiving and prayer.

"I especially want to thank the American people, who have been through so much with us and stood behind us. That's what has really helped. That and my neighbors, of course, who have just been wonderful."

"I still can't fully believe it. It all hasn't sunk in yet," said German, 45, smiling as she sat with her three children on the family-room couch in front of the television set where they have spent much of the last week.

"Until I can see him, touch him and hug him, it won't be over. I know when I finally do see him I'll

probably get hysterical," she said.

German said she is considering traveling to West Germany to see her husband, despite advice from the State Department that the families first give the hostages some time to recoup.

"I don't agree with that," German said. "I feel I know my husband a little better than they do and I think he'll want me there. But we'll see what he has to say when I talk to him tonight.

"If he wants me to come, I'll be on the next plane out of here."

German said her 17-year-old daughter, Debbie, has already packed a suitcase for her for the trip.

"She keeps telling me, 'Mom, he's going to want you to come and be with him, Mom,'" German said.

"I probably would have gone over there already, but the timing of this thing has been so impossible — first they're on the plane, then they're not on the plane, I wanted to be sure before I went."

German said she disagrees with psychiatrists who have said the hostages will need time by themselves to deal with their release from captivity.

Debbie displays a sign she made as soon as she heard that Bruce was on the plane, enroute to Greece from Tehran, Iran.

Bruce with his entire family celebrating being reunited

Weekly Reader

EYE Edition 9 • Vol. 59 • Issue 18 • Feb. 27, 1991

My Dad Is HOME

Chris makes the cover of the
Weekly Reader magazine when
he is interviewed after
Bruce was released.

**Fifth grader Chris German
talks about his dad,
a former hostage.**

See pages 4-5

Chris featured with his dad on the cover of the Weekly Reader (a weekly educational
classroom magazine designed for children).

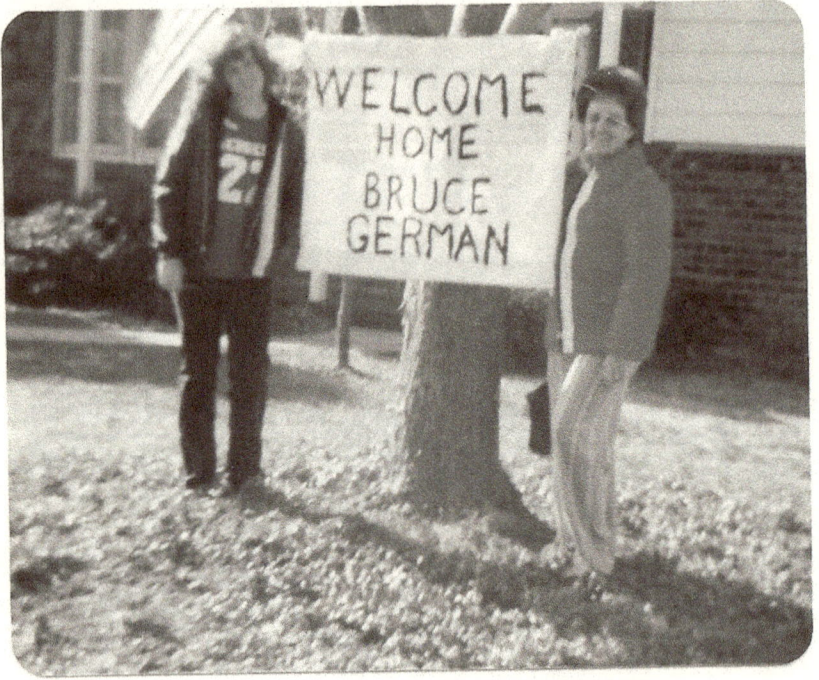

Debbie and Marge letting everyone know that Bruce was free.

Bruce surrounded by his children on a plane to New York for the ticker tape parade

CHAPTER 15

NOT HAPPILY EVER AFTER

Saturday, June 12, 1982. Bruce woke me up at 7:10am to go to Baltimore for jury duty. I went into the bathroom to wash my face and when I came out, I saw his suitcase. I came into the kitchen and asked, "Are you going somewhere?"

He said, "To my mother's."

"Why didn't you tell me?"

"There's no need!" he responded.

I was gritting my teeth as I responded, "There *is* a need! I need to know if you'll be here or not so I can plan accordingly."

He said, "Well, I'm going to my mother's."

"Why, is it time for your breastfeeding?"

"I told you I wanted to leave," he responded

"Whether you want to leave or not, that's no reason to treat me like this. I don't deserve this!"

He sort of agreed, saying, "You're right; I have no right to treat you like this. Come on, I'll take you to Baltimore."

I told him to go to his mother's—that I could find my way to Baltimore myself. I had done it before—I could do it again.

Sunday, June 13, 1982 Bruce returned home from Pennsylvania.

"You must think I'm crazy," Bruce said to me.

I began, "Do *you* think you're crazy? Are we making you crazy? If so, are you in therapy? What are you doing to prevent it? What are you doing to help yourself? I don't believe you're crazy. I believe you have a choice about what you're doing. You have a choice!

These are your children, too. I didn't have them alone. Do you know what you're doing to Chris, Matt, and Debbie? Do you think this isn't affecting Matthew? Just because he's quiet do you think he's not torn up. What about Chris? He's 11-years-old, the same age you were when you lost your father. You should know how he feels. But the difference is your father did not choose to die. You are choosing to leave. Do you think they'll ever get over this? They'll never get over this because you are choosing to do this. As for Debbie, her emotional well-being is at risk because of this. College is hard enough without this turmoil. She has a special relationship with you and she can't understand why you are treating us this way.

You helped to bring these children into this world and it's your responsibility to protect them—not to cause wounds and scars that will never heal. They waited for you, they love you, they've been proud of you and want you to be proud of them, but you are choosing to reject them. You don't talk to them; you don't want to live with them. Bruce, we don't deserve this kind of treatment.

And what about me? What's going to happen to me? Do you think I ever prepared for my life without you? At one point in my life I would have died for you—no questions asked! I've never loved anyone else. There isn't anything I wouldn't have done for you. You are destroying your whole family—you don't have to do this. Why are you doing this? We aren't your enemy—we're the ones who love you. I can't even think, I can't concentrate, and I'm not prepared for a career. And no matter what you've ever done, I've supported you in your career.

You are going to have to tell the kids not only that you're leaving, but also why you're leaving. You must tell them what it is about them or about me that is so awful that you cannot love us or want to be with us. You can be sure that this, for us, is overwhelming rejection of us—a family who is worthy of your love. We don't deserve this!

If you really think there's something wrong with your mind, then get help, but don't abandon and destroy your family. You may think we may get over this, but we never will. We have loved you and waited for you and have no way to understand not being loved in return. Is it that you've become so much of a celebrity that we've become worthless to you? Do you feel that you are so important that we are an embarrassment to you?

All the years I've known you, I've done my very best to do what was best for you and the kids. We were partners. I don't know what's happened to you. I don't know what to do, but if you leave without trying to get help or trying to understand our feelings, it will be devastating. How can you reject us like this and cause this kind of pain? The scars will never heal. It's not enough to tell the kids you're leaving. If they can't understand it, if they don't know why, they will think that they are not lovable and are not worthy of your love; that they are not good enough for you. The damage to them—losing their father in this way, by his own choice, will last a lifetime.

You asked me to promise that I would not turn the children against you, but you are doing a good job of that yourself. How many times have you run up to "mommy" and left us here by ourselves—rejecting us even then? You preferred your mother to your children. When your mother came to visit specifically so you could take her back home during the Christmas vacation, you wouldn't even let us come with you. You could have spent time with your children that week that they were off from school. They were devastated. You are mean and selfish!

And did you act at your mother's the way you acted here on your birthday? Did you tell your mother you didn't want any singing? Did you refuse to come out and even see your birthday cake the way you did here? Then you say your mother is not involved? And don't lie to me and say that your mother didn't have a party for you. Your mother succeeded in breaking up our marriage and God does not sleep. I shudder to think what lays in store for her.

You may think we're stupid, but believe me, even our 11-year-old knows when he's being rejected. And what about your commitment to God? You promised many things while you were in captivity. Now that you're safe and free, you've forgotten Him. He hasn't forgotten you, Bruce. And when you tell me to get a job, you aren't being realistic if you think I can. My skills are obsolete. I've been out of the job market too long. I'll need training to compete in this world.

You said you weren't good at hiding your feelings and yet in the next sentence you say the letters of love from Tehran were lies. How can that be? You must have been hiding your real feelings pretty good then.

I'll ask you again, Bruce. Do you have a girlfriend? I must know the truth— or perhaps the stay in Iran really changed you and you have a boyfriend. Your actions tell me there's someone. Be honest - no matter how painful it will be - instead of being deceitful. I can handle the truth; it's the lies that I can't take.

Is the reason you are acting this way due to delayed reaction to the crisis? Is it depression? What are you really worried about—what is too scary to confront? It makes me feel that you never cared about the kids or me. You have to respect the emotional feelings of your children. If this was just you and me it would be different, but with children, we have a responsibility to them. The kids and I went to great lengths to show you that you were not forgotten. Now you are deliberately showing us you are unconcerned about us. Everything that's happened has embarrassed us; people from your office calling here, you lying to them and us, and then me finding out you've been lying to me. You're a shadow around the house, acting devious and deceitful, like it's a secret. You put us in an embarrassing position."

He chose to not make any comments whatsoever while I said all of this to him. When I was finished, he only had a few things to say. "It crushes me to think you might think I am gay. That really hurts!" He also said the crack I made about his mother was uncalled for. "My mother would never do anything to hurt you." I said, "Oh, Bruce, you have no idea." He replied, "Don't tell me, I can't handle it right now." I said, "You don't know, that's right." Most of his other comments were, "I don't know why." Or he just didn't comment.

Sunday, June 27, 1982 I went to church and found another letter from Bruce on my dresser when I got home. I told him I wouldn't read it unless he was there with me. He was getting ready for bed and I decided that that was the opportune time to read it. I made comments as I went along and asked questions. He gave me some vague answers and some direct ones.

I asked, "What is it that I did to you?"

"Well," he started, "first, you ruined my career. Secondly, are you even satisfied with your appearance because I'm ashamed to be seen with you. And third, I'm tired of not having money. I want out. I don't want the responsibility of a wife and three kids." I told him, "There is no way I could have ruined your career. Because I had spoken to Sheldon Krys about Bruce's lack of promotion, Bruce blamed me for his career being ruined. As for the money, we have bills to pay. We must pay our bills first before spending money on anything else. We also have three kids who we must provide for."

June 28, 1982, I met with Lori again and told her of the latest events. She was pleased to know I finally got a reason for his actions. I relayed his wish to meet with her soon, so we could tell the children. The next day I met with Heidi Hoffman at A Woman's Place and worked on my resume. I need to get a job quickly since it seemed I would be alone soon.

June 30, 1982, I had an appointment with a lawyer to find out what my entitlements were. He said the children are not to be moved from their surroundings and the law in Maryland states that I can stay in the house with them for three years after the divorce is final. I told the lawyer that this was a trial separation. He responded with, "I hope you realize that most trial separations end in divorce—only a few are ever reconciled. I hope yours is one of them."

He asked me a lot of questions about the children, how this would affect them in my opinion, whether there would be a custody battle, and how we were financially. I told him I thought the children would really be affected since Bruce didn't want the responsibility and restrictions of child custody. He asked if we had any savings. When I answered yes, he suggested that I go to the credit union and take it all out. I told him I could never do that. He said, "If you don't, he will." I said that I thought I knew Bruce well enough that he would never do that. He shook his head and said, "I've seen it too many times."

July 18, 1982, I found a note on my dresser saying he was moving some of his clothes out to Will Robinson's. Somehow, I just didn't believe him. I went to church by myself, leaving the kids at home so that he could tell them he was leaving. He went to St. Jude's and when he returned and found the kids were here, he paced back and forth and then left. He was back at 2:30 pm. That surprised me—I thought he'd be out all day. Later, he said he couldn't find his shot record and when I didn't offer any information, he said he looked in the fireproof box and it was empty. He asked what I did with the insurance policies. I told him I put them away.

"Why?" he asked.

"Because you have something of mine."

"What?" he asked.

"Some letters and tapes," I told him. He looked shocked that I had caught him, and he said, "I'll give them back to you." When I asked why he took them, he didn't answer. Instead, he went into the bedroom. This was his way of ignoring me and letting me know that that was the end of the conversation, but I went after him.

I said again, "You still haven't answered my question."

He responded, "Marge, I don't know why I took them. I do a lot of strange things and I don't have an answer for why I do them."

"I never thought you'd be so sneaky," I said.

Agitated, he answered, "Well, you won't have to put up with me too much longer. I'll be gone—out of your way." He had to express righteous indignation as his defense—still playing the "poor me—a hostage and you don't care" card.

July 22, 1982 The phone rang. It was Ben. He asked to speak to Bruce, so I handed the phone to him and went down into the rec room. After Bruce got off the phone, he came downstairs with a contrived pained look on his face. He was such a poor actor it was almost funny. I asked what was wrong. He said his mother had received another citation for selling liquor after hours and that this time it was very serious. She was going to be arrested and would have to go on

Tuesday to be fingerprinted. Since Bruce's name was on the license, he would have to appear also and be fingerprinted. The lawyer said that if they said they were going to sell the business; it would be better. I didn't believe a word he said. The whole mess sounded very fishy to me, especially after the way he had been acting. It was another excuse to go to Pennsylvania. I began to think he really had some emotional problems.

While we were in the rec room, I brought up the child custody situation. We talked for an hour and a half about how we would handle it. I suggested split custody: he'd have the kids for six months and I'd have them for six months. Bruce said he'd like that arrangement but wondered how he would do it. I replied that I'd live in the house for six months and then he could live in the house for six months. That way the kids would not be moved out of their environment. He asked how that would work. I replied that we would really have to work at it. He continuously would ask me if I had found a job yet. I told him that I was too old to start a career since I was having a hard time finding a job. I had no idea how I could support myself. He said it was the economy and maybe I should start a bakeshop. I said, "Oh, you mean you still like my cooking?" He said, "Sure—that would be a hell of a reason to leave."

He mentioned our appointment with Lori Gordon which included the kids this time. Lori insisted that Bruce not be allowed to walk out of our marriage and our life – things had to be settled first.

I asked him about the love letters he wrote, telling me of his love and he answered that he probably meant them when he wrote them. That didn't explain why he suddenly changed into this very distant, hateful, sneaky, and deceitful person.

July 24, 1982 When I returned home from a family's member's funeral, I noticed that some of Bruce's clothes were gone. He also took all his hostage memorabilia. That surprised me because he said he wanted to forget all that. When I asked him about it, he said he put it in storage someplace. Another lie.

I asked him when he was leaving, and he answered, "Sunday."

"What time?" I asked.

"I wanted to do that while everyone was in church," he answered.

I put my foot down. "You will NOT do that to your children. They will really think that you've abandoned them." Again, he was playing the poor me victim, "I can't face them." I was having none of it. "You have to. They'd never forgive you."

When I asked him what else he took from the house, he said some books because he needed something to read. Then I asked how long he'd be staying with Will. He replied, "I'm afraid that will be very temporary. He's a nice guy and he's willing to help out, but I feel funny about it."

"Did the kids see you taking your clothes?" I asked.

He said, "No, they were sleeping when I left."

"Did you take all your papers out of the night table?"

"Yes, I just put them in my briefcase. I don't even know what's in there."

I had to finally realize that he had become a pathological liar. Every time he opened his mouth, out came lies. I looked around and found the toothpaste, razor blades, and other toiletries I had just purchased were gone. He was like a damn thief. If he wanted this separation, the least he could do was be man enough to face me and tell me what he was taking. He took the blue and white bath towel set that I bought when I worked at Sears, Roebuck, and Company and the homecoming album that I had put together with pictures of me with Metropolitan Iakavos while we were in New York, something that meant nothing to him.

July 26, 1982 I called Bruce at the office to ask him what happened to the deed to the house. He said he didn't have it. While we talked, I told him, "For someone who was getting reacquainted with God, he wasn't doing very Christian things."

He complained, "Boy, you're really giving it to me today!"

"If you think you need help," I said, "get it."

Again, he said, "You really are giving it to me!"

I asked, "Why? Because I said if you think you need help you should get it. I don't think that's giving you anything. I feel like I've been stabbed in my heart!"

When he came home from work, I went to Rosie's and picked up Deb. We ate in almost total silence—no one really wanting to talk. Bruce finished eating and left the table. When everyone was finished, I went into the bedroom and found him reading his bible. I said, "Now is the time" and called the kids into the living room. Bruce told them that what he had to say would be very difficult.

He started by saying, "You all know I've been having a lot of emotional problems, and I haven't been totally truthful with you. But I want you to know I love you guys—I really do."

"I need to leave because I need answers that I can't get here," he told them. "I hope you'll understand. I feel like I'm still a hostage, but the future has something better for me and I have to find out what it is."

I could not believe my ears when he said that. Better than what? Here he had a wife and three wonderful kids, and he wanted something better? The kids just sat there looking at him. They didn't say a word. Finally, Bruce said, "Do you have any questions for me?"

Debbie spoke up, "What's going to happen to us?"

"You're going to stay here and live here," Bruce answered.

"Is this just temporary or is there going to be legal stuff?" Deb asked.

"Deb, we really don't know," he told her.

Debbie had tears in her eyes and asked if that was why he had his clothes in the car when he went to see Mr. Robinson.

"Yes," said Bruce.

"Will you be living with him?" asked Deb.

"I think that arrangement will only be for a short time. He has his own problems," Bruce said.

Again, I felt that he was lying. I just couldn't believe anything he said anymore.

At that point, Debbie got up and started to sob. She put her arms around her father and he embraced her and cried. I had been crying throughout the whole ordeal and I went and put my arms around Chris and he started to sob. Matt had tears running down his face and kept looking toward the window. Bruce put his arm on Matt's shoulder, but Matt pulled away. Then after a few moments, Bruce sat on the floor near the loveseat and said he was sorry that Jim Mayer didn't come by or call anymore and that it was his fault. I asked him what he meant. Bruce responded, "I didn't make him feel very welcome when he came by and I'm sorry for that."

Then he said, "I'm going for a ride," and looking at Debbie, he said, "Do you want to come with me?" She said yes and they left. He never even asked the boys to come along. What a bastard! Matt went into his room and locked the door and didn't come out for two hours. I was really worried about him.

Chris said to me, "Mom, I had some questions but I didn't ask them."

I asked him, "What were they?"

"I wanted to know if he'd be here for Debbie and my birthdays."

I answered, "You forgot about Matt."

He said, "Well, his is a long way off, ours are soon."

July 28, 1982, I picked Debbie up at her friend's and headed for the hospital for her arthroscopic knee surgery. She had injured it during welcome activities at school. We went to the short stay unit and Deb signed in. We sat for about 50 minutes and then she was called to the pre-op waiting area. At 1:10pm, Dr. Schonholtz came out and said that everything went well. There was no torn cartilage, but there was inflammation. He had cleaned it out and also removed the band in her knee, which he said sometimes gets irritated.

I called Bruce to let him know she was okay, but he wasn't at his desk. I left a message with the secretary. I went to the cafeteria for some lunch, then I came back to the waiting room and called the house. Chris wasn't home. I called a few more times and still no answer. I was beginning to worry about him. I called Bruce again. He still wasn't there. I gave the secretary the number of the pay phone I was using and asked her to have him call back. A few moments later, Bruce did. I told him about Deb and that I couldn't get in touch with Chris. At 1:45pm, he called back to let me know that Chris was home. It was difficult trying to be in two places at once. I just couldn't split myself in half.

After waiting and waiting, the nurse finally came to say that Debbie was being released. I brought the car around and the nurse helped Debbie get in. She looked very pale and groggy but seemed to be in good spirits. She said she was starving! We got home about 4:00pm and Chris came out to help her with her crutches. She made it into the house without them. I felt so exhausted; I flopped on the bed and fell asleep until 5:00 pm. I hurried and made some spareribs to go with the leftover lasagna. After dinner, Rosie and Evelyn stopped by to see Deb, then her boyfriend Jeff came and took her for some ice cream.

Thursday, July 29 Despite the fact that we were headed for divorce, we still shared the same bed. Bruce did not want the kids to know that we were actually going to be separated. I woke up and reminded Bruce we had a family meeting scheduled with Lori on Saturday. I wanted to make sure he didn't say he forgot because he was very good at "forgetting" or "feeling ill". He left me another note that morning – I was up before he left for work and he had the note written, but instead of giving it to me, he said, "I wrote you another note and put it on your dresser." He walked from the living room to the bedroom to do this. After he left for work, I read the letter. I called him later at work and we talked for about half an hour again—mostly about money. His note said he'd give me $1,300 and that was for two mortgages and other expenses. I told him it wasn't nearly enough. Two mortgage payments would be $700 plus $300 for one month of utilities would leave us with $300 to live on for two months for four of us. That would be less money than poverty level families had. Finally, we decided on $2,000 to hold me over until he got back from his three-week trip to the Far East. We left it on that note.

July 31, 1982, We had the family meeting with Lori. She asked the children if they knew what was happening and why. They said, "No." She said, "Well, we'll start with some background material and work forward. She drew a chart on the blackboard as she got information. She asked Bruce about his childhood and wrote in his mother and father's names. She asked me my mother and father's names and about my siblings and where I was in the lineup. We talked about when Bruce and I met and when we married and then when each of the children were born. Then she asked about Bruce's career. He was in the Navy for three years and three months and then worked for the Central Intelligence Agency. I worked for Acme Supermarkets and then for Bell Telephone Company of Pennsylvania in the accounting department.

At that point, Lori said she felt there had been a lack of communication between us. After getting the background information she said, "Now I usually have personal contact. She came to Bruce and said, "Turn your chair around and face Chris. Take his hands in yours and look at him. Tell him what it is you want him to know. At that point, Bruce balked. "I have three children and I treat them all the same—I can't pick one over the other."

"Well, okay," Lori said. "Debbie and Matthew, turn your chairs around and face your father. Chris, you sit on your father's lap. Now, Bruce, take Matt's hand with that hand and Debbie's hand with this one."

Lori then took Chris' hand and put it on Bruce's chest. She asked, "Bruce, how does it feel to be touching your children?

"Great!" he answered.

"Now, what is it you want to say to them?" Lori asked Bruce.

Silence. Then finally, "I don't want them to think I'm abandoning them."

"Look at them and tell them. Don't tell me," Lori instructed.

Looking at the kids, he started, "I don't want you to feel I'm abandoning you. I love you all. If you ever want me, just call. I'm as close as the telephone."

"What is it you'd like to tell Debbie?" Lori continued.

"That I'm proud of her."

"Tell her. Look at her."

"I'm proud of you, Deb. You never had to prove anything to me. I loved you the way you were."

"You said 'loved' as if it's in the past," Lori inquired.

"No, I was thinking of when she was a little girl," he said.

"Tell Matthew your thoughts about him."

And so, it went. Bruce sharing with Matthew and Chris what they meant to him.

"Matt, you're bright, you're determined, and you are quiet in a way that I see some of me in you. I'm proud of you. If you ever want me just call and tell me what you want and I'll be there." To Chris he shared, "Chris, I'm proud of you and your accomplishments, and want you to know that I'm here for you. If ever you need me, just call me."

When Lori said it was my turn for Bruce to speak to me, all he could muster was, "What I have to say is between us. I don't want to discuss it now."

"Why?" Lori investigated. "Do you think your children won't understand?"

"It's between us," Bruce repeated.

"Do you feel they'll blame you?" she asked.

"Yes."

"I'm trying to understand and I'm trying to accept this," I cried to Bruce. "But it's difficult. I always thought of you as my best friend, but I'm finding out you aren't. It hurts!"

Tears were streaming down my face and he got a tissue and gave it to me. At this point, Bruce became agitated and shared how he felt interrogated. We left there and came home - the tension was horrible. He said he would never go back there again. If either one of us were the least bit violent in nature, there very well may have been bloodshed. Bruce said he wasn't going to have dinner because he was going out with Ben. He left about 6:30pm and got back after midnight.

Sunday, August 1, 1982

Bruce got up at about 6:15am and I got up just as he went out of the bedroom. He had some breakfast and then went downstairs, and I heard him rattling around in the rec room. I came downstairs and he dropped something and came toward me saying, "There aren't any more beer mugs." I said, "They were all on the shelves and now the shelves are empty, so I guess you have all of them." I stayed close to him because I felt he couldn't be trusted. I didn't know what he was trying to hide. He started to pack his clothes and I looked at his dresser and asked him if he was going to take his wedding ring with him. He said yes rather emphatically, and then started to cry.

"I said I wasn't going to do this," Bruce said.

"I'll wake the kids."

"Why?"

"So, they can spend some time with you before you leave."

I woke them and Bruce asked if they'd like to go to pick up Ben. Deb wasn't too enthused and he really didn't tell the boys. I did, though. They left at 9:00 am and didn't get back until 11:15am. I was in the bedroom when they came back but walked to the kitchen. Ben came in and we made some small talk. They didn't make a move to leave, so I asked Bruce if he was leaving.

"I thought I'd wait until Matt leaves," Bruce said. Matt was going to Karate camp for two weeks.

"No, you'd better leave first," I said. "I want Matt to see you leave."

"Oh, Okay." He called Ben to help get his suitcases and took them out to the car. He came back in and picked up his suits and came over to me and hugged me and cried.

"Take those out and come back in," I told him.

"Okay."

He came back in and held me and we both cried. As he left, he said, "You'll be okay, you're stronger than you think."

"I'm not strong enough for this."

With that, he walked out the door. I took Matt to meet the bus that would take him to camp. He had a splitting headache, one of the many he had been having most of his teen years. I spent the rest of the day trying to act as normally as possible for Chris' sake. That evening, I was sitting on the couch in the rec room and Chris came over and sat on the floor by me.

"I miss Dad," he said. "Why did he leave?"

I replied that I missed him, too, and I was sorry I couldn't really answer why his dad left.

August 6, 1982 Today was the holy day of the Transfiguration. I went to Church to bless fruit. It also was the 12th anniversary of my mother's death. It was very emotional, partly because I wished I could talk to her about my situation and partly because I was so depressed about my separation. My mother never interfered in my marriage. Whenever I talked to her about any problems, she'd always say, "It's your life and you have to make your own decision." Then I'd ask, "But if it was your decision, what would you do?" Then she'd tell me what that was, but always ended with, "But that's what I would do; that's me not you" or she'd say, "That's my opinion."

I had a meeting with Lori Gordon later that day. We talked about mediation and the fact that Bruce cancelled the meeting, so I decided to get a legal separation. I didn't think mediation would do me any good since Bruce didn't seem to be in any hurry to get anything down on paper. I called Bruce's office thinking he was out of town, which was the reason he gave for not coming to the meeting, but he answered the phone. It was 3:00pm. I told him he had mail here, some bills, and asked him where to send them. He said to send them to Will Robinson's house. I know he wasn't staying with Will. He had stated earlier that he was staying with Will, but later admitted that was not true. The lies just got bigger and bigger. After I talked to him, I felt myself going into a deep depression.

August 8, 1982 When I went to church, I got a lot of compliments on my appearance after my hair appointment. That made me feel a bit better, but it didn't really mean anything. I think everyone was just being kind. Deb went out with Jeff, and Jim stopped by to take the boys to the game room. They stopped at Mother's for some pizza and brought it home to eat.

I noticed this week that Chris had been crying a lot. The slightest thing seems to set him off. Debbie moped around and not knowing what to do with herself. I know they both missed Bruce and they're having a hard time adjusting to him not being here again. But this time it was different from when he went to Tehran. This time it was more frightening. I was glad that Matt had been away at karate camp because it kept him busy; however, he really suffered with tension headaches.

August 9, 1982 I decided to go to visit my brother John in New Jersey. I thought a change of scenery for all of us would be good. I called and asked if he'd like company and told him we'd be arriving the next day.

August 10, 1982 We arrived in Beachwood at about 3:00pm and the boys immediately went swimming. They loved visiting their Uncle John because he had an in-ground pool and it was always fun. I had a nice visit with John and Ceil, talking and talking about my separation – hoping they could shed some light on what happened. They both said that they always thought Bruce and I had the best marriage of anyone they knew and they were totally shocked by his actions. The next day was their anniversary, but they hadn't planned any celebration. Ceil had to work and John had a doctor's appointment. To pass the time, I took the kids to a shopping center.

August 12, 1982, I called Bruce's Aunt Mildred and asked if we could come to visit her since she was only two hours away from Beachwood, NJ. She lived on Long Island and although I wasn't familiar with the area, I didn't have any trouble finding my way. Aunt Mildred and Uncle Bill had always treated me as family and I loved talking with them. Uncle Bill had been a Captain in the Merchant Marines and had traveled all over the world, especially during wartime. He was a soft-spoken, Southern gentleman with a great sense of humor. Aunt Mildred looked very tired but was as cordial as ever. Uncle Bill was his pleasant self but had become hard of hearing and had a terrible time hearing us. We stayed for three hours and then started back to Beachwood.

August 14, 1982 My hip and back were worse, but I went crabbing with John, his son, Bruce, and the kids. I caught three crabs and Chris caught one. It was something that we had never done before and was a lot of fun. We learned something new. On the way back to John's, my hip started to bother me again. It was getting worse.

August 15, 1982 I was awake most of the night in terrible pain. I couldn't turn over, sit, lay on my back or right side, nor stand. I thought I was having a stroke or slowly being paralyzed. The boys packed up the car while I lay on Johnny's lounge chair on my left side—the only position that was bearable. I was thankful that Deb drove from Beachwood to beyond the Harbor Tunnel, and then Matt, who had his driver's permit, drove the rest of the way. I couldn't have driven even one mile. When I got home, I searched for some pain medication and found some Tylenol #3 left from a tooth extraction. It helped.

August 16, 1982 I called Dr. Bresler and made an appointment for 10:30am. He examined my back and said I probably had a herniated disc. He asked if I was ready to go to the hospital for traction and I said yes with no hesitation. I just could not function with the pain that I was in. It was unbearable. Dr. Bresler gave me Tylenol #4 (with codeine) to get me through the day until I got to the hospital.

I arrived at the hospital at 5:00pm and tried to get settled. The maintenance people came and put the traction apparatus on the bed and I had 15 lb. weights at first, which was changed to 25 lb. weights during the day and 15 lb. weights at night. I was to keep the weights on all day and only get up to go to the bathroom or to sit up to eat my meals. My hospital stay lasted 15 days.

That evening, Debbie tried to find Bruce. He had called the children from somewhere "near Philadelphia" before we left for New Jersey but didn't leave a phone number. Deb called Will Robinson who told her he had no idea where Bruce was, although Bruce had told the kids he was going to live in Will's house for a while. After calling multiple people, Deb finally called Pennsylvania and Bruce's stepfather Al answered the phone.

"Hello, this is your granddaughter, Debbie. I'm trying to find my father. Is he there?"

Al said, "No, he's not here. Do you want to talk to your grandmother?"

"No, that's okay," Deb said. "Thank you."

She never did get in touch with him that day. She had called the office before I left for the hospital and the secretary said Bruce was expected back but hadn't come in. Deb told her to please tell him to call his daughter – it was urgent.

August 17, 1982, I got a call from Bruce asking me how I was and what happened. I told him the events and said, "No one was able to get in touch with you."

He said, "I know. I had all kinds of messages on my desk to call my daughter. Then Will called and said to call Debbie and then Gary came across the hall and told me that Deb was trying to get in touch with me. Everybody was after me."

"Well," Bruce continued. "I was going to see the kids anyway tonight, so I'll bring them by to see you and then I'll take them for something to eat." He never did say where he was or why he never let his boss know how to get in touch with him.

August 18, 1982 Dr. Bresler came by early to say he had the results of the tests and had some bad news. I had a slipped disc as he thought, but I had three problems, not one. The other two were: a spur between my 4th and 5th vertebrae, and also a narrow channel in the 5th vertebrae, probably because it didn't grow enough when I was a teenager. He said he wanted a second opinion and he suggested Dr. John Lord.

Later that evening, Bruce came to visit by himself. Most of what we discussed were the needs of the children and money. He wanted to know what bills I had. At that point, I couldn't even think about anything but the pain I was having.

August 20, 1982 Dr. Bresler had not been able to get in touch with Dr. Lord but had left messages for him to come to Holy Cross hospital to see me. I had been in traction for five days and was feeling slightly better. The time at the hospital passed slowly, but I wasn't anxious to go home. I knew I could not function properly as I was. There was so much to do, but I just couldn't tackle it just now.

I received a lot of cards, phone calls, and visitors during those 15 days I was in the hospital. At least other people cared about me, especially those from my St. Mark family. Bruce had come that second day with carnations. Deb, Matt, and Chris brought three red roses, and I received a beautiful arrangement from Jim and another one from Pat and Gary Lee.

Elaine came down on the first Thursday and stayed until Sunday. She canned some tomatoes for me and then baked a blueberry pie for the kids. I felt better that she was with the kids. I didn't like them staying alone for all these days. Yet she did this while leaving her three children, so she could help me out.

Fr. Basil stopped by a few times to see how I was doing. Mike Karas called me since he had been in traction for 11 days in June or July and so he gave me the benefit of his experience. Johnny Petro took Matt driving on Sunday, August 29th for 2 ½ hours. Later Matt and Chris went to the Mikuluks who took them to Valle's where they both had two lobsters each. I was surprised that they could each eat two lobsters! I was very thankful for my friends. What would I do without them?

Tuesday, August 31st Dr. Lord came to the hospital and asked if I was ready to go home. I was! He made arrangements for me to be fitted for a corset. I called Sue to see if she'd take Matt for his driver's test, so she picked him up at 8:00am and had him drive to Gaithersburg. She called me at about 10:30am to say he passed his test and was getting his picture taken. Afterwards, they came to the hospital to get me and drove me to Silver Spring to be fitted for the corset. When I got home, I made my way to the family room where the kids had put the brown lounge chair from the rec room so I could rest in comfort.

CHAPTER 16

Sept. 13, 1982 Bruce called this morning, *not* to see how I was but to say, "We'd better get in touch with Lori 'what's her face' because there are things to settle. I know you haven't had time to think about it."

I said, "You're right. I didn't have time to think about it. I've had other things on my mind, such as the six weeks bedrest that I'm on."

He was surprised to find out I needed that. I also told him the kids had a harrowing experience with crank phone calls at 3:15am & 3:20am and that someone hit the car. He didn't seem interested.

"I'd like to see the boys tonight if they don't have karate. I'll be there about 7:00pm. Maybe I'll take them for a ride or something."

After I got off the phone with him, I felt really depressed. He didn't give a damn about me or the kids. Then he asked me if I felt okay."

"Yes, I'm on codeine."

When he came over that night, I made a point of telling him I was in the hospital for 15 days and paid $90 for the back-brace corset. I tried to read his face to see if he really cared—he didn't. I noticed he was growing his mustache again. His only comment was he bought three custom made shirts in Bangkok for $15 each.

Again, he said, "We have to get in touch with Lori 'what's-her-face' because there are things to settle, like the All-Savers certificate and whether we should take it out or let it ride for another year. And I'll have to get tags for that car in Virginia."

I said, "They can't do anything to you if you don't—you're not the sole owner of the car."

"Well, I don't want to get a ticket."

"There is nothing they can do to you legally."

I don't think he appreciated that comment. I wasn't jumping through hoops just because he said something. He took the boys for ice cream and then came back and watched the Redskins game that we had taped yesterday. He left at 9:00pm with a "so long." Despite being unable to handle everyday things on my own, he wasn't bothered to help in anyway.

Sept. 15, 1982 I called A Women's Place and spoke with a lawyer who dealt with mediation. A one-hour consultation was supposed to cost $20, but the lawyer I was referred to had a different rate—15 minutes free and then the rest pro-rated at the hourly rate of $75 - $100 per hour. I couldn't afford to go over 15 minutes. When I called A Woman's Place, she recommended I get a lawyer quick. I needed someone who would watch out for my interests and to ask about the Government's liability in this.

I again called A Woman's Place to see if I could hire the lawyer I had spoken with on the phone, but she said no because that would be a conflict of interest— as if she was drumming up business for herself.

Later, I called Aunt Mildred to see how she was doing. We chatted about our respective illnesses and she asked if I had a slipped disc. Evidently, Bruce didn't tell her. We discussed my situation and I began to cry again. The emotional pain I've been feeling was unbearable and I wished I had died before Bruce came back from Iran so I would never have known this pain, rejection, degradation— feeling like some kind of vermin or scum. My character had been assassinated and the vile feelings I had sometimes scared me. We talked about the fact that my mother-in-law did not call the kids while I was in the hospital, nor had she called to see how they were doing while I was on bed rest.

Sept. 25, 1982 Deb called to get a ride home after the football game. She complained about the food we had for dinner because they were leftovers. All she did was complain. I asked her to help with the dishes and she carried on something terrible.

She ranted, "I'm tired of you making me do work every time I come home. I do work at the dorm. I don't have to do it here.

I said, "Look, Deb, I can't do it and it's not going to hurt you to help."

She retorted, "I won't come home as often."

I said, "Good, stay there!" I couldn't believe how ungrateful she was. I knew she was stressed out over this situation, but she should have realized that it is worse for me, especially with my constant pain.

Sept. 27, 1982, I had an appointment with a lawyer about a separation agreement. As I sat there, I was very uncomfortable with pain in my back. He said my expectations were realistic, but after we talked about fees I almost died: he wanted $2,000 retainer and $100 per hour. He did give me some tips on what to do in the meantime.

FINDING THE RIGHT LAWYER

Sept 28, 1982 I spoke with a paralegal that gave me a few names of lawyers that I might want to call. The first two I called seemed to want me to make a decision immediately, with one asking me if I wanted an appointment or not. The third one impressed me. Her rate was better - $65 per hour and $750 retainer. She even offered to come by the house to see me if necessary. Her name was Ellen Pattin and her office was located on Georgia Avenue in Olney, about three miles from my house. I decided to go with her.

Sept. 29, 1982 At about 11:30am, the phone rang and it was Bruce.

"Hi! Boy, what a day!" he started. "I've been on the phone to University of Maryland and the credit union because Deb called and said she'd be put out of the dorm if her bill isn't paid by Friday afternoon. What a mess! I tried to call her and there's no answer, so tell her she's supposed to go to the Bursar's Office and speak to Paula Noll. She has been in contact with the credit union and she'll handle everything. The credit union says the check was mailed on the 22nd or 23rd but Maryland can't find it, so that's the problem."

I think he wanted to impress me with all he had done by giving me all the details of the phone calls. This was my way of life, so it was good that he had a little taste of it. He had refused to take responsibility for anything lately. That was the most he'd talked to me in months. He did ask how I was feeling and asked how the boys were. I told him they were fine.

He said, "Well, they didn't call me." Again, trying to put a guilt trip on them —sounded just like his mother. He had a dial on his end of the phone, too.

I said, "They thought you'd be here to take them to bowling, but you didn't show up."

He answered, "Well, I thought they'd call me."

"I'm not going to make them call you."

"I know," he said. "But I thought I'd come by tomorrow and see them. If they want to do something special, they can call me.""

Later I told Matt and Chris and asked if they wanted to call him. Chris said, "Yes." Matt just shrugged his shoulders.

I went to a lecture on the new laws on divorce and separation in Maryland with Ann Weiss and when I came home, Chris was already home from karate. Matt came in later. I reminded them again about calling Bruce. Finally, Chris called and talked to Bruce for a while and called to Matthew to come and talk but he didn't come out of his room. Finally, I said, "Matt, are you going to talk to your Dad?"

Matt said, "I don't know." Then he came out of his room to take the phone, but by that time Bruce had hung up. It would be just like Bruce to blame Matt. What he should have realized was that the kids didn't feel comfortable with him anymore, not since Bruce told them he wanted to get "away from everybody." Last week when I asked each of the kids if they wanted to go and live with Bruce, Deb said, "Mom, he said he wanted to get away from all of us."

Matt asked, "Why?"

I answered, "These are questions that have to be answered for the separation agreement."

I had been trying to be open and frank with them about this rotten mess. I wanted to prepare them for whatever happened. Sometimes I wanted to kick Bruce so hard he wouldn't be able to sit for a month. He was devious and sneaky and he couldn't be trusted.

GETTING RID OF HURTFUL REMINDERS

Oct. 2, 1982 I looked through my closets and decided to get rid of anything that reminded me of Bruce, his mother, or his brother. His mother had bought me two winter coats and he had bought me a coat and some boots. Everything was in perfect condition, but I would rather do without them altogether at this point. I gathered them up and put them in a box to go to the clothing drive that was being held by St. Nicholas Orthodox Church in Washington, D.C. I found a few other items and added those. Items that Bruce had not taken were packed up to go to the dump, which Debbie and the boys hauled away later that day. I felt a lot better having the stuff out of the house.

Oct. 3, 1982 After so many weeks away, I was finally able to go to church again. Since I normally went to church every Sunday or Holy day, I really missed it. The people at St. Mark were great as usual. John Dennis, one of the parishioners who I knew from St. Nicholas Orthodox Church, talked to me for a while and then as Matt was standing near me, John asked, "Where is your Daddy these days?" Matt turned around and walked away. He was deeply hurt.

I told John, "Bruce and I are separated. He lives somewhere in Arlington."

John offered his condolences. Many people came up to me and said they heard we were separated and how sorry they were. They offered prayers for both of us.

Oct. 4, 1982 The mail came and there was a notice from State Farm Insurance Company stating that the insurance on the Ford Escort was cancelled as requested. I read that and was angry. Bruce was continually doing things without telling me. I was so mad at him I wished he had never come back from Iran.

I had gone out for a 15-minute walk in the morning, but I went out again to walk off some of my frustrations after reading that. I wondered how he could do that without notifying me since my name was on the title.

OUR ALL-SAVERS CERTIFICATE

Oct. 5, 1982 Lori Eisenburg Gordon called to respond to my call yesterday about Bruce canceling the insurance on the Ford Escort. She said I should get a lawyer at least until we got to mediation. I asked her what she thought I should do about our All-Savers Certificate that would be maturing in a few weeks. She agreed that asking for half was fair. I told her I needed money for a lawyer and she said to call him and ask for it.

So, I called Bruce and told him I needed money. He asked, "For what?" and I said, "For a lawyer." He seemed shocked.

"I thought we were going to Lori," Bruce said. "What's the use of paying two people?"

"We still are going to Lori, but in the state of Maryland, I still need a lawyer to be sure the documents are legal according to Maryland law," I told him. "Lori can help with the incidentals, the lawyer with the official document."

He asked, "How much do you need?"

"$750."

"My God!" he exclaimed. "Well, you don't need it now, all at once."

"Yes, I do. I need it by Friday. When are you coming by to see the boys?"

"I don't know," he answered. "It's a long weekend so I'm going out of town."

"Matt called you on Sunday and there was no answer."

"Where did he call, at home?"

I said, "Yes."

"I was home Sunday evening," Bruce said.

"This was in the afternoon."

"Oh, I wasn't home."

I retorted, "That's obvious!"

Oct. 8, 1982, I got up early because I had the appointment with my lawyer, Ellen Pattin. After I finished getting dressed, I called Bruce. He was out of the office – again. The secretary asked for my phone number and I told her he knew it – I was his wife. When he called back, I asked him what I was going to do about the money for the lawyer.

"I don't understand why you're doing this," Bruce said.

"Because Maryland law says there must be a lawyer to do the legal papers."

"I thought we were going to Lori. What's the sense of going to both?"

Sometimes I thought he really *was* dense.

"Lori will take care of the incidentals," I reminded him. "It's better than paying a lawyer to do that. They charge you for phone calls by the minute."

"Well," he said. "I'm not going to pay for a lawyer now. I know I'll end up paying for this, but not now.

"All lawyers ask for retainers," I informed him. "Have you called a lawyer?"

"No."

"Well, I have. They all take retainers. Separations and divorces are very expensive. You're the one who wanted this damn separation."

"Yes, that's right," he said. "But I don't understand why you need a lawyer."

"I'm entitled to representation. You've been doing things behind my back and I'm damn tired of it. You act as if we're already divorced and you don't have anything to do with us."

"Don't start shouting or I'm going to hang up this phone."

"You won't have to; I'll do it for you!"

Oct. 14, 1982 I called Bruce to let him know I needed money again. He said very sarcastically, "I figured as much when I got this letter from your attorney. What gets me is where she says I should make regular payments. That's what I thought I was doing."

'Bruce, you always wait until I call you and then you ask me how much I need and get upset when I tell you."

"Well, we need to get this straightened out."

"Are you going to call Lori?"

"No, you got your lawyer," he said. "I'll get my own. I'll come by with a check tonight. I had an appointment, but I'll have to cancel it."

After I hung up, I called the credit union to tell them I forgot to put an account number on my letter that I sent them about splitting the All-Savers certificate. It was then I found out that Bruce had taken $4,000 out of our regular share account and had written a letter saying he wanted the total amount of the All-Savers certificate to be made out in his name only. I told the teller that it was a joint account and he said that since Bruce was the employee, the check would be made out to him. I called Ellen Pattin and told her about it.

Bruce came by about 7:00pm. He looked at me with disgust and said, "Well, how much do you need?"

I said, "I have $590 in bills; I need at least $900. He wrote the check for that amount. He took the boys to Dairy Queen and they were back by 8:15pm.

Oct. 15, 1982 Ellen talked to the attorney at the credit union and told him there would be a lawsuit if the check was made out to Bruce alone. He said there were three options that we could use: It could be divided equally between us, it could be put into our joint account with neither of us being able to withdraw on it, or it could be turned over to the courts where it could stay for months at a low rate of interest. She told me to call Bruce and see if he was agreeable to splitting it. I came home and called him at the office and was told he left for the weekend—he had gone away.

Oct. 18, 1982, I prayed really hard before I picked up the phone to call Bruce, but finally I made the call and explained the situation. "I'm calling about the All-Savers Certificate. I understand you wrote a letter asking the Credit Union to make a check out to you for the total amount."

"Yes," he replied.

I bet he flipped out knowing he got caught being sneaky. This would be the second time he did this, and I wasn't going to stand by and let it happen again.

"Well, about two weeks later," I said, "I wrote asking for half of the amount to be made out to me and the other half to you, which I thought was fair. Now, the money is considered to be 'In dispute' and they won't make the check out to either of us. There are three options" I outlined. "1.) We divide the money in half; 2.) The credit union puts it in our account but neither of us can touch it until the courts decide what happens to it; or 3.) The money is handed over to the courts where it will sit for months and make only 3% interest. My lawyer suggested that it would be best to come to an agreement without involving anyone else; otherwise, it will cost money."

"Oh, yes, I know it will," he responded. "Well, do whatever you want. How will we do this?"

"I'll call my lawyer and have her call the credit union attorney."

I called Ellen Pattin and told her what Bruce said, so she called the credit union attorney. They decided to have us both sign an agreement to keep everything legal.

Oct. 18, 1982 Two packages arrived—one for me and one for Debbie—from Bruce. To say I was flabbergasted was an understatement. Why would he do this? After our latest conversations, this was the last thing I expected from him. I waited until after lunch to call him. All that went through my mind was, "why was he doing this?"

"I'm calling about a package I received," I told Bruce when I phoned him.

"What kind of package?" he inquired.

"A package from you! I opened it and it's a beautiful crystal bell. There's also a package for Debbie here."

"Oh, those were supposed to be for Christmas."

"Oh, I sent Deb's over to her with Rosie."

"Well, I guess it could be for her birthday," he said.

"Did you pick it out?" I asked.

"Yes."

"It's beautiful," I told him. "Thanks so much! I appreciate it. I'm sorry I opened it—I didn't know."

"It doesn't matter," he said. "I'm glad you like it."

After I got off the phone, I tried to weigh his behavior. First, he took $4,000 out of our savings account, then he tried to have our All–Savers certificate money sent to him and nothing for me, but now he bought me this beautiful crystal bell because he knew I had a bell collection. Talk about mixed signals. Maybe he was hoping his actions would cause me to become unstable.

Oct 25, 1982 Ellen Pattin called to tell me the check for the All-Savers Certificate had come into her office. I told her I'd be in to pick it up. The phone rang about two hours later. It was Ellen again, telling me she had received a call from Bruce's lawyer, who she described as particularly obnoxious. The lawyer had said that Bruce and I had been having marital difficulties before he went to Tehran and that's why he took the assignment in Tehran – to get away from me. I felt like a knife went right through my heart! She asked me if I had lied to her about our marriage and I told her that everything I told her was the truth.

I went to her office to pick up the check and we chatted a bit more. She said Jeff Krause, Bruce's lawyer, asked her if she had ever heard of the Iran Hostage Crisis. Jeff was going to use the "poor hostage with a bitchy wife" scenario to defend Bruce.

When I got home, I told the kids about it. Jeff also told Bruce to give us less money. Chris and Matt were both very upset. Matt was so distraught that he got a splitting headache and couldn't go to karate. I felt so badly for him. He took everything to heart.

Oct. 26, 1982 When the boys came home from school, Bruce called. He talked to Chris and then Matt and said he'd be by to take them to Mother's for pizza. In the meantime, John Petro called me to ask if I could bring the car up for him to look at. I told the boys to watch for Bruce so he wouldn't have to come in the house. I left and got back at 5:50pm and they were gone. When the boys came back, Matt gave me the envelope with the check and there were other papers sticking out. When I looked inside, I saw that Bruce had paid the electric bill, the car payment, and had a note attached to the phone bill saying it would be paid by the end of the month. Also, a check for $500 was enclosed for me for November. I suddenly realized that he had the mail transferred to his address. Now I knew why I wasn't getting any mail. He never said a word about it to me. He was trying to drive me into an early grave.

Oct. 27, 1982, I met with Ellen so we could come up with a proposal to present to Bruce's lawyer. I had a list of things I wanted to ask her, so I went through it and also told her about the $500 check that he gave me. She said his lawyer said Bruce would pay the mortgage and utilities and give me money for food. I read off a list of bills I paid including hospital, dental, and school related expenses.

I spent about one-and-a-half hours with Ellen going over points to consider. Rehabilitation alimony for six years was discussed. She said surely Bruce would know that I couldn't work. I told her not to bet on it. Next, I went to see Lori Gordon and bring her up to date on the latest developments. She was appalled at the crap Bruce was pulling. I talked about Bruce being a father for about one-and-a-half hours per week for 12 days. She just shook her head in disbelief. She commented that I must have had a really hellish time these past weeks with 15 days in the hospital and six weeks bed rest.

Oct. 29, 1982 While I was out, Debbie called Bruce at his office but was told he was gone for the day. She told me she got an "A" on her Mythology test and wanted to tell Bruce. She was very proud of herself and I was proud of her too. I was glad she succeeded because it would certainly boost her morale.

Debbie showed me her class catalog and discussed some courses she could take next semester. She said she'd like to take a course on the Holocaust but didn't know if she could handle it. I told her that her father would probably be a big help to her, if he were around. She didn't answer. Bruce was very interested in history, especially World War II. I really think he would've been a big help to Deb if he took the time.

Matt seemed a little antsy today. He mentioned something about Bruce and the fact that he didn't enjoy the time spent with him. Matt didn't come right out and say it, but I got that impression. Matt continued, "He only spends about two hours with us when he does come. What is this? A part time job?" I laughed because it just struck me funny the way he said it.

Sept. 24, 1982, I had an appointment with Dr. Lord, my neurosurgeon. He was happy with my progress, especially the fact that the pain in my right leg had stopped. When I asked him if I could drive to Virginia on Wednesday, he said, "No, put that off for a few weeks." I then asked, "Could I go for a job interview?"

He replied, "Not yet. You have to get yourself well first. We're talking about a recovery period of up to a year. Don't be in a hurry to put a lot of stress in your life."

I thought to myself, that's a joke! I've been under stress for three years! He also said he wanted me back in three weeks for another check-up.

When I got home, there were letters from Bruce's Aunt Betty and Colleen Knight, shocked by what was happening to us. Hearing from them made me realize just how much they cared about me and what was happening in my life.

A DATE THAT WILL FOREVER BE ETCHED IN MY MIND

November 4, 1982 It had been three years to the day that the Iranians overtook the American Embassy in Tehran and three years since my life changed. I had taken two sleeping pills my doctor prescribed and fell asleep almost immediately. I got the boys off to school and went back to sleep. I didn't get up until 1:00pm.

I set my sights on going back to school and taking classes to learn new skills. I decided to see some counselors at Montgomery College to ask about computer courses.

Nov. 8, 1982 I went to New Phase and did some work on scholarship research. Then, I called the Maryland State Senators and Congressman Mike Barnes offices for Matt's nomination to the Naval Academy in Annapolis and later I got Chris his Social Security card. It was a lot of little things, but they needed to be done.

Nov. 11, 1982 Pat Lee called. She was in a blue mood. Things were not going well between her and Gary and she was crying. She said he hadn't come home from work one day last week and wasn't home yet - and it was 8:00pm. She talked for a while and poured her heart out. Pat and I had been through so much these past months and we shared a lot of our feelings with each other.

After about an hour, Gary came home. He had been drinking. He asked Pat who she was talking to. He grabbed the phone out of her hand and said, "Hi Marge, how are you doing?"

I replied, "I'm okay – some days good and some days bad."

"I know, Marge, and I wish I could do something but I can't," Gary said. "There's nothing I can do to change things, but I want you to know that I think he's not treating you right. What he's doing to you is rotten. If he's going to be involved with another woman, he should just get a divorce. Fish or cut bait. It's not fair."

"Did he tell you about the woman?" I asked incredulously.

"No, I have my own ways of finding out," he said.

"What's her name?"

"I don't know. He never told me. All he said was that he was madly in love with an old flame—a high school sweetheart. He got involved with this girl about one and a half years ago. I'm not sure but I think it's all over now. I don't think he's involved now. But if you ever tell him I said so, I'll deny it."

"What hurts is he told his lawyer that our marriage was in trouble for a long time and he went to Tehran to get away from his wife," I told Gary.

"Now wait a minute," Gary said. "I'll call him on that. I happen to know that's not true. We spent five weeks together in Tehran and all he talked about was you and his kids. He was counting the days until he could come home on his visitation. He cared too much for there to be someone else. So, if it ever comes to it, I'll back you up in court."

Many things were beginning to fall into place, though I felt deeply hurt.

Nov. 17, 1982. I called Bruce this morning.

"Hi, I need money."

"You didn't have enough?" Bruce asked.

"No. You gave me $500 and I've already spent almost $600. I have nothing left. I had $65 in prescriptions."

"I'm paying all the bills," he said.

"You're paying the mortgage and utilities," I told him. "There are a lot of other bills. I've paid these bills for 21 years. You don't know how much it costs to run this house. I told you before that we were just making it. Do you expect four of us to live on $500?"

"Four?" he asked.

"Yes. We have three children or don't you remember that? I give Debbie $25 per week plus some groceries to take back to the dorm – unless you'd like to do that." No comment from him.

Sarcastically, Bruce said, "I take it you haven't looked for a job."

"Yes, I have. I went for a physical yesterday but I didn't pass it."

"Why?"

"Because of my back. Anyway, the doctor said I shouldn't work for about a year. That's how long it'll take to heal. I have put my application in at a few places, but I haven't heard anything. This is not the time to find a job with so much unemployment and my skills obsolete after being out of the work force for almost five years."

"If you can't maintain the house, you'll have to sell it. That's the only option."

"No, it isn't," I said. "It wouldn't be right to uproot the kids. They've been through enough."

"I see you're still paying for organ lessons," Bruce brought up.

"Yes, just for Chris," I answered. "$28 isn't going to make that much of a difference." He wanted the kids and me to stop all activities so he could be free to spend money on that bimbo of his. "By the way," I continued. "I was humiliated on Sunday. I went to buy something on VISA and it was refused because you closed the account. The least you could have done was to tell me." At that point, he changed the subject to voice his complaints about what happened to him.

"I got a few surprises, too," he said. "I got a long letter from the lawyer and one from the retirement section at the State Department. Was that a surprise!"

"What letter? From the lawyer?"

"The letter telling all your demands."

"You never asked me what I wanted. It was all what *you* wanted. I didn't even know you had a lawyer."

"I had to get one," he said.

"No, you didn't. We were supposed to go to mediation and a lawyer was needed for the legal documentation."

"And you expect me not to have my *own* lawyer? HUH!"

It was useless to try to talk to him in a civil tone. He wanted to know why I contacted the Retirement Department at the State Department. Early on in our separation, he told me I should find out what my entitlements were and now he was mad that I contacted the Retirement Department. He was really getting nasty. He never ceased to amaze me.

"When's the last time you called the boys?" I asked him.

"When did they call me?" he asked back.

"You're the one who left – it's up to you to call them! They feel rejected and you should at least call them to see how they are and how they're doing in school, AND we should be having communications between us for their benefit, but you're not in the least bit interested. You've spent less than 16 hours with them in the three months you've been gone." Again, he changed the subject.

"Well, I'll see what's left in my account and I'll send you a check."

"I'll need at least $400-$500 to get through the month. Call me to let me know."

"Okay, I will."

After I hung up, I thought about the conversation and thought of the many times Bruce changed the subject when I made my points about things he did that he shouldn't have, or things that he didn't do that he should have, and realized he always changed the subject when it got uncomfortable for him.

CHAPTER 17

LEARNING TO FIGHT BACK

Nov. 23, 1982, I called Debbie while she was away at college to wish her a Happy Birthday.

"Mom," she began. "My roommates said that some detective was here looking for Dad with a summons. Was that your doing?"

"Why?" I asked.

"Well, the girls said he came about five minutes after we left and said he had a summons for Bruce German and that he stayed around the apartment—walking back and forth. He looked really shady. Was that your doing?"

"Yes," I replied.

"Why?" Debbie asked me.

"Because he wants a divorce and now, he'll get it."

"Well, he was really P.O.'d! He got really white when he found out and he took off."

"Did he get the papers?" I asked Deb.

"Not unless the guy caught him down in the parking lot."

I was terribly upset by the ineptitude of the process server. I had told Ellen exactly what time he should be there. Why didn't he follow instructions?

Dec. 2, 1982 I had another appointment with Lori. She saw how depressed I was about the latest check Bruce sent for only $250 and about things in general. She offered to call Bruce if I thought it would help. I said, "Okay, but he probably won't talk to you." At that point, I left. Lori called me later to tell me that she had talked to Bruce and he was willing to come in and talk to her.

I then called him to ask about the check. He said it was for expenses.

"If $500 wasn't enough," I started, "what makes you think $250 will be okay?"

"I'm so strapped," he responded. "I can't give you anymore."

"That's not enough for food and there are karate lessons due plus other things."

"Well, I can't help it."

"Well, there's no way that I can give Debbie any money. You'll have to send it to her," I told him.

"Well, I guess I'll have to send it because you fixed it so I can't give it to her. You sent a process server on me."

"What did you expect? I'm tired of being kicked in the teeth and stomped on."

"Well, I didn't appreciate it, especially on her birthday," Bruce said.

"It wasn't planned for her birthday," I defended.

"Well, it's done now and I didn't appreciate it and neither did she."

"I'm not about to get kicked again."

It seemed it was always about him. It's amazing how he always turned everything into something I did to him—he wouldn't be in this situation if he acted decently.

Dec. 3, 1982 Sue Petro called saying that her daughter, Marie, had gone for a job interview. Unfortunately, Marie didn't have enough experience in accounting, but Sue thought I might be a good fit for the job.

I went for the interview, filled out an application, and left a resume with Mr. Sieling. It was a family construction business and the whole family was involved. His daughter, Cheryl, took care of the office but was expecting a baby any day, so they needed a replacement for her. It would only be a temporary position, with hours from 9:00 a.m. to 3:00 p.m., and paid $6.00 per hour. I needed anything I could get. On Monday, Mr. Seiling called about the job, and I started on Wednesday.

Dec. 10, 1982 I was usually busy at work. I was glad to have a job but I wasn't too fond of the fact that everyone in the office smoked and I could hardly breathe. Also, the family cat liked to climb on the desk and bite me. It had been declawed, so I guess that was the only way it could protect itself. But I wasn't paying attention to it, so I didn't know why it bit me. I know I wouldn't stay on this job too long.

A Matter of Trustworthiness

Dec. 13, 1982 Today I went to mediate with Bruce at the Family Relations Institute for about two hours. Lori started right in with mediation. Bruce gave vague answers when he discussed his finances. He lied about insurance and didn't mention the $4,000 he took out of our savings account. He told me he fell on the ice by his place and heard something crack. He had Band-Aids all over his hands and wrists. I think he was looking for sympathy.

Bruce said he was upset about his retirement and the fact that when it split between us, he would lose $2,600. He wanted me to let him take all the money and he'd pay me, but I couldn't trust him. If I couldn't get money out of him now, I'd never be able to later. He must have thought I was born yesterday. He stated that two pay statement totals were his monthly income but I corrected that. The truth is that he received 26 pay periods per year, so his monthly total was more than those two statements. He also said we owed about $30,000 on the house, and I told him that was impossible—it was closer to $43,000. I'm the one who had been paying the bills all during our marriage, and he just came up with these figures off the top of his head. A few days later, I called Columbia First, the company that held our mortgage, and confirmed that the balance was $41,070.

Bruce also said he wanted to see the kids more but didn't know how to arrange it. Lori said, "I understand the children will live with Marge." He said, "I guess so." She suggested he take them every weekend or every other weekend over to his apartment. He said he had nowhere for them to sleep. She said to get them sleeping bags

Dec. 21, 1982 Bruce came by at about 6:30 p.m. to give the kids their gifts. It was rather strained because he stayed at the house with them until about 10 minutes to 8 and then took Matt and Deb to Crown Books. Chris had gone to basketball practice. He dropped the kids back home and wished them a nice Christmas. I could have choked him! He preferred to spend Christmas away from his kids. It was embarrassing to receive Christmas cards from various people telling me that he was seen with another woman while he was in Pennsylvania.

Dec. 24, 1982 Christmas Eve was always a busy day. I did the usual preparations of special food for Holy Supper. We had our Holy Supper, but it had lost much of its significance. It was hard to think spiritually when your heart was broken. I love my children, but I ache for them. This was so much worse than the Christmas Eves while he was a hostage.

Dec. 25, 1982 – Christmas Day Well, this was the fourth lousy Christmas. Somehow, I couldn't find any spirituality in it. I knew Christmas was not about gifts, but it certainly was about family. I just felt we were not a complete family. The children and I got up early and opened the gifts, but there was a big void. It didn't seem to have the same meaning as it did years ago. We went to church and I came home with a terrible headache and laid down for a while, but the kids kept coming in to ask me questions so I didn't really get any rest. I got up and made dinner. Jim Mayer and Jeff joined us. Just as we were about to sit down, the phone rang and it was Ben. Matt answered and had a look of total disgust as he talked. Chris talked to him next, and then Debbie. She asked if her father was there. Theresa and Ben said he wasn't—he was gone someplace. They also said they sent Christmas cards which the kids would probably get on Monday. Ben also forgot about Debbie's birthday and Theresa was in Germany so that's why she didn't send a card. Even though Uncle Paul and Aunt Rose got postcards from Theresa from Germany, she didn't send any to the kids.

Dec. 27, 1982, I went to work and felt I was getting to know the system a little better. I applied for my own credit card and called VISA to see if it had been processed. I didn't really have any income to report so I wasn't sure I'd be approved.

I called Trudy Wiekoski at the State Department's retirement division about Bruce's retirement and the difference in the annuity benefits when they're divided between us. I also told her about Bruce's suggestion that I waive my benefits and he'd pay me from his check. She said I would be very foolish to do that. Once I signed those papers, I would get nothing. If he walked out the door tomorrow and got hit by a car and died, the children and I would get nothing.

I called Pennsylvania at 9:30pm to ask Bruce for the check he was supposed to have sent. Al answered and said he was "at the wake." He didn't mention who's. I told Al to tell Bruce I was waiting for the check he was supposed to send me.

A NEW YEAR – A NEW BEGINNING?

Jan. 1, 1983, I told Matt that this should be a new and better year.

He said, "Mom, you've been saying that for four years now."

I answered, "Well, it's bound to get better. We have had the worst!"

I didn't even make it to church today. I had started to clean my room yesterday, but didn't finish it so I tried to do a little more. I kept thinking of the old adage my mother used to tell me: "If you have a dirty house on New Year's Eve and it carries over into the New Year, you'll have a dirty house all year long."

I called Jim Leo in Texas and told him of Debbie's travel plans to visit him and Lydia. She was to leave on Wednesday, but he said he hoped she'd arrive on Tuesday. I called the airlines and they put her on a waiting list for Tuesday. She'd have to call tomorrow to see if she'd be able to change the date. Jim said he'd take her into Mexico and she was flying high! He also said he got in trouble because she gave him a Redskins Christmas stocking and took a picture of him holding it. That for a Dallas fan is unforgivable.

Jan. 3, 1983 The boys were back in school and there are no other holidays until January 15th. I felt a bit unnerved on the job. I was expected to know everything but hadn't really been trained. Debbie was going to Texas the next day. Jim and Lydia paid for half of her ticket, so we arranged for her to fly from Washington National to Houston and then on to McAllen.

Bruce stopped by to bring Debbie money for her ticket ($100) – that was a bit more than half of the $174 total. He stayed only a few minutes and chatted with the kids. He told them he had a nice time in PA and for them to write notes to Theresa and Ben letting them know they got the money gifts.

Jan. 4, 1983 I took Deb to the airport at 2:30, but she didn't get her ticket until 3:45 pm. The plane was due to leave at 4:05. I got home about 4:45 pm, concerned about her traveling alone. I had forgotten to tell her not to talk to strangers and I waited anxiously for her to call me when she arrived in Texas. I called Lydia and Jim at about 6:30 to tell them she was on her way. She had a stopover in Houston, and then would go on to Mission where the Leos would pick her up. I went to bed, but didn't expect to fall asleep until I heard from Deb. At 12:40 am, the phone rang and it was Jim Leo, calling to tell me that Debbie hadn't arrived. I almost had a heart attack. I was shaking like a leaf and asked him if he had checked to see if she had gotten the flight from Houston. Then he laughed and said he was just kidding and I could hear Lydia laughing in the background. I was *not* amused. My heart was pounding almost out of my chest. What a stupid thing to do! Debbie came on the line to tell me some older man was trying to get her to go to Mexico with him. I asked her why she didn't tell the stewardess he was annoying her and she said she didn't want to be rude. She said when she got off the plane, she took off running to where the Leos were waiting for her. I shudder every time I think of it. This was not funny and I didn't appreciate Jim pulling a stunt like that. After that I couldn't go back to sleep until after 3:00 am.

Jan. 5, 1983 My current job was getting on my nerves; I still didn't totally understand the system. Elise Rothchild from A Woman's Place called me about a part time job as an accounting and bookkeeping clerk at Tri-Services Center. I made an appointment for an interview and was told they wanted me to work for them. It was a center for people with learning disabilities. I would be getting in on the ground floor of the automated accounting department. I was pleased to know that they wanted me, but I was also feeling guilty about quitting the job I had. I had to pray for guidance on this.

Jan. 7, 1983 I went to mediation today. It was quite a session. I didn't feel that I was satisfied with the way things were going, but I was willing to see where this would lead. Bruce said that he called the retirement department at the State Department and was told $2,500 would go to me.

I said, "I called them, too, and was told the $2,500 were survivor's benefits and were taken off the top. When I told them that you wanted me to sign a paper saying you could collect all of the money, I was told it would be a very foolish decision because if you died, I wouldn't get any survivors benefits."

He shrugged his shoulders as if he had to accept it. There wasn't anything he could do about it. We started to go over some of the forms and Lori and a lawyer named Kirk conducted the session. Lori said, "Marge will have custody of the children" and Bruce became annoyed. She said, "Well, they'll live with Marge in the house.

Kirk interjected, "It could be shared parenting." Lori asked Bruce how often he wanted to see the kids. He said as often as he could. She wanted a schedule and he hemmed and hawed.

"They need to know you'll be there on schedule," Lori told Bruce. "Something they could count on. Do you think you could take them for a weekend?"

"I don't have room," Bruce said. "I have three rooms, bedroom, living room, and kitchen."

"Well, you have a lot of room," Lori continued. "The boys could sleep in sleeping bags. Is there a couch?"

"Yes, there's a couch in the living room and if push came to shove, one of them could sleep on that."

"We have one sleeping bag and a folding cot that he can take when he picks up the boys," I said.

"What weekend can you take them and what would be the time frame?" asked Lori. "Friday to Sunday evening?"

"Well, after a long day at work, I'm pretty tired and it's a long ride over."

"Well, how about Saturday morning to Sunday evening?

"Yes," I interrupted. "He could pick them up on Saturday and take them to bowling and bring them back Sunday evening about 8:00 pm. So tentatively he'll take them the first weekend of February."

Bruce wanted to get the financial segment done so we both would have money to survive, and he wanted to retire as soon as he was able.

"When my three years are up, I'm gone! The Department has done nothing for me—I owe them nothing."

"Where are you going?" I asked. "What are your plans?"

"I don't know," he answered.

"What am I supposed to do? I don't like the uncertainty."

"Well," Bruce's lawyer, Kirk, started. "You can be separated for a while or you can go for divorce."

"Well, we're heading in that direction," Bruce said.

"Is that what you want?" I asked.

"Well, we're heading in that direction," he repeated.

The truth may hurt," Lori said. "But it can be dealt with, so for the other person to build a new life you have to tell them what you plan. Are you saying you want a divorce, Bruce?"

"Yes, I guess that's what I'm saying."

"Well, look Marge in the eye and tell her."

He turned to me and said, "That's what I want."

We ended the conversation by talking about the children's tuition and necessity money. He gave me a check for tuition and food and asked what I did with the other money he gave me. Sometimes I wonder how he got to be a Budget Officer—then I remembered— I taught him my job.

BRUCE'S LOVE INTEREST REVEALED

Jan. 18, 1983 Elaine called to tell me she found out who Bruce was seeing in Pennsylvania—a Mrs. Hahn who was separated from her husband and had been having affairs with other men. She had an apartment in Swoyersville, PA and had been running around with the principal of Wyoming Valley West until the principal's wife told her to stay away from her husband unless she wanted trouble. Mrs. Hahn's son had his appendix out and was talking to a boy who shared the room, whose mother knew Mrs. Felch, my mother's neighbor. (That's a small town for you!) Her son was asked why his mother didn't come to the hospital to see him and the boy said, "She's too busy with her new boyfriend. He was a hostage, and his name is Bruce." When Elaine told me this, I couldn't believe it! Some of the rumors she found out were that the boy's father had custody of the children because the court judged her to be an unfit mother. The husband was a mail carrier and she worked at Wyoming Valley West School a few days each week. That's how she got involved with the principal until Bruce came along. She and her husband had been separated for about 3 – 4 years but not divorced, and the principal was not her first affair. She'd had a few. She also traveled in high political circles. I wasn't sure how much of the rumors were true and how many were just that—rumors.

Jan. 20, 1983 In the two years following Bruce's release, I never would have guessed I'd be where I am now. Elaine called to tell me there was a picture of Bruce hugging Lovey in the paper—the same one they used for his homecoming. He was interviewed, but said he didn't think about Iran anymore and that he'd be in the Far East for the anniversary. The article also said that his mother— who ran into the street ringing a cowbell and screaming, "My Bruce is free, my Bruce is free!" — was unavailable for comment.

Elaine called the newspaper and talked to the reporter. She told him the story was incomplete. Where it stated that Bruce was the father of three children, she said it should have also stated that he deserted his wife and children and only sees them for short periods about once a month. She also said that Mrs. Lodeski was probably ashamed of herself and her son.

Feb. 19, 1983 We had another mediation meeting. Bruce was really belligerent. He said he couldn't afford to pay the mortgage and that I shouldn't be surprised to get a letter from the mortgage company. He told Lori that he wanted the house sold and for me to move somewhere else. Lori discouraged that idea because she said it wouldn't be good for the boys to be uprooted. He wasn't too happy with that. He also complained about paying on the car. Lori had a few suggestions and the last one appealed to him—I would get the Ford Escort and he would get the Fairmont, and then trade it later. He would sign over the house to me and let me live in it and pay all of the bills on half of his salary. When Lori mentioned that the boys were under a lot of stress and moving them from their environment wouldn't be good for them, he retorted, "You want to see stress? I'm the one who has stress! I give her money and she's always asking for more and I'm going to have to dip into my savings and she won't touch hers." He was referring to my half of the CD that matured, which he tried to cheat me out of.

I calmly said, "That money is in case I have to go to the hospital because I won't have any health insurance. I will not go to a charity ward!"

The Psychologist Visit

March 6, 1983 I took Matt and Chris to see a psychologist. Matt was really mad at me for making him go. I was trying to do what was best for both him and Chris and yet I could understand his feelings. Matt didn't want people to know he ever saw a psychologist.

All three of us went into the office first and then Pete, the psychologist, said I could leave, so I did. I drove to Larisa Looby's for the luncheon to honor past officers of the St. Mark Women's Guild. When I returned to the office, the boys were outside the office and said Pete wanted to talk with me. He told me they were handling the situation as well as some other boys in the same boat and better than others. He didn't recommend that I bring them back unless they wanted to see him. He also said that Matthew had a lot of anger inside him but felt that making him face it right now wasn't the wise thing to do. Also, that Chris had not accepted the fact that Bruce was not coming back.

March 23, 1983 Today was another mediation day. Lori started with the list of items that she thought were settled only to have Bruce deny he had agreed to any of it—*again*. He started in on selling the house again. I got angry and got up and walked out. As I was leaving, I said, "You are not putting me out of that house with those kids." Then I added, "You can afford to go away every weekend."

I went out and as I was closing the door, Lori said, "Wait, let's discuss this." I answered, "No, I don't think so." As I came out to the reception room, Joan, the receptionist, looked surprised and I said, "I walked out. I'm getting screwed in there and I'm not going to take it."

She came around to where I was standing and put her arms around my shoulders. I had started to tremble and couldn't stop. She told me, "Please, sit down and I'll make you a cup of coffee or tea." I knew I couldn't drive home at that instant—I was too upset. I sat there for a while and Kirk came out and talked with me. He said that maybe we could just discuss other topics since the house is such a volatile one.

I went back in and Kirk listed all the expenses and asked if we had any suggestions as to how we could manage. Bruce just sat there. Lori talked about visitation. Bruce is supposed to have the boys every other weekend, at least one or two weeks in the summer and stay with them every Thursday while I go to school and study or do whatever I want until 9:30pm.

Bruce came over early on the 27th to get the furniture for his new apartment. He took the chest of drawers, double dresser, night table, desk and chair. These were all things that belonged to him when we got married. Then he asked, "What about the bar?"

I said, "You didn't tell me anything about wanting the bar. You should have told me sooner."

"Well, I thought as long as the truck is here—I thought I might as well take it."

I replied, "But I didn't clean it out."

Again, he said, "Oh, well, I thought as long as the truck is here…"

I answered, "Okay, I'll clean it out and you can take it, but you should have told me sooner."

I was not going to make it easy for him. I cleaned all the liquor, glasses, and coasters out of the storage area so the movers could take it apart to get it out of the house. They took it and the three bar stools to the truck. I didn't really want the liquor but I was determined not to give him anything more that I had to. If he wanted it, he'd have to ask. There were many times while the kids and I were in church that he took stuff out of the house like a thief. My neighbors would tell me later that they saw him taking bags and bags of stuff out.

I went upstairs and woke Debbie up and asked her to come downstairs. I told her that her father was here to take his stuff, and he'd probably want the big projection screen TV. But if she were downstairs, he wouldn't ask for it. So, she came down and talked with him for a few minutes and then he left. I felt that he could afford to buy a new TV; I couldn't. Now, I didn't have any bedroom furniture for my things since I had given my bedroom furniture away after we got married. I only had a bed, so my clothes were stacked on the floor.

April 6, 1983 It had been two weeks since Bruce came for his stuff. At nine minutes before midnight the phone rang and Chris answered. He said, "Oh, Hi. How are you? …. Yes, I'm okay… Yes, she's here." He handed me the phone and mouthed, "It's Dad." I took the phone and said, "Hello?"

He answered very dramatically, "Hi, are you all right?"

I said, "Yes."

"Thank God!" he exclaimed.

I asked, "What's the matter?"

He said, "Oh, I had such a terrible feeling that something happened to you. I just had to call."

"Where are you calling from?"

"Okinawa. I just wanted to make sure you were okay." I told him I was fine and we chatted for about 3 minutes and then hung up.

I didn't know what to think about this latest event. Why was he calling from Okinawa? Why was he so dramatically concerned about whether something had happened to me or not? He didn't say what he thought had happened nor why it mattered to him, especially after he had been so hateful during our mediation sessions. Those mixed signals were coming on again. He was making me nuts!

Apr 15, 1983 - Palm Sunday Bruce called to ask how we were and if he could come over to talk. I hesitated, and he asked, "Don't you want to talk?"

I said, "Well, I guess we could talk one more time."

He came over at 2:00pm and asked, "What would it take for us to get back together?" I was flabbergasted. He asked for a hug, so I hugged him. I told him for us to get back together we would have to go to counseling because there had been too much hurt in the past two years and that until we got everything out in the open, there was no chance.

He came over Thursday after he had an appointment with Dr. Ballon, his psychiatrist, and seemed happy. He asked if we had plans for Easter and said he didn't want to be alone. I asked if he was going to PA and he said "No." He asked for another hug.

He came over on Holy Saturday and took Chris to bowling, had lunch with us, and stayed and talked to Deb, Chris, and me. Matt wasn't home. Bruce seemed to enjoy the time spent here and Debbie said she enjoyed the talking and laughing with both of us in the same room. I wondered how long this would last.

April 24, 1983 The doorbell rang, and Chris called me to sign for delivery—13 red and white rosebuds in a vase. The card said, "Happy Easter. -Bruce. Sorry these are late due to an error by the florist." I called Bruce to thank him.

I said, "Hi, I got a surprise today."

"They finally got there!" He explained that he had ordered them last week and wanted them delivered on Friday and had called the florist about three times on Saturday and again on Monday and today. I told him they were beautiful and thanked him. But he was still confusing me.

April 26, 1983 Bruce came by about 6:15pm and ate dinner with us. He told his shrink that we were talking and Dr. Ballon asked how he felt about it. Bruce told him that since he had made the effort to reconcile, he felt pretty good. He didn't stay long but he saw the bouquet of flowers and seemed pleased with the arrangement and picked up the rest of his Easter stuff. He said he was going north for the weekend because his mother was depressed, and he also had to get some things settled. He didn't say what they were. I didn't have a good feeling about it.

Life went on and at various times Bruce would call me to ask if we "could talk." I usually would agree to meet with him, but after the meeting, things would turn sour again. It seemed every time I had an exam, I would get news from his lawyer that upset me, so much so, that I couldn't focus on my studies. The stress was killing me.

CHAPTER 18

WHO IS THIS DEVIOUS PERSON?

Apr. 3, 1983 Pat Lee called and said, "I don't know if I should tell you this, I've debated about it all afternoon." She continued to tell me that Bruce was in Virginia on Thursday and back at work on Friday. Gary told her that there was a birthday party for him at the Firenze restaurant in the C&P Telephone Company building on Glebe Road and that Gary was invited. Gary said he went around 8:30pm and that he thought most of the people there must have known Bruce from the Agency, but that he also had a "lady friend" with him. Pat asked me the name of the person I had heard about and I said, "Theresa." She said Bruce introduced Gary to a "Terry." I thought that if he had her there on Thursday, that meant she spent the night with him and probably went back to PA when he went up. I wish I had known sooner so I could have had a detective follow him.

Apr. 7, 1983, I called Bruce at the office and he wasn't in. I left a message for him to call me back. At about 2:45pm, he called and said he was on his break and didn't have too much time to talk. I asked what kind of break. He said he was taking a word processing class and that he had to return to it soon. I told him I was calling to see if he was coming by tonight.

He asked, "Tonight? What's tonight?"

I said, "Today is Thursday and since no one has heard from you, I didn't know if you'd be by."

"Well, no one has called me. I didn't get a card or a phone call."

At that comment, I exploded. I said, "Now wait one damn minute! Both Matt and Deb called you and you weren't in work."

He said, "Well, I was home."

I retorted, "Wrong! They called you at work and at your apartment and there was no answer. Your birthday cards are here. They asked me if they should mail them to you and I told them to do whatever they wanted. They thought you went to PA early."

He said, "I didn't. I didn't go until Saturday morning."

I remarked, "Well, how were they supposed to know that? They're not mind readers!"

Then he said he would be by, but he'd have to stop by the apartment first. He came by and got his gifts that night. He really made me furious.

Apr. 9, 1983 Bruce came by around 9:00am to take the boys to his apartment. He told them they didn't have to bring any sleeping bags because he had a sofa that opened into a bed. Debbie and I left for PA to go to my godchild, Lovie's, bridal shower. It was nice to get away and I enjoyed seeing some of my relatives who I hadn't seen in years. The shower was great and the bride-to-be got many beautiful things. We stayed until 4:00pm and arrived home about 8:00pm. The boys were home and there was no sign of Bruce. I asked them what time he dropped them off and Matt said 2:15pm. I was furious because he was supposed to have them until 8:30pm. I called Bruce and asked why he dropped them off so early, and he said he had things to do and that the boys said they had homework. He made my blood boil.

April 29, 1983 I called Bruce to tell him we had received the income tax refund and to meet me at the credit union at the State Department so we could split it. He made these big, important movements as he filled out his deposit slip and asked for the check, so I gave it to him.

He said to me, "You didn't sign it."

"I know, I'll do it later." So, he signed it and then said, "You'd better sign it," so I did. While we stood in line, he looked everywhere except at me. When we got nearer to the teller I said, "While we're here, we'd better sign the stock certificates because who knows when we'll be together again." He went to ask someone who would be able to do it and came back and said he had found someone. When we got to the teller, he told her he wanted to deposit $1,354 and wanted $150 in cash and the rest to be made out in a check for me. She said the balance would be $1,490. I stated emphatically, "Oh, no, my check is supposed to be $1,495.27." The teller said, "Sir, that would leave you with $145 cash." He said, "Whatever!" Again, he tried to cheat me out of a few measly dollars that mean so much to me and so little to him! I'll bet he was furious that I spoke up, but he didn't say anything. I hope he was embarrassed.

Afterwards, we went to the woman who transferred the stock to me. We signed the certificates, had them notarized, and as soon as that was done, he went running out ahead of me. I asked, "Which way are you going?" He said, "Oh, back through the cafeteria." I started to walk out that way and said, "I hope my meter hasn't expired. I don't want a ticket." He said, "I'll go and stand by the car—I'll run out now." He went running down the hall and was gone in a flash. He really was ashamed to be seen with me. When I got outside, he waited until I was about 10 feet from the car and walked away, saying, "You're lucky, it was already expired."

May 5, 1983 When I came home from my class, I found a note from Bruce saying I would be hearing from my lawyer because he decided not to continue mediation and that he had a new lawyer.

May 16, 1983 Matt was inducted into the National Honor Society. I was so proud of him. Despite all that has happened, Matt had kept focused on his schoolwork and it paid off with this honor. Bruce met us at Peary High School and again the process server missed him and he wasn't served. Matt's induction was very nice. He was elected Secretary/Treasurer of the National Honor Society and out of 24 students was one of five that was selected for a possible National Honor Scholarship Award. Bruce was so impressed that he told Debbie to take his picture with Matt. Why? Did he think Matt's intelligence in some way reflected on him? When it was over, Bruce dashed to his car and took off.

May 23, 1983 Chris and I went to Parkland Jr. high for the Gifted and Talented Students meeting. Chris had called Bruce and told him about it and asked if he'd be here. Bruce told him to call him back and remind him. I wasn't sure whether he'd show up or not. We got there at about 6:45pm and he arrived about five minutes later. He sat next to Chris and chatted for a few minutes and then I asked him if he had received the PEPCO bill and water bill. He said, "Yes."

I responded, "Oh, when I go up to PA for the wedding, Debbie and Matt are going to a concert at the Capital Centre and Chris will be alone on Friday night, so come and get him right after work."

He said, "I can't."

I looked at him and repeated, "You can't?"

He answered, "No, I can't."

I sat there seething. I had told him three months in advance about the wedding and he pulls this crap. Damn him, damn him, damn him! Chris looked at me and said, "What's the matter, Mom?"

I just said, "Nothing, Chris, I'm just upset."

Bruce then said, "I don't see why you can't take him with you to the wedding."

Chris replied, "Dad, when Mom filled out the card that asked how many people were coming, she put '1' because we were supposed to stay with you."

May 27, 1983—22 years since our wedding. Not an anniversary to celebrate.

ELAINE AND I BECOME DETECTIVES

June 8, 1983 I left for my niece's wedding in Pennsylvania at about 10:50am on Thursday and arrived at 3:00pm. It was a good trip with beautiful weather. We decided to walk around the stores in Nanticoke to look for some clothes for me. It was nice just doing that with my sister – something we had not done in years. At about 6:00pm we went to Swoyersville to look for Bruce and the Ford Escort. Since Bruce had been seen around there with a woman, we decided to look for the house or apartment where she lived. We went up and down Watkins Street but didn't see it, so we went to Edwardsville and looked to see if he had come to his mother's. Sure enough, the car was there. I said to Elaine, "Let's go to the shopping center and come back about 7:30pm."

We came back at 7:30pm and the car was gone, so we went back to Watkins Street. There was the car parked on the corner of the street just off Watkins. We looked at the house number—170—and went back to Elaine's and called the phone company for her phone number. They said it was a private number.

I asked Elaine, "Are you sure that's the Theresa Hahn at 170 Watkins Street?" to which she replied, "Yes." On Sunday, we went back to see the name of the street that the car was parked on and saw that it was Gillespie. At one point in our investigation, we called the Post Office to find out how to get to Watkins Street and we were asked for a house number. Not knowing what to say, we made up a four-digit number and the guy said, the numbers didn't go that high, but told us that if we went up Wyoming Avenue and turned left at a certain street then go up about two blocks, it would take us to Watkins Street. It went to the left and right from that street, and maybe we could find the house that way.

As Elaine and I were driving around Watkins Street, we were almost giddy, trying to decide if I should get out and drive the Escort to Elaine's house. I would have done it except there was an older gentleman sitting on the porch across the street on Gillespie and I didn't want him to see me drive it away. We had visions of Bruce calling the police to report his car stolen and having to tell them from where. The car was registered in both our names, so I couldn't be accused of stealing my own car. How would that look to the police? I wanted to do it so badly, but didn't really have the guts. It would have been such a shock to him to find out I knew where he was committing adultery. I thought to myself, "How could Bruce just throw away that meaningful, holy sacrament for some scum?" I tried hard not to refer to her as a slut and a whore, but it was very difficult. Those words were never in my vocabulary until a few months before.

When I got home on Tuesday, I found a letter from Ellen Pattin telling me a Mr. Harvey Jacobs, Bruce's new lawyer, contacted her and wanted to postpone our court date because he had not had time to prepare any proposals. I went to her office and we went over my financial statement and tried to bring everything up to date. She reviewed the original proposal and came up with a new one and sent me the draft, which I received on June 11, 1983. I added a bunch of comments and additional proposals and sent it back to her.

June 14, 1983 - Father's Day I had asked the kids if they planned anything for Father's Day and they said he probably wouldn't be here. Deb asked for suggestions and I told her that she'd have to decide for herself because I was not included in this.

Later, I saw that the James Bond movie *Octopussy* was showing and suggested they take him to that. So, Deb called him at the office. I left to go to the store and when I came back, she reported that Bruce initially claimed he wouldn't be here, but then he said he'd be busy in the morning, so he'd be here in the afternoon. I asked if he was going to meet them someplace. She said, "No, he's coming here, although he's reluctant to come here because of all the things you're doing to him."

I said, "Oh, poor baby, time for a pity party."

Deb retorted, "I don't want to be in the middle." It seems that he can say things that I'm doing to him, but I'm not supposed to say anything because then she would be in the middle. Something was wrong with this picture!

June 30, 1983 Today I took Matt to have his picture taken at Sears because he needed them for his applications to the Naval Academy. On the way home, I happened to mention out loud that I wondered if his father left for Pennsylvania today to start the 4th of July weekend early. Matt said, "Who cares? Knowing him, he probably did."

I looked over at him with raised eyebrows and he said, "What? Am I supposed to care?"

I answered, "Well, I guess when you don't see him too often you can't really miss him."

"That's right—he sees us maybe one hour every three weeks."

"Well, he did go to the movies with you on Father's Day."

"And don't forget the ride home. That was at least another minute!" He said it with a touch of sarcasm, but no malice in his voice. I know Matt is really hurting inside. His senior year was coming up and I'm sure he wondered if his father would be part of it. I felt especially bad for him.

July 15, 1983 I was back at school and back to working at the Legal Counsel Office at Montgomery College. I had my midterm yesterday and felt pretty good about most of it, but yet I didn't want to get my hopes up. I called Mr. Weldon, my instructor, and he told me I got a 91 plus five bonus points, for a total of 96. He also told me I had the highest grade in the class. I couldn't believe it. I was so happy; I could have screamed. I called home and Chris answered. When I told him how I did, he said, "That's great, Mom! Congratulations." When I told him, I got the highest grade in the class, he exclaimed, "You did?" When I got home, Debbie said with a grin, "When did you become such a brain?"

Going to college at my age was scary and I kept telling my kids that I had an "old" brain and it didn't function like it did when I was in high school. I told them to get as much of an education as they could while they were young and didn't have a lot of other responsibilities. It's too hard to go back after being away from studying for over 25 years.

I was enjoying class very much and I hoped it continued to be my best effort. On the other subject, I sent Bruce bills for prescriptions, doctors, clothes, and other things and all I got from him was the usual $150 check. I also got a credit union statement that said he hadn't made a payment on the Ford Fairmont in two months. I'd have to call Ellen on Monday to tell her.

HIRING A DETECTIVE

July 24, 1983 John Gabriel, the private detective I hired, called to tell me he got some good pictures of Bruce and Theresa Hahn. John Gabriel lived in Wilkes-Barre, PA and I hired him to follow Bruce on his weekend trip to Pennsylvania to see his girlfriend. I told John how I found out where she lived and how to get to her house. He told me to leave the detective work to him.

He said that Bruce was observed kissing Theresa on the upper arm on July 16th. I think we have what we need against him to charge him with adultery. I hope these pictures would do. I had the report and pictures sent to Ellen because I didn't want the boys to see that stuff.

July 29, 1983 I went to see Ellen and read the report from the detective and saw the photos. The report stated that Bruce and Theresa went to a church bazaar and then they came back to her apartment. After about 10 minutes, the light in the bedroom went on and then off. After 30 minutes, the lights went back on and a few minutes later Bruce left.

The pictures turned my stomach. I thought to myself, "And he asked me if I was satisfied in my appearance?" Then I remembered that it wasn't that part of her anatomy that interested him. I couldn't sleep or keep my mind on my studies. I had a very bad weekend, still thinking about those pictures.

August 5, 1983 I met Ellen at the new Judicial Center in Rockville at 9:00am and waited ten minutes until it was ready. We chatted a few minutes and then I hopped in the car and drove up I-270. The trip was pleasant, and I arrived at Gabriel's Detective Agency and left the summons at 1:35pm. I gave Elaine's phone number for him to call me when he got free from the testing he was doing. He called about 3:00pm and I explained that the summons had to be served on Theresa Hahn as soon as possible today. He said he'd do his best. I said that I wanted to be sure Bruce and Theresa had a "nice" weekend.

He laughed and said, "What is that? Your 'woman's scorn' coming out and you're using me as an instrument?"

I said, "You bet!" Elaine and I sat anxiously waiting for him to call back. We just sat down to dinner and the phone rang. It was him! John said, "It's done."

I responded, "Good. Tell me what happened."

He said, "I read it to her as required by law. And she said, 'What is this?' I read it and she said again, 'What is this?' I said, 'You can read,' and handed it to her. Then I smiled and said, 'You know what this is all about.' And turned around and left."

I said, "John, I wish I could be there when Bruce finds out."

"He was there," John said. "His car was there."

I snickered and asked, "Do you think that that ruined their weekend?"

He answered, "I'll bet it did."

John said he'd send me his bill and we hung up. We went up to Lovey's after dinner and gave her all the details

August 18, 1983 Again, Lori said that the part of Bruce that was a husband and a father had died, that he had abdicated that position and didn't want to be reminded of those responsibilities except for the periodic check he sends. She was more convinced than ever that his mother and brother were behind his affair with Theresa Hahn, that his mother probably arranged their meeting after telling Bruce something about me and that once he got involved there was no turning back. I told Lori I didn't believe his mother would be so venomous especially to her three grandchildren.

Lori said, "When you're dealing with someone who is so self-centered as she seems to be, there is nothing they won't do to serve themselves. She sounds like a sick person, mentally, and it's unfortunate that she has such a strangle hold on Bruce. For some reason, in his eyes, she can do no wrong. He has transferred all his anger from the Iranians to the people who love him most and without reservation, his wife and his children."

CHAPTER 19

◆————————————————————————————————◆

THE HEARTACHE AS MY MARRIAGE ENDS

Aug. 24, 1983 Debbie called the credit union to see about her student loan. They said it was just signed and returned from University of Maryland, and would take about 10 days. She said, "Mom, I guess I'll have to call Dad and ask him for money for my books."

When I went into the kitchen and saw that she was on the phone, I went back into the bedroom to give her privacy. When she got off the phone, she said that Bruce said he'd send her a check for $100. She also told me that he said he had hoped "one of you guys" would call him. She told me she replied, "Well, Dad, you could call us." He responded with "I guess it does work both ways." She asked when she and the boys would see him again and he said he didn't know. He also said he hoped the problems between he and I would be solved soon. When she asked what that had to do with them, he said I used them to get to him because I had him served with a summons when he came over to see the boys. Then, she mentioned Matt having his teeth pulled and he said, "Yes, his wisdom teeth, right?" After she hung up, I asked her if he mentioned talking to Matt to wish him well on his surgery. She said, "No."

Later I told Matt that Deb had talked to his father and he asked, "Didn't he even ask to talk to me?"

I said, "I suppose not."

It angered me to see the hurt on his face. Later he mentioned it again – that he thought Bruce would have called. Matt and Chris had no contact with him since Father's Day. The more I thought about it, the madder I became.

Aug. 26, 1983 Matt woke me up at 4:00am. He was in severe pain and had tears running down his face. He said he didn't want to wake me because he knew I was tired. By this time his face had started to swell and he was really hurting. I got him ice and pills and got him settled back into bed.

I got up at 7:00am and got dressed to go to Pennsylvania for the deposition of Theresa Hahn. I hated to leave Matt at a time like this, but I couldn't get the date changed. I called Sue Petro who offered help if Matt needed it. Matt got up, had some Jell-O and his medicine, and went back to bed. As I left, I told Deb and Chris to help Matt in any way they could. I picked up Ellen and we went on our way to the United Penn Bank for the appointment and waited for the required one-half hour to take the deposition. Theresa Hahn never showed up.

Ellen looked really surprised. I informed her of the many people who had called my sisters about Theresa Hahn's affair with my husband and the fact that she had many other affairs.

We talked for a while and then went to Atty. Elliot Edley's office. We explained to him that Theresa Hahn had not shown up for the deposition and he said he'd process the papers through the Pennsylvania courts.

I called home and the boys told me that Bruce came by at lunchtime for about 15 minutes to see Matt. For Matt's sake I was glad that he did stop by.

We had lunch and then left PA around 4:10pm, much later than I had wanted to, but Ellen drove, which I found incredibly helpful. When I got back about 8:45pm, Matt, Debbie, and Chris were relieved. I never came home this late from a trip and they worried that I was in an accident. I told them that this was how I felt whenever they arrived home late too.

September 2, 1983 Today I got the copy of the interrogatories from Bruce. He said we had an understanding about the separation. I'd like to know what kind of understanding there was if he said he was leaving and there was nothing I could do about it. He also said he had not had intercourse with anyone, but I knew better. He wanted the house sold "because the two eldest children will not be living at home by September 1984." Where he got that idea, I'll never know.

Deb asked, "Mom, where does he want me to go?"

Matt asked, "What happens if I'm not accepted into the Naval Academy? Where will I go and what happens if I don't have any place to live?"

The interrogatories were not signed which I'd take to mean he doesn't want to perjure himself.

Depositions and Accusations

September 14, 1983 Today was deposition day. I left the house at 9:20am and got to the office of Harvey Jacobs at 9:40am. He's located on Rockville Pike across from White Flint Mall. I parked at White Flint and carried my Xerox box full of receipts across the street. I was shaking really badly and thought that if I could sit for the 20 minutes before we started that I might be able to calm down. Bruce came into the office and I didn't even look at him. I was going over the deposition questions and wanted to be sure I remembered what I had said in the answers. I looked up and Bruce looked at me and started to smile. I just glared at him and went back to my papers. When Ellen came in, she was called into Mr. Jacobs' office. She was in there for about 20 minutes, after which Mr. Jacobs summoned Bruce, and Ellen summoned me. They went into one room while Ellen and I went into the library. Ellen said Mr. Jacobs hoped we could come up with a solution we could both live with. She told me Bruce offered to give me $1,400 per month. I said we couldn't survive on that. She went back in and told him that. He told her that Bruce said I squandered $60,000 while he was in Tehran. I almost had a heart attack! How could he say that? Ellen told me Harvey Jacobs' first suggestion was $1,200—that was $357 below the poverty level.

After each proposal, Ellen consulted with me, then would go back and talk with Harvey Jacobs; then he'd go and tell Bruce and then come back with comments. Some of Bruce's comments were: "If she can't live on the money I'm offering, she'd better stop living so high on the hog."

The changes went by so fast that at the end of the two- and one-half hours, I wasn't really sure what I had agreed to. The final offer was $1,642 per month and he won't pay for any of the kids' tuition. He also said he'd pay $100 for their books. Together, we agreed that the hostage stuff is *his* and that if he wants to leave it to the kids, it will be his decision, not mine; we'll trade cars, the Acacia insurance policy is my responsibility after he brings it up to date; he'd pay off the Ford Fairmont, and he'd pay me the money he owes me.

September 15, 1983 I felt really lousy about the agreement and really shouldn't have accepted it. I know Bruce is lying about his salary. He must have thought that he was pulling a fast one. My mind kept going back to his accusation that I squandered $60,000. It had me extremely upset. If he had stabbed me in the heart, the hurt wouldn't be any more painful. Why would he ever say such a thing? I felt betrayed.

September 19, 1983 The weekend went badly. Bruce met the boys at the bowling lanes yesterday, saying he wouldn't meet them here. I told Chris to be sure that Bruce saw the condition of his sneakers. So, after bowling Bruce took both boys for sneakers. Matt also told him he needed new shoes, but Bruce ignored it.

Bruce told the boys that once the agreement was signed, he'd see them more often. I told them he was making excuses. I was really upset over the weekend, repeatedly thinking of Bruce's accusation that I squandered $60,000 while he was in Tehran. It bothered me so much that I told Ellen I wouldn't sign anything until he proves it or apologizes for the accusation. She said she'd write a letter to Mr. Jacobs to let him know the agreement was in jeopardy.

BRUCE GOES TO THE FAR EAST LEAVING US WITHOUT MONEY FOR FOOD

September 28, 1983 I didn't receive a check today. I had called Bruce's office on Monday because Chris needed money for a school trip and for school pictures, and that's when I found out he'd be gone to the Far East until the 10th or 11th of October. I called again today to find out if he gave the checks for me to someone in his office. I talked to a Joanne and a Mr. Tyson. Neither of them knew anything about it, but Mr. Tyson said Bruce would be in Jakarta on Monday and that he'd send a cable on Monday morning to see if Bruce could make arrangements for the money. I'm sure he'd have a fit about the cable. Joanne asked me if I thought Bruce might have given the checks to his mother to send to me and that maybe I should call her first. I told her that she was not speaking to me.

October 12, 1983 I had called Ellen to tell her that I had not gotten a check from Bruce since he left for the Far East. She was furious. She called Harvey Jacobs to let him know that she was resetting the date for the deposition and support hearing, and that she was starting proceedings to have Bruce's wages garnished. Bruce called to tell me he had no idea that I didn't get any money while he was away –that he had sent a check from Bangkok. I asked him why he didn't send me the money when he left and he said he didn't have it then. What a liar. He had his advance, which was more than enough to cover his trip and our measly few dollars. I'm sure the reason Bruce called me was that he knew he was in real trouble now and hoped I wouldn't go through with the court action. Ellen told me that Harvey Jacobs was so furious with Bruce he told him that his chances in court were blown. He told Bruce that when you leave your wife and children without money for food, the judge –in his words - "will crucify you." It seemed now that we had the upper hand, but still I can't count on that.

Deb called that evening and said that Bruce had called her and was acting strange. He asked her if she had talked to me, if I knew she had talked to him and if I knew he was seeing her this weekend. She answered "Yes" to all the questions. Then he asked her what I said about him seeing her and she said, "Nothing." She didn't understand the questioning.

October 14, 1983 Deb was home for the weekend and said a little bit more about Bruce's visit. She said he told her that, "Grammy wasn't spreading rumors and she shouldn't be blamed for what happened. No one should be blamed. It was just something that happened." Now that confused me. She tells people Bruce and I were divorced because he was having an affair, but it was just something that happened? How was it I was blamed for ruining his career among the many other things he'd blamed me for? Again, he said that Grammy wanted to be close to them again.

Debbie said, "Mom, Dad doesn't love you anymore," and the way she said it really tore me up. I felt like I was kicked in the stomach. I spent the rest of the weekend in tears. Bruce said he didn't come around to see the kids because he had trouble separating them from me. I felt that since he said he didn't love me anymore; he was also saying he didn't love them. Deb said he was all choked up and had tears in his eyes. I remember that – it's a good act! He should get an Oscar.

BRUCE WANTS TO MEET TO TALK, MOSTLY ABOUT HIM

October 24, 1983 I went to the bank to cash the checks from Bruce and when I got home, Matt said, "Mom, Dad called and wants you to call him back."

I just looked at him in disbelief and said, "He wants *me* to call *him*?

I called the office and Bruce answered. "Matt said you called."

"Yes, could we meet someday this week?" he asked. "I have a problem and I have no one else to turn to."

"What's the matter?"

"I don't want to say over the phone."

"I can meet you on Wednesday and maybe we could go someplace and have a cup of coffee," I said.

He asked where and when I could meet him. I told him somewhere near Montgomery Mall around 1:00pm. I didn't have a clue as to why I was the only person who could help him with whatever this problem was.

October 26, 1983 Bruce called at 11:45am asking when he should meet me because he had to arrange his lunch hour. I told him to meet me at 1:00pm, but he suggested the place Hamburger Hamlet in Bethesda. I arrived at 12:55pm and he was already there. We had to wait about 10 minutes for a table and we made some small talk while we waited. After we were seated and had ordered, I began, "Well, what is this problem you have that only I can help you with?"

"I have something to show you," he said." "But promise me you won't show it to anybody."

He reached inside his jacket pocket and pulled out a letter written to me. He said he could only turn to me because I knew him best and he was scared of everything. He was very nervous and was close to tears. He thanked me for coming about six times.

I read the letter. It said he wanted to put the divorce action on hold. I was the person who knew him best and it was only logical that he would turn to me. He wanted a relationship with the kids and wanted me to help him. It seemed as if he wanted reconciliation, and yet, I couldn't really feel that. I was getting mixed signals.

"I hope you'll help me," he said. "But I understand if you say no."

"How do you want me to help you?

"By listening to me and asking questions."

"Bruce, I offered you help before and you didn't want it."

"I know," he said.

"Well, the offer still stands."

He looked relieved. We talked a little more and then he said he had to get back to work. He walked me to the car and I asked him how often he wanted to talk to me, "Once a month would be fine," he answered. He was going to Pennsylvania "to tie up some loose ends." My antenna warning for additional problems seemed to come to the forefront. Could I believe he wouldn't go back to his nasty ways? We said goodbye and went our separate ways. He said he'd stop by on his way back from Pennsylvania.

Later I re-read his letter, and although I tried hard to feel sorry for him, I thought it sounded very self-centered. My intuition told me to be careful.

Bruce called me and said he felt better than he had a right to and felt better than he had in months. He seemed almost like his old self. Still my sixth sense told me not to put much faith in this latest meeting.

October 30, Sunday Bruce stopped by on his way home from Pennsylvania and said he didn't feel good and wanted postpone our talk for a few days. I said, "Okay." He left saying he'd call. I had a feeling this "change" was going back to his deceptive ways.

Nov 3, 1983 I had another appointment with Lori and told her of these recent events. She suggested I call him and meet with him that evening at his apartment so we'd be able to talk without interruption. I had second thoughts about it, but I called and told him I was in VA and if he wanted, I'd wait for him to get off work. He told me to meet him at the Roy Rogers at Loehmann's Plaza.

He came into the parking lot at about 5:30pm and pulled up next to me. He opened the door to the Fairmont and asked me if I wanted a cup of coffee because he needed something to drink. I expected him to ask me to go inside for it, but he went in, got the coffee, and came back and sat in the car. We talked for about 1½ hours, but he didn't say much that I hadn't already heard.

"I received the marital agreement from my lawyer," he said. "It looked okay."

"It's not worth the paper it's written on," I said.

"Why?" he asked.

"Because of the discrepancy in your financial statement.

He looked at me as if he didn't know what I was talking about. The kind of look he always gave whenever he didn't want to remember. He said that the one thing he and his lawyer changed was about the cars. I asked what he meant

"After Ellen and I left my attorney's office," he started, "my lawyer asked me if I wanted the Fairmont. I told Mr. Jacobs "no," so he said we'd just change it."

So much for a legal agreement, I thought. Well, they can shove it because there is no way that they should change something that was already decided on. He also mentioned the car loan—that he had agreed to pay it and that he asked Mr. Jacob's why it wasn't in the agreement and he said Mr. Jacobs said he just left it off. I was trying hard not to show how mad I was getting because I had given my word that I'd help him overcome his problems, so I said nothing. I left there after a few more bits of information. For instance, I learned that he carpooled to work, so there was no way that he spent all that money on gas except for his weekly trips to Pennsylvania. He did tell me to think back to all the things he did—always taking the easy way out for himself and not caring who it hurt.

"What am I supposed to do?" I asked him.

"Just help me reestablish a relationship with the kids. Don't get me wrong, I'm not asking to come back. I hope you don't think that's why I wanted us to talk."

That confused me because the letter he gave me when we met at Hamburger Hamlet asked if we could put the divorce action on hold. So, what sense did this make?

Nov 4, 1983 – That Infamous Day – Four Years Later Will my life ever return to *normal* or will it forever be wrapped around the aftermath of the Hostage Crisis? And how long would this last?

Bruce called in the afternoon but didn't seem too bothered by the date. He said he'd come by on Saturday and meet the boys at the bowling alley. As it turned out, Matt had to work and so he met Chris there, brought him home, and they had lunch here. Deb made Bruce a sandwich and then the three of them went shopping. He did tell me that he needed somebody to be with him the night before—that he had a bad time. I asked him why he hadn't called. I would have talked to him. He said he had thought about it.

When he called me on Friday afternoon, he asked me for Deb's address at school and I said I didn't know it. He said Ben called him (he hadn't heard from him in months) to thank him for the birthday card Bruce sent. Ben wanted Deb's address at school. Bruce suggested that he send any mail to the house, Ben said he'd rather not. He also said that Ben was trying to reestablish a relationship with Debbie. I thought that was strange, especially the word *re-establish*. I had heard that a lot lately. I told him to call Deb to get it. Later Deb called and asked why Bruce called to ask for her address at school.

November 7, 1983 Deb called, furious at the letter she received from Ben. He said a lot of rotten things to her, including how I had alienated Bruce's family. He ended with wishing her well in her life, school, career, and growth. He also wished her a happy birthday a month early, saying she may not hear from him for some time.

Debbie told me she showed the letter to her father and after he read the first two pages, he said he didn't see what was so terrible about it.

She said, "You don't think the stuff he said about Mom was rotten?"

His response was, "Oh, that."

I told her that she should consider the source and not let it bother her, but I know she was hurt. I related the comments from the Iran Working Group workers who thought Ben had emotional problems and to try not to let it bother her.

For the next few months we went on living our lives without any other contact.

HIS FEELINGS OF GUILT

March 13, 1984 – Meeting with Bruce I had another meeting with Bruce tonight. He called me yesterday and asked me if we could meet. This was the first I had heard from him since he stopped by before Christmas to see the boys and even then, he only gave me a nod and a hello and that was it. The plan to meet with him once a week back in late October to talk never did pan out – just as I had suspected would happen. When he asked me to meet with him, I said okay. He arrived at the house about 20 minutes after six and came in and Debbie sort of ignored him. When I got my coat on, I asked her if she was going to talk to her father and she said, "For what? He doesn't want to talk to me." But she did say "Hi, Dad" before we left. We went to Roy Rogers's restaurant in the Aspen Hill Shopping Center. He had a cup of coffee and I had a cup of hot chocolate.

We sat and he did most of the talking, and for a change I didn't jump in with comments just to keep the conversation going. I just sat it out and waited. He was very nervous and he cried off and on for the hour and a half that we were together.

He started off again by saying that he was scared, that he hates the thoughts of going overseas, he was frantic that he was scheduled to go on the 29th and he wouldn't be back until the middle of April. He had trouble sleeping, saying he slept maybe for three hours and then he'd be awake.

Then he told me he was put on medical hold for an overseas assignment, but that didn't make any difference because he didn't want an overseas assignment. He said physically, there wasn't much wrong with him – he had high blood pressure and he had deep depression. He also had terrible pains in his right hand and his knee but they couldn't find anything wrong with him. He said it might have been psychosomatic.

Then he said, "I've even been going to a shrink." I asked him how long he had been going and he answered, "A couple of months."

I asked, "How often do you go?"

"I was going every other week, but now I'm going every three weeks."

"Well, if you're as bad as you say you are, you should be going at least once a week."

"Well, I'm going to start that up, Bruce said. "I think I'll be going every week. I have no one to talk to. I can't talk to Mom.

"Why?" I inquired.

"Well, after talking to the shrink, I realize she's my problem."

"Oh? In what way?"

"It stems back from when I was little, when I was younger and she remarried after my father died. She laid a guilt trip on me. She said she married Al for me, for my benefit. After asking some probing questions, the psychiatrist showed me that my mother has me on a guilt trip. She's had me on a guilt trip all these years."

"Well, it's good that it's out on the table," I tried to reassure him.

"Yes, but I'm 48 years old. How can something that happened so long ago still be affecting me—still be a monkey on my back?"

"If it wasn't handled properly in the beginning, then it's got to come out sometime. It stays dormant for a while until something triggers it and you can't stand it anymore."

"I love her dearly, but she has really put me on a guilt trip. And then there's my dear brother."

"What about him?"

"He can do no wrong!" he exclaimed.

"By whose standards?"

"My mother's."

"How do you feel about that?" I asked him.

"Guilty," he said. "Guilt that I have a brother. Because it seemed like my father died, and as far as I was concerned, it was like my mother married the next day. And the third day I had a brother. I resented that and I feel guilty because I resented it.

"If you are able to at least face the truth, and start dealing with it, that's part of the battle."

He talked about his stepfather Al, telling me that for all the years his mother was married to Al, he was never a son to Al; he was always "Theresa's kid." But Bruce said, "At least he was somewhat of a father to Ben. But suddenly when I became a hostage, then I became "My son, my son" to Al. He'll tell anyone who will listen, but you don't hear that too often now that it's all over. Where was he when I needed him? Where was he on my birthday and Christmas?"

I said, "Maybe in his own way he did the best he could"

Bruce said, "No, he didn't. He only hears what he wants to hear and only does what he wants to do. But I CANNOT stand when he says that."

"There's resentment?"

"You bet! My father is dead and when he says, 'This is my son,' I pack my suitcase and I leave, not that night, not the next day - right then!

He talked for a while and was very nervous and then he'd cry. Luckily, I had a lot of tissues with me. We used plenty. He said, "I do a lot of this anymore."

Then he said something again about his mother and guilt and I said, "Well, what can I say about this situation except that I knew you were always very close to your mother. I don't know what else I could say."

"She has me on a guilt trip!"

"I think I told you that once."

"I wasn't listening—I didn't hear that. I didn't want to hear it. I didn't want anyone saying anything."

"I know that."

He mentioned again the guilt he felt about his brother.

"Did the shrink say that I was a problem?" I asked. "That I caused you problems?"

"No, only that I was closest to you, and that I blamed you for everything."

"What else do you have guilt about?"

"Everything," he said. "The kids. I don't know how to handle it for now. I'm having enough problems trying to handle these things, and I can't handle that yet. The last time I had the boys, I ran out of things to say. That's terrible."

"Yes, considering the fact that when you came home from work every day, they wouldn't shut-up, and would follow you into the bedroom saying 'Hey, Dad, guess what happened in school today.' All three of them. And you'd say 'Hey, Guys, give me a chance to change my pants.'"

"Yeah, and I loved every minute of it."

"Well, you can call them," I suggested.

"Well, Chris called me a couple of weeks ago and said that he needed sneakers and I sent him the money. He never even called back to say what he got."

"Bruce, why didn't you come and take him shopping. Then, you won't have to ask what he got, because you'll be there with him."

"Yeah, I know." This was his very common answer to many of my questions.

Well, they don't want to be in your way, but they feel like they are," I told him.

"Debbie never calls me anymore.

"She told me the last time she called you that you weren't interested in talking to her.

"Boy, it's a vicious circle, isn't it?"

I agreed with him. "Yes, it sure is."

During about the last 15 minutes of our one and one, half hour meeting, he asked, "Well, what are we going to do about us?"

"What about us?"

"What are we going to do about our situation?"

"I don't know. Bruce, you're the one that wants the divorce."

"Oh! Well, I've got to have it," he said. "There's just no way that I can be a family man anymore."

I sat there thinking, "Then what the hell are we doing here?" I asked him, "When was the last time you talked to your lawyer?"

"About three weeks ago, when your lawyer filed a motion of some kind."

"Yes, a motion of discovery."

"It had something to do with last year."

"She asked for your latest pay statement and a copy of you W-2 form, and she told your lawyer that if she didn't hear anything by February 28th, she'd file a motion of discovery. She hasn't heard from him, so that's what she's doing. She's called him a few times and he doesn't answer or return her calls. She writes to him and he doesn't respond to that, so you're going to have to figure it out with your lawyer.

"For all the money I pay him," he said, "he's supposed to be looking after me."

"Yes, and every time my lawyer has to do something like this, it costs me money. I owe her almost $1,000. Once in a while I pay her about $25 a month."

"Well, I never wanted to hurt anybody." He repeated, "I never wanted to hurt anybody."

"Well, you have."

He brought me back to the house and before I got out of the car, he told me to tell the kids he loved them. I said, "Why can't you do that for yourself? I think they'd like to hear it from you."

"I don't know if I could handle that."

"You can give each of them a hug," I suggested.

"Yeah, I could do that."

When we pulled up to the house, Jeff's car was there.

"Do you have company?" Bruce asked. "Is somebody here?"

"I don't know," I said. "Maybe Debbie's boyfriend, Jeff?"

"Oh, then I'm not coming in. Do you think that's his car?"

"Yes, it's his."

"Well, I'm not coming in," he said. "It's no use."

And with that he left. I decided that I was not going to meet with him anymore. It only tore me up and did nothing for our situation. He was, and always would be, self-centered.

CHAPTER 20

THE AFTERMATH

When the crisis first ended and Bruce returned to us, we thanked God for His goodness and mercy for a happy ending to a terrible situation. Bruce was home alive and well, and we looked forward to resuming our normal lives.

After he was home ten months, problems began to surface, rather subtlety at first with Bruce acting strangely and giving us the silent treatment. Then, he started lying to me and the children, doing very devious and sneaky things behind our backs. The biggest shock of all was adultery. He was having an adulterous affair with a married woman.

Sometimes I wondered if I had known the heartache I would endure after the stress of the hostage crisis and other events in my life, would I have done things differently? Would I still have written Bruce over 300 letters and cards, or sent sports papers, books, cookies, and toiletries for those 14 ½ months? Would I have forced myself to go to all the meetings at the Department of State, become secretary of FLAG and mail chairman, meeting with Mr. Slim de Bagha at the Algerian Embassy, and begging him to have our personal mail go through their diplomatic pouch? Would I have begged everyone going to Tehran to deliver mail to Bruce and the other hostages and have them ask to see Bruce if it was possible? Would I have done all of these things? Would I have still married Bruce? If I had not married Bruce, I would not have my three wonderful children and seven grandchildren? This must have been in God's plan for me. I must have been destined for this life, but why? Why did I have to endure the terror of the Hostage Crisis and then experience the destruction of my marriage?

During the separation, I was most worried about the children. I didn't want them to know that their father was committing adultery. How do you explain that to children (ages 12, 16, and 19) who idolize their father and could never believe he would do something sinful after preaching high moral standards all their lives?

I tried to shield them from the rumors and the facts, but if I didn't tell them and they would only hear it from someone else, they would lose trust in me. With a very heavy heart I broke the news to them as gently as I could, explaining that there were many rumors going around in Pennsylvania about their father and a woman by the name of Theresa Hahn who he knew from high school. I told them that my sisters and brother-in-law had seen their father and Theresa holding hands and acting like lovers. I also told them that I knew nothing about her, except that she was married with children and was separated from her husband.

After I told them, there was complete silence. It was a hard pill to swallow— to know their father, whom they loved and respected, was doing something they never thought he was capable of doing.

Our separation lasted three years, and despite all the times Bruce asked to put our divorce "on hold" and the many attempts at reconciliation, it became apparent that it was time to end our marriage. The hurt, the distrust, and all the lies had taken their toll on my emotions and I could no longer live in a state of uncertainty. I could never trust him again.

When it became apparent that my marriage was over, I had to learn to fight for the children and for myself because otherwise Bruce would have left us destitute—another trait I never thought I'd see in him. Here was this person who worried that we wouldn't have enough money to survive while he was a hostage, now cheating us out of every cent he could get away with. He was no longer a decent human being. Whether it was by his own choice or whether his mistress and his family were goading him into it, I didn't know.

While the children were growing up, there was never a doubt in my mind that they would all go on to college to further their education, but now with the divorce, Bruce refused to help them with their college tuition. He said they could get jobs and work for their college expenses. The only help he would give was to pay $100 for books per semester, which barely covered one book for some courses.

GOING TO COURT FOR THE DIVORCE

On **March 14, 1986** Ellen, my lawyer, and I proceeded to the courthouse in Rockville, MD and terminated my marriage of 24 years and 9 months. Even at the courthouse, the details of the divorce were still unsettled. Ellen and I arrived prior to Bruce and his lawyer, Harvey Jacobs. When Bruce came into the waiting room where I was sitting, he looked over and smiled. I gave him a disgusted look and turned away.

Ellen went to negotiate with Harvey Jacobs and said that Bruce would pay me alimony and child support for Chris until he graduated from high school, and that I could have the house and he'd pay one half the arrearages. The support would be called "family support." I didn't care—I was so damned mad at Bruce and his lawyer for putting me through hell for the past three years that I was not willing to make any deals, deciding I'd rather take my chances in court. I had reached the saturation point where no matter what they said, I was not going to agree to it. I wanted the whole world to know just what Bruce had done to us. When I got into court, I was going to tell them just how Bruce got the Budget Officer job – because I taught him MY job in Frankfort, Germany! I could have had the Budget Officer career and been making the kind of money he was, and he probably would have remained in a file room!

At that point, Ellen said, "I don't want to talk you into anything and I will fight for you as long as you want me to, but I think this is an offer that you might want to consider. The laws have changed and wives are no longer granted the house and alimony for life. It is a sad testimony of the so-called Women's rights, and you have to realize that depending on the judge, you may not get as much."

The "family support" which was a combination of alimony and child support would be $1300 per month and Bruce would be able to claim that as alimony for tax purposes and I would have to claim it as income. Of course, the fact that he would not pay anything for Matt or Debbie since they still lived at home when they weren't at their dorms and still needed to be supported, was another issue. Finally, after ironing out a few more details, we went before the judge and he went over point by point what I had agreed to.

My divorce became final on March 14, 1986. It was a relief. I thought my life would now become more normal. I would be through with Bruce and could concentrate on my own life. The one detail I missed in the divorce agreement was that Bruce would pay child support for Chris until he graduated from high school instead of his 18th birthday. Chris would be only 17 years old when he graduated. When I told Ellen that after we left the chambers, she said, "Oh, you should have reminded me. Well, when the time comes, we will go back to court and have that rectified, because Federal laws say that a child doesn't reach the age of majority until they are 18, so we'll try to get the other six months' worth of support."

Not having any contact with Bruce didn't last long. When it came time for our income taxes to be prepared, Bruce thought he could claim the children as his dependents along with claiming all of the money as alimony. That is not what the Family Support statute meant. It meant that I had to claim the money as income, but I claimed the children as my dependents because it was for the purpose of supporting them. As usual, Bruce was being devious. I let him know, in no uncertain terms, that I was not about to let him get away with that. I threatened to report him to the IRS if he tried to claim the kids, especially since he wasn't giving any money toward support for Matt and Debbie.

Throughout the years, we've had more of the same problems that we had during our separation, so being divorced did not make it any easier for me. As for Bruce saying he wanted to see the children as often as possible, that too, went by the wayside. He had the boys one weekend and never even took them for the two weeks in the summer as he had promised. As for keeping in touch by phone, that was the biggest joke. Over the years, the kids continued to call him for his birthday, Father's Day, the 4th of November, and the 20th of January, only to get his answering machine - and he never called back. I know that there were times when he was listening to the kids on the answering machine but wouldn't pick up the phone to talk to them. At one point, Debbie called him and left a message. When he didn't call back, Debbie called him again only to find the number had been changed to another unlisted number. Evidently, his mistress had had it changed. The next time Debbie was able to get in touch with him at his office, she asked about the new phone number, and he gave it to her. At that point Debbie said, "If I call this number will she have it changed again?" He assured her that it would not be changed.

During these years, my mother-in-law never called the children to see how they were doing, though she was always telling Bruce she wanted to be "close" with them again. One day. Debbie asked if I'd be upset if she visited her grandmother. She said she didn't want to have a guilty conscience if her grandmother died before she got to see her. As time went on, all three of my kids went to see her, and although the closeness they felt when they were young never returned, it was certainly an improvement over the previous 16 years without any contact at all. It was at that time that I wrestled with my own feelings toward her and the family as a whole. When Bruce left, I decided to get rid of everything that reminded me of him or his mother. I told the kids I never wanted to see their father, grandmother, or uncle again, nor did I ever want them in my house.

Ben Called me about his Mother's Illness

In 1998, Ben called asking if Bruce had let me know that their mother was in the hospital with a blood disorder, and was very ill. He had not. Ben gave me a few details about her condition, but emphatically stated that she did not have cancer. He asked me to tell my children. I suggested he call them, but he said he'd appreciate it if I told them. When I called them, they wondered why he even bothered to tell us since they had not heard from him in the past 16 years.

Although I was adamant that I wanted no contact with my former in-laws, I guess God had other plans for me. After I found out that my mother-in-law was very sick, and while I was visiting my sisters in Pennsylvania, I thought about going to see her. She was now home from the hospital and after much thought and prayer, I decided to stop by for a few minutes to wish her well. After all, I would do the same thing for an acquaintance.

I went to the flower shop in a grocery store and stood looking at the flowers for about 20 minutes, debating on whether I should get her a potted plant or some cut flowers. I couldn't make up my mind. I thought to myself, "God, help me decide. I don't know what to get." Finally, I settled on a small vase of yellow roses.

I drove to her house and went in the back door, which she never locked.

I called out, "Hello? Anybody here?"

She answered, "Who is it?"

I answered, "It's me, Marge" as I went into the dining room where she was in her recliner.

She exclaimed, "Oh, Marge, how nice of you to come." I held out the vase of flowers and said, "I brought you a few roses." At that point she was overjoyed saying, "Yellow roses! That's my favorite flower. I carried yellow roses when I got married to Al." I said a silent, "Thank you, God, for your guidance."

I talked with her for about an hour bringing her up to date on my children's and grandchildren's activities. By that time, it is was already after 3:00pm and I had the long drive back to Maryland so I said "goodbye."

She said, "Please, come again. You are always welcome in my house and if you need a place to stay, you are welcome to stay here. You'll always be my daughter-in-law." That comment surprised me.

When I got home, I told the children that I stopped by to see their grandmother. I think they were glad that I did but didn't say much. I also called my sisters and told them that I stopped by to see her. Their comments were: "I knew you would. You can't stay mad at people no matter what they do to you."

That was the beginning of my reconciliation with my mother-in-law. Although the feelings of closeness never returned, I tried very hard to be as amiable as possible so that my children would not feel they were betraying me if they decided to have a relationship with her. It was important to me for them to have a grandmother they could remember. My mother died while I was pregnant with Chris, and Matt was only four years old at the time. The only one who remembers her at all is Debbie.

I grew up without knowing my Mom's parents because her dad died long before I was born, and her mom died when I was 4 years old. My father's mother, Anna, died when I was about 12 and his stepfather left our house on unfriendly terms. Besides, Anna didn't speak English, which made the relationship very aloof. According to her, children should be seen and not heard, so there was never any closeness. I don't ever remember my father's mother hugging me or even talking to me. However, when we visited my Mom's mother—though she didn't speak English either— I would give her a hug, and she would chuck me under the chin and have me say "AAAH," which made me giggle at the funny noise I made. Then she'd give me a sand pail full of lollipops, which I had to share with my siblings and any cousins that were visiting. Those are fond memories.

As the years passed, my mother-in-law had a knee replacement done, which I was told the doctor botched. She was unable to walk without using a walker. She was in rehab for three weeks, and the day she got home, she tripped and fell backwards and hit her head on the TV. She was barely able to crawl to the telephone and pull it down onto the floor to call 911. The paramedics wanted to take her back to the hospital, but she refused to go. Because of that, her recovery was very slow.

Debbie invited her to come down to Maryland for Thanksgiving, but she had no transportation. Since I was picking up Lovey and Richard in Wilkes-Barre to attend my cousin's wedding in New Jersey the weekend before, I offered to pick my mother-in-law up and drive her down to Maryland when I was on my way back. Instead of staying at Debbie's house, she stayed at my house – in my bedroom – for Thanksgiving week. I expected Ben to come to take her home, but he called to ask when I was bringing her back, so I drove her home.

Since the drive was four hours each way, she and I had plenty of time to talk. She asked me all kinds of questions about Bruce and our divorce. I told her everything he had done to us. She kept saying that he was not brought up like that and she was very upset. She asked why I didn't call her for help. I told her that this was between Bruce and me. During this conversation, however, she denied knowing anything about his adulterous affair, and said she didn't know Theresa Hahn was coming to her tavern to see Bruce. Somehow, I doubted that.

Bruce always drove his mother to the doctor and to her hair appointments, but she had to be careful not to get him mad or he'd refuse to take her. Then, she'd have no transportation. The days when he took her to get her hair done, he would just drop her off and she would then take a bus home. As that got more difficult for her to do, she would have to call someone else to pick her up. One day she asked Ben if he thought I'd come up and stay with her and take care of her for a few days, but I did instead.

While I was there, Bruce called to say he'd be by to take her to her hair appointment, but she told him not to bother, that I was taking care of her and that I would take her to the hairdresser. I wish I could have seen his face or at least read his thoughts about that. Besides taking her to the beauty salon, I took her to the mall and out to dinner. I pushed her around in a wheelchair, which was not easy for me with my bad back, but I managed. When it was time for me to return home, she told me to please come back and stay anytime I wanted.

Debbie, her children, and I went up to see my mother-in-law for Easter, which happened to be on March 31st, Bruce's birthday. Our Orthodox Easter was much later, and we had just begun our Lenten fast, so we were not eating meat. She was upset that we couldn't eat the ham and all the fixings that had been prepared, but we told her not to worry about it – that we were fine with the vegetables.

Debbie called her father and, as usual, got the answering machine. She informed him that she and the children were at "Grammy's" and then put Zachary on the phone. She tried to explain to Zachary that he would be talking to the answering machine and that his grandfather wouldn't answer him, but that he should talk to his Grandpa Bruce anyway. I sat there with tears in my eyes as this little child talked.

He said, "Hi Grandpa Bruce. This is Zachary. I'm here at Grammy's house and I wish you would come and meet me. I love you, and I miss you. Bye. Love, Zachary." I thought to myself, if that doesn't get some kind of response from him, he might as well be dead. He never responded!

During that trip, Ben had come in from New York and Art, Bruce's cousin, and his girlfriend, Audrey, had come over to see us. It was nice to see them, but my feelings toward them were more as acquaintances than family. Audrey kept telling me what a really wonderful guy Bruce was.

Hostages Twentieth Mini Reunion Jan. 2001

Bruce Laingen called asking for Bruce's phone number. I told him I didn't have it and asked if there was a specific reason he wanted it. He said he just wanted to get in touch with him. About two days later, David Roeder called asking the same thing. He said he was trying to get in touch with the former hostages for a mini reunion, and that he wanted Bruce's phone number. I told him that Bruce and I were not on speaking terms and that I didn't have his phone number, but his children did. I told David that Bruce would get very upset if they gave his phone number out. I also commented that Bruce Laingen had already called me two days before and wondered why he hadn't told Dave that he had called me. Dave said that sometimes Bruce L. forgets. Dave said, "Let me give you my phone number and you can call Bruce and have him call me." I said I'd have Chris call his father.

Dave asked me if I had gotten any information on the reunion, because I should have as a former hostage wife, but I told him I had not. He said it had been sent via email, and if I had an email address, he'd send me all the information and that I should let him know if I would be interested in attending. I asked when it was being held, and he said Saturday. I asked, "What Saturday?" He answered, "This Saturday."

After I got off the phone with him, I told Chris about the phone call and asked him to call his father. Bruce actually answered, for a change. Chris told him that Bruce Laingen and Dave Roeder were trying to get in touch with him, told him of the reunion, and gave him Dave's phone number.

In the meantime, I read the emails from Dave and decided to attend. On Friday, Pat Lee Palmer called me to say she had some information for me and didn't know how I'd take it. She had a phone call from Mike Metrinko, at whose home the reunion was going to be held. Mike asked her how well she knew me and when she said she knew me quite well. He said he had a dilemma. Bruce did get in touch with Dave and said he'd be attending the event with his "significant" other. He just wanted me to know.

When Pat told me that, I said that I had changed my mind and I wouldn't be going. She said, "Don't let him ruin your plans. I was looking forward to seeing you, and you know more people there than he does. Dana and I will be there, so we could be together."

I wasn't sure I wanted to go. I had no idea what his mistress looked like, and after some of the nasty comments he made about my appearance (he didn't like the way I dressed or wore my hair and thought I was out of date with my style of clothing), I didn't want to be embarrassed. Finally, Pat's argument helped me to make my decision and I decided to go. I would not let Bruce spoil my plans. I called Mike and asked if I could bring Chris along to do the driving. The event was for hostages, spouses, and significant others – no children. Mike asked how old Chris was and when I said 30, he said, of course he could attend. I didn't know my way around Virginia and driving at night would be a challenge.

Chris and I arrived at Mike's house at about 6:50pm and a few people were already there. It was great to see the people who were so involved with us during the crisis. About 15 minutes later Chris said, "I recognize a head of white hair coming through the door, so I guess Dad is here." They came inside, and Chris waved to Bruce and Bruce acknowledged him half-heartedly. He was directed to take their coats up to the bedroom and to come down and help themselves to drinks and snacks in the kitchen. When Bruce came down the steps after putting their coats away, instead of coming over to Chris, who he hadn't seen in many months, he and his mistress went through the dining room into the kitchen, specifically avoiding us.

After about 15 minutes, when it was evident that Bruce was not going to acknowledge his son, Chris said, "I might as well get this over with," and headed for the kitchen to speak to his father while I waited in the living room. He came back a few minutes later and related the conversation to me.

Chris said, "Hi, Dad, how are you? Nice to see you," and Bruce answered with "Hi. Chris, this is Theresa, Theresa, this is Chris." There was no hug or "Happy to see you" or "This is my son, Chris." Chris told Theresa he was pleased to meet her. He asked Bruce, "How was the trip down?" He responded, "It was long, but okay." That was it. End of conversation.

I saw Gisela Ahern, Barbara and Barry Rosen, Donald Cooke, Kevin Hermening and his wife, among many others. As Wallapa Tomseth came by, I said, "Hi, Wallapa, do you remember me?" She gave me a quizzical look and I said, "Marge German!" She exclaimed, "Marge, how are you? And WHO is that in the kitchen with Bruce?" I explained that the woman, Theresa, was Bruce's significant other. Wallapa said, "What is she doing here? She doesn't belong here." I told her that it was okay for hostages, spouses, and significant others to attend. She asked, "What did Bruce say to you?" and when I told her he went in the opposite direction, she said, "Well, let's go into the kitchen and fix that!"

As we were making our way into the kitchen, we spoke to Billy Gallegos and Rocky Sickman, who had recently arrived, and finally got to Charles Jones, who was standing against the sink next to Theresa and Bruce. I held out my hand and said, "Charles Jones, how are you?" He looked at me and I could see he was trying to put a name with my face, so I said, "Marge German." He said, "Oh, Marge, it's good to see you." At the point when I said my name, Theresa's head swiveled like it was on a spindle, and I gave her a very blank look and turned my head. Bruce was talking to someone at that time and I could tell that he wasn't paying attention to the person he was talking to. He had a very guilty and embarrassed look on his face.

As more people came into the kitchen, I spoke to Penne Laingen and Alan Golacinski, asking about his mother and sisters who I hadn't kept in touch with for years. I asked him to remind me of his Mom's phone number and promised to call her in the next few days. At that point, Mike announced the buffet was ready and for us to go into the dining room and enjoy the food. As Pat, Dana, Chris, and I went into the dining room and going around the table, Theresa and Bruce started to come into the dining room and then did an about-face, as if to say, "SHE's in there! We can't go in there now!" For the rest of the evening, they made sure they were not in the same room with us.

The reunion was held to inform the former hostages and spouses about a lawsuit that had been filed on our behalf to sue the Iranian Government for the incarceration of the hostages for 444 days. Representatives from the law firm of Langford & Reed were there to present us with the details of what had already been done, conducting a short meeting as we ate. Many questions were asked and answered about our chances of getting any kind of compensation since our Government signed the Algiers Accords before the hostages were released, stating we would not sue the Iranian Government. How that came about I don't know, because no State Department official ever asked me, or anyone I spoke with, what we thought of the idea and if it was agreeable to us or not. They certainly didn't ask the hostages themselves!

A few former hostages who couldn't make it to the reunion sent messages to let everyone know they were sorry to miss the reunion, but we were all in their thoughts. After about 45 minutes, Mike announced that dessert was ready and we headed for the dining room. Pat, Dana, Chris, and I had our desserts and then just hung around in the dining room, talking and taking pictures and remembering events of the Crisis. After about a half hour, Chris came and said, "Dad left."

Chris said he saw Bruce and Theresa coming toward the dining room to have dessert but because I was there, they decided not to come in. Poor babies didn't get their dessert! When Chris took his empty glass into the kitchen to put into the sink, Bruce came by and put his in the sink also. He had his coat on and turned around to leave without a word to Chris.

Chris said, "Dad, are you leaving?" Bruce said, "Yes," and with that turned and waved over his shoulder at Chris and left. I was furious. What a scumbag! He didn't even give him a hug or say anything about how nice it was seeing him or when he'd see him again. Chris was hurt and said, "I can't believe my father did that to me! I can't believe my father did that to me!" I didn't know what to say to ease his hurt; I just commented that his father had problems. The thoughts I was having about Bruce weren't anything I wanted Chris to know.

Before we left, I went to Mike Metrinko and Dave Roeder and thanked them for inviting me to the reunion. At that point, Dave informed me that his conversation with Bruce put him in a dilemma. When he told Bruce that I would be at the gathering, he asked if Bruce had any objection to Dave telling me that Bruce would be there. Bruce said, "I'd rather if you didn't tell her." At that point Dave said he didn't want me to be blind-sided, and since Bruce knew that I was going to be there, I should also be informed that Bruce would be there with his mistress. To keep his word about not telling me, Dave asked Mike to call me to let me know. Since Mike didn't know me well, but knew Pat through her second husband, Steve Palmer, he called her and ask her to call me. Both Dave and Mike did not think too highly of Bruce at that point.

CHRISTMAS 2003

As time went on, and as my mother-in-law became less mobile, she began to have problems taking care of herself. So, a visiting nurse started coming by two or three times a week to take care of her – making sure she got her shower, her meals, etc. I'm sure it was difficult for her to know that she was not the strong, self-sufficient person she used to be.

Ben took her to New York for Christmas 2003 and while there, she became sick and was taken by ambulance to the hospital on New Year's Eve. She was there for a few days and before she returned home. Ben brought her back but worried that she couldn't stay by herself. A few days later, while Bruce and Audrey were with her, she had an episode where she seemed to lose control of her bodily fluids and they called 911. She was taken to the hospital and remained there for some time, after which Ben decided that she could not live by herself. He had her admitted to the Little Flower Manor Nursing home where she remained until she died. She never forgave Ben or Bruce for putting her in a nursing home. I visited her a few times and she would say to me, "I'd never do that to my mother! I'd never do that to my mother!"

That made me think back to when Bruce and I were married, and he would always tell me that his mother was going to come to live with us. I asked what about Al, her husband, and Bruce said he didn't care where he went.

Now I wondered why he didn't take her to his house, and then I remembered that she and his mistress were not on speaking terms. God moves in mysterious ways. Had we still been married; I would have been expected to take care of her.

THERESA'S DEATH AND FUNERAL, FEBRUARY 21ST, 2005

The phone rang at about 12:30pm. It was Ben telling me that the Little Flower Nursing Home administrator had called him to tell him that his mother had died just a few moments before. They asked if they should keep her body in her room until he got there so he could spend some time with her, or if he wanted them to contact the funeral director to come and get her. He was in New York and it would take him at least two and a half hours to get there. He didn't know what do to. I asked him if he wanted to spend time with her at the nursing home and he said, "No, not really." I suggested that he have the funeral director come for her. There would be plenty of time to spend with her at the funeral home while he made the arrangements. He said he'd let me know of the arrangements as they developed. I told him that Chris had gone to Las Vegas on Sunday - the day before, to attend a Real Estate Convention held by Keller Williams Realty and that he wouldn't be back until Friday - but I'd see if he could change his flight plans.

I called Debbie, Matt, and Chris to let them know their grandmother had died and that she would not be buried until Wednesday or Thursday, maybe even Friday, because the funeral director would need time to get her ready.

Ben called to say he tried to have the funeral on Thursday, but that there was another funeral that day from Kopicki Funeral Home, so it would have to be on Friday. I called Chris and asked him to see if he could change his flight to get in early on Thursday. From there, I could pick him up at BWI (Baltimore Washington International Airport) and we'd drive to Pennsylvania from there. He tried to get a flight out at 11:30am, but they were all booked and so the earliest was 4:00pm CT arriving here at 7:00pm. His original flight would have brought him in at 11:00pm on Thursday night.

Matt's stepfather-in-law, John, had just died the previous week and Matt, Danielle, and the children, Rachel and Joshua, had gone down to Florida to take care of things and to help Danielle's mother, T.J, since she was having some problems with John's children from his first marriage. Matt wasn't sure if he'd be able to take off from work again, but he knew that he'd have to fly up by himself. He called back about an hour later to tell me that an airline ticket would cost $800, so I told him not to bother coming up. Matt and his family came up in January and saw Grammy in the hospital, which was more important.

Debbie and Carl decided to go up to Pennsylvania on Wednesday evening, so they would be there for the Thursday viewings. Deb called to tell me my three sisters had come to the viewing to pay their respects even though the weather had become really bad. Ben and Bruce were very surprised but pleased that they were kind enough to come. All three had long conversations with Bruce, talking about old times. Theresa Hahn was not there. Ben told me that his mother said she did not want Theresa Hahn at her viewings or funeral.

When Chris and I finally arrived at the funeral home the next day, Ben came over and hugged me and cried, thanking me for being so nice to his mother. I went over to the casket to say a prayer and turned toward where Bruce had been sitting as I walked in, but he was gone. At that point, I asked to use the restroom, and by the time I returned, the priest from St. Hedwig's Roman Catholic Church had already started the service. He then asked the friends to come forward to pay their last respects, so I went up with everyone else. Bruce didn't get up, but I touched his hand and said I was sorry. I went past the casket and then went out to my car. Chris and Carl had been asked to be pallbearers, so they stayed behind to carry the casket to the hearse. It was bitterly cold while I sat waiting for Chris to join me, so I started the engine to get the heater working. It suddenly occurred to me that although I cry over sad movies or even if someone tells me something sad about a friend or relative, I didn't cry at all during this time.

We drove the short distance to the church and I stood inside the vestibule while Chris went to the hearse. I waited for the family to come in after the casket. As the pallbearers went by, there were Timothy and Zachary pushing the casket down the aisle. After Ben, Art, Bruce, Debbie and her family were in their pews, I went around to the side aisle and stood in the pew next to Zachary. Debbie, Carl, Melanie, and Timothy were in the pew in front of us. Art, his girlfriend, Audrey, Bruce, Ben, Zachary, and I were in the second pew. Off and on, Ben would break out into sobs and Zachary would look over at me with tears in his eyes.

Ben and Bruce went up to receive communion and came back up the aisle where Zachary and I were standing. We stepped aside to let them pass and as Bruce went into the pew, he was sobbing. Again, I touched his hand and said I was sorry. When I saw that he had tears running down his face, I took a packet of tissues out of my purse and gave them to Zachary to pass on to his "Grandpa Bruce." Later, Ben told me that Bruce had leaned over to him and said, "I knew I could depend on my ex-wife."

As we left the church, again Zachary and Timothy were right there pushing the casket with their great-grandmother's body. We drove to the cemetery and were ushered into a small building where they held the last memorial service before the burial. As we were leaving, I asked Bruce for directions to the restroom and he directed me to the back of the building. Of course, Melanie,

Timothy and Zachary wanted to go with me, and by the time we came out, the hearse was already gone and the casket had been lowered into the ground. Debbie was calling to us to hurry because everyone had already left to go to the repast meal that was being held at the Knights of Columbus in Luzerne, a town near Kingston. When we got there, the funeral director drove Bruce back to the funeral home to get his car while we all went into the dining area. There was one table that had "Reserved for Family" and Ben came up to me and said, "You're sitting with us. You're family." I was a bit surprised. It was a round table with Debbie, Carl, Zachary, an empty chair, Melanie, me, Timothy, Ben, and Chris all seated when Bruce came in. There was another empty chair between Debbie and Chris, so Debbie said, "Over here, Dad, you sit between us."

As dinner was being served, Ben filled our glasses with water. Lifting his glass in the air. Timothy said, "To Grammy! To Grammy!" It was priceless. Then Melanie started to sing "Happy Birthday" because she had heard someone say that Grammy's birthday was the next week. That is something I'll never forget.

As we ate, Debbie and Chris had a nice conversation with their father. They talked about sports, careers, and then went on to TV programs. Chris said his favorite program was *24* and Debbie mentioned her favorites, too. Bruce asked them if they ever watched any of the British sitcoms. Chris said, "Mom likes those. She likes the British humor; *Are You Being Served* and *As Time Goes By.* As he said that, both Bruce and I said in unison, "That's my favorite show." Debbie looked at Chris and he looked at her, they looked at Bruce and then at me and I could just see the wheels turning in their heads – "Oh ho, they still like the same things!"

At that point, I excused myself to go to the restroom and Melanie came with me. We walked down the hall past the entrance and went into the restroom. Melanie, at three and one-half years of age, had become very self-sufficient and insisted she didn't need help. She was growing up so quickly! As we were returning to the dining room, Bruce was standing near the entrance talking to two or three people who had come to the repast meal.

Bruce called out to me, "Marge, can I talk to you for a moment?

I stopped dead in my tracks and tried to search for words. I stammered, "Yes, I supposed so." I couldn't imagine what he'd want to talk to me about. We had not talked in years and those talks had not been pleasant.

He said, "Marge, today is my day of atonement. Do you think you could possibly forgive me for everything I ever did to hurt you? I mean **everything** I ever did to hurt you." He was gesturing with his hands to stress "everything."

I was dumbfounded. I stood there trying to respond for what seemed like a long time. Words would not come out of my mouth. God says if you expect to be forgiven you had to forgive others, but I wasn't sure I wanted to do that. Finally, using his exact words, I said, "Yes, I think I could."

He responded, "Oh, thank you. You don't know what that does for me. You don't know what that does for me."

I replied, "It's been a long time coming."

"Yes, I know it has."

At that point, I was still at a loss for words and didn't know what else to say, so I asked, "How have you been all this time?"

He said, "I'm doing okay except I have a problem with my knee. I had surgery on my one knee and it is fine. I had surgery on my second knee and it's not fine. It has been bothering me ever since the surgery back in September."

"Well, I've had a bit of a shock myself. I found out I'm a diabetic less than a year ago." "I'm sorry to hear that," he answered.

"Well, my mother was diabetic, so I guess one of us had to end up with it."

At one point, Carl walked past us and went into the dining area. I'm sure he was surprised to see us talking to each other without any shouting or having any lethal weapons in our hands.

I asked Bruce what he thought of his grandkids and he seemed very impressed with them. He said that Zachary was just like Matt, Timothy was like his father Carl, and Melanie was another Debbie. We talked about them for a little bit and then people started coming out of the dining room to say "goodbye" so Bruce went over to thank them for coming.

I saw him go over to Debbie and guessed that he was telling her that I had forgiven him. He was smiling from ear to ear and I read her lips as she told him how glad she was. He then told Ben and he, too, was glad.

As we were leaving the restaurant, Ben gave me the earrings Theresa had on in the casket. I looked at them and recognized them as the ones I gave her for Christmas a few years ago. Ben asked Chris and me to come back to the house for a while since Debbie and her family were staying there, so we followed him back to the house. Bruce didn't come—he said he was going to church for the "Stations of the Cross" that the Catholic Church holds on Good Friday.

Back at the house, Art and Audrey and a few of Ben's friends were there, and we socialized for a while. The main topic was Bruce asking for forgiveness. Everyone was pleased and surprised. I was still in shock.

During the conversations, Art and Ben discussed Bruce's girlfriend, Theresa Hahn. Evidently, while Bruce and I were going through our marital problems, she called them all the time, sometimes being on the phone for hours. Ben mentioned that Theresa had a few affairs prior to the one with Bruce, including one with the principal of the school where she used to work, until the principal's wife threatened her and told Theresa to stay away from him. Then, along came Bruce, and she turned her attention to him. Art said that at one point, when Bruce decided to try to reconcile with me, Theresa called Art and was crying that she loved Bruce and couldn't live without him. Art's answer to her was, "If you want him, go after him." I sat there, not believing what I was hearing. This whole family was in on the destruction of my marriage. They all knew what was going on and encouraged it.

On Saturday, Ben asked us to come by to pick out any things we wanted from the house, so Chris and I went over about 11:00am. We stood around in the kitchen for a few minutes and Chris showed Bruce some of the photos from our trip to Germany. He glanced at them a little but didn't show much interest. Then he said he had to go. He always had to go. Debbie called the kids to give him a hug and when Zachary and Timothy tried to give him a kiss, Bruce said, "We don't do that." He gave them each a hug. But he did give Melanie a kiss and a hug. He also hugged Debbie and Chris and shook Carl's hand and sort of waved to me. Then he was gone.

About two weeks after Bruce asked for forgiveness, I was still thinking about the conversation, word for word, when it hit me. He wasn't really sorry or repentant; he was asking to ease his own conscience, otherwise he wouldn't have said, "You don't know what that does for me."

On **March 31ˢᵗ**, Debbie and Chris went up to Pennsylvania to get some furniture from their grandmother's house. Since they would be up there on Bruce's birthday, they called him to ask if they could meet with him and take him to lunch. Chris asked him where he'd like to go for lunch, but Bruce didn't have any suggestions. Chris finally said that since he didn't live in the Wilkes-Barre area, he had no idea where a nice place was. His one comment was, "Work with me here, Dad, I don't know the place." It was decided that they'd pick a place when Chris, Debbie, and the kids got to PA.

When they got to Pennsylvania, the boys drove around the neighborhood trying to find a restaurant. Once they found one, they called Bruce to meet. By the time the boys arrived, Bruce was already there waiting by his car and holding a cane. They asked him what happened, and he said he had fallen. They had a nice lunch and then went up to the cemetery to see their grandmother's grave. While Chris was with the kids, Bruce was talking to Debbie and gave her the letter I had written him after the funeral.

Bruce showed the letter to Debbie, but she didn't tell him that she had already seen it. He was very upset and said, "Your mother thinks I had an ulterior motive when I asked for her forgiveness. I don't want anything to do with her and I don't ever want to see her again." So much for the sincerity of his "Day of Atonement."

All during my married life, Bruce wanted me to be a-stay-at-home mother. Now, he was pushing me to get a job. The economy was not good, and jobs were hard to find. My prospects for a career with decent pay was slim. But that became my focal point—to make as much money as possible, as quickly as possible. I had to support my children and myself. To make myself more marketable, I enrolled in a few courses at Montgomery College. I never had the opportunity to attend college after high school and worried that any job I got would not have any potential for advancement or it would be very limited. However, my career turned out to be more than I ever thought it could be.

In 1983 I was hired as an Office Manager for a college student financial aid company where I learned a little bit about computers. Although it only paid $4.00 per hour, I was able to work around my class schedule. In the meantime, I applied for a position at Bethesda Naval Hospital and after many months of waiting, I was hired as a temporary Clerk Typist, GS-4. While at orientation, I met Diana Maykowskij, who had been working in Government for a few years. While we stopped to have coffee at the break, she gave me some very sound advice: to get ahead quickly, I had to be willing to move from job to job as the opportunities presented themselves and to always look for jobs that had promotion potential. In my case that meant a job starting as a GS-5 with potential to GS-7/9 over a period of two years. Some government jobs have one step while others have multiple steps (a promotion ladder). GS-5 was the lowest step, and over two years I could potentially make it to a GS-9, but I was very skeptical that I would ever qualify for that.

I began in the Orthopaedic Clinic where my supervisor was Claire Radeloff, who became a very good friend as time went on. I hated typing, but I knew that was the only way to gain access to a government position. My job was making multiple copies using carbon paper and various colors for different departments. As luck would have it, a new computer was brought into the clinic where the chief warrant officer was trying to learn to use it. I asked him to show me how to turn it on and load it. This gem of a computer was called a "Winchester," which had to have the operating system installed every day with a 5" floppy disc; but at that time, it was a precious piece of equipment. After he showed me, I was able to use it to do most of the typing.

Captain Lichtman, our director, gave me a three-page memo to type, which I typed, printed out, and returned to him. He read through it and apologized to me that he wanted to change two sentences on the second page. He asked if I would mind retyping the document to fix them. I made the changes, printed it out, and gave it back to him in about 10 minutes. He looked at me and said, "I wanted the changes made." I showed him the old and new copies. He was impressed and so was Claire. She said, "We have been living in the dark ages!" Needless to say, I felt pretty good about myself.

I loved working in the clinic but constantly looked for any job listings where I could get a permanent position, preferable working in budget or accounting to use my past experience. I had to count on getting a full-time, permanent job with benefits and promotion potential to be able to support myself - the sooner the better. I applied for an accounting tech position and was told I was accepted and was to start the job on a Monday, but late in the day on Friday afternoon, I was called to say I did not qualify because I was a temporary employee – not because of my experience. How do you get a permanent job? That was a question no one seemed to be able to answer. Finally, I applied for a permanent clerk typist job in the OB/GYN clinic, where I managed to survive for a few months until I applied for a budget analyst position in the Finance Office.

Claire was very helpful in getting me an interview, and I was accepted and started there as a GS-5. This position had promotion potential with the possibility of a GS7/GS9 in the next two years, if I did a decent job. I felt that I was on my way to a great career. Getting to a GS-9 was more than I could possibly have dreamed. After many changes of bosses due to the normal rotation of personnel by the Navy, I reached my GS-9 and decided to look for another position with promotion potential and found it across the street at the Library of Medicine at the National Institutes of Health (NIH) as a budget analyst GS-9/11/12.

From there I went to the *National Institute of Arthritis, Musculoskeletal and Skin Diseases (NIAMS)* and I received promotions and awards in a timely manner. I still marvel at the fact that I actually got to a GS-12 in less time than it had taken Bruce to reach a GS-9 since he had also gone to night school for 12 years of our married life. There was no doubt in my mind that God was watching over me and my career.

For most of my career, I had excellent reviews and received awards for a job well done. However, the last two years of my career with NIAMS I had a supervisor who I could not please in any way, shape, or form. They made my life so miserable that it began to affect my health. After eight years in that office, I decided to retire as soon as I was eligible.

For a year after retirement, I tried to catch up on all the things I was unable to do while I worked and went to school. While browsing through the local *Gazette* newspaper, I saw an ad for a part-time Program Director with the Department of Recreation in Montgomery County Government of Maryland. I applied and was hired as a Program Director, planning and organizing activities and events for senior citizens at the East County Community Center. I enjoyed working there but was annoyed with some of the policies governing my job.

In 2002, after a few years of not working outside the home, I began working at St. Mark Orthodox Church as an Admin Assistant to the Treasurer. It was two days a week and did not have the stress level that the other jobs had. Suzette Eremin, another parishioner, and I worked as a team, she with the bulletin and *Evangelizer* newsletter, and I with the financial portion – sorting the mail, preparing the bills for payment, and checking to see that the checks and bills matched by amount. During the three years I worked there, we oversaw the renovation of the church, the addition of the classroom wing, and the expansion of the altar/kitchen wing. There were many days when the dust and dirt were overpowering, along with the noise level and freezing temperatures in winter, and suffocating heat in summer. In December 2005, I retired, but returned to the job at St. Mark in 2007 when my replacement retired. I worked there until October 2014.

Matt's Graduation, Commissioning, and Wedding

Matt was in the last graduating class (1984) at Peary High School before the County closed it due to low enrollment. He was offered one ROTC scholarship with the U.S. Navy and one with the U.S. Air Force and. After much thought, decided to take the one from the Air Force. He earned a Bachelor of Science degree in Aerospace Engineering and was commissioned as a 2nd Lieutenant in December of 1988. It was a very proud moment for him, and I was even prouder. The one unique thing about the aerospace graduating class was that when that class was announced, they all threw paper airplanes into the air to signify the specialty of their curriculum. It was a very joyous occasion.

At Matt's commissioning, Vietnam veteran and family friend, Fred Downs, administered the oath and I was to pin Matt's 2nd Lieutenant bars on his shoulders. Bruce, who had done nothing for Matt during his college years, except pay $100 for books per semester (which hardly covered the cost for one book), came right up there as a proud father and grabbed one set of bars and pinned them on one shoulder as I did the other. Then, he grabbed the ones for Matt's hat and I stopped him. I told him Fred was going to do Matt's hat. Bruce had hardly kept in touch with Matt at all during college and here he was trying to be Mr. Big Shot!

Matt was able to get a job at Bethesda Naval Hospital while he waited for his Air Force assignment. Finally, his assignment came, and he was to report to Tyndall AFB in Florida the day before his birthday. Being the mother of a very shy son, I was having a hard time coping with the fact that he would be so far away without any family nearby. Matt had always been a very quiet, reserved person and I worried just how he would manage. I decided to drive to Florida with him. So, with his little car packed as full as possible, we headed off to Tyndall Air Force Base.

When it was time for me to fly back home, saying goodbye at the airport was extremely difficult. I'm sure Matt will never forget how emotional I was. I think I embarrassed him because all he could say was, "Mom, Please, Mom, please" as I cried and cried.

While at Tyndall AFB, he met his wife-to-be, Danielle Walker, and they married on November 21, 1992. In April 1993, Matt and Danielle were blessed with a baby boy, Jordan, who was three months premature and weighed only 2 lbs. 2 oz. Unfortunately, he lived only two short days. It was a very sad day for all of us. In 1995, Matt and Danielle were blessed with a beautiful daughter, Rachel Lauren, about a year after the loss of Jordan.

DEBBIE'S GRADUATION, WEDDING AND CHILDREN

Debbie graduated from the University of Maryland with a degree in Spanish Translation and began working at NSA as a Linguistics Specialist. She was preparing to go to Mexico City for a tour of duty following in her father's footsteps in the Foreign Service, but after the plane crash at Lockerbee, Scotland, she decided she did not want to go overseas.

During Matt's years at Tyndall, Debbie said she wanted to live with him for the summer and work at a resort restaurant. It was there, while working at the Seven Seas Restaurant, she met a young man named Carl Firestone. Somehow, I knew this was different because she didn't say much about him to me. Usually if she saw a handsome guy, she would pat her heart and say, "I'm in love!" But before long, she would have moved on to the next one. This time she just said she met someone—no other comment.

She returned to Maryland after her summer in Florida and invited Carl up in October so I could meet him. He was very mannerly—a real southern gentleman with a southern drawl. I began to suspect there would be a wedding in the future. I was correct. Debbie flew down to Alabama to spend Thanksgiving with Carl and his family and he proposed.

She decided to move to Alabama and enrolled at the University of Alabama at Birmingham to earn her Master's degree in Elementary Education. On August 21, 1993, Debbie and Carl married at St. Mark Orthodox Church in Bethesda, MD. It was difficult for me to plan the wedding with Debbie in Alabama and the wedding being held at St. Mark in Maryland. Debbie wrestled with the invitations, wondering if she should put her father's name on them, not knowing if he would be glad or mad. I told her it was her decision – I could not help her with that. She called him and left a message on his answering machine, telling him she wanted him to be part of her wedding and to please call her. When he didn't call in a week, she wrote him a letter, again telling him she wanted him to be here. Since she did not hear from him, she decided to leave his name off the invitation.

The wedding was beautiful, and Debbie looked stunning. Right up until she walked down the aisle, she thought her father would be at the church, but he never showed up. On what should have been one of the happiest days of her life, she was very saddened that her father never came – and never responded to her invitations. I let it be known that he resented not having his name on the invitations.

Debbie and Carl worked hard to make a go of it in Alabama, but they were finding it impossible to make ends meet. In 1995, Zachary Kyle was born in

Birmingham, but Deb and Carl were struggling to survive. Although Debbie graduated with high honors, she was unable to get a teaching job. I asked them if they'd like to come to live with me for six months until they could get on their feet. Debbie was ready to come home, but Carl was leery. Carl discovered that he was able to transfer to a Loomis Fargo office here in Maryland, so the move was beneficial to them both. They made the decision to move and Debbie got a teaching job at St. John's Catholic School in Silver Spring. She loved teaching, but the pay was not good and she continued to try for Montgomery County Public Schools. After about three years, she was hired at Wheaton Woods Elementary School as a second-grade teacher, which she loved. It was also the school she attended when she was young.

I was becoming a grandmother by twos. First, it was Rachel Lauren born in May 1995 and Zachary Kyle in November 1995. Then, it was Joshua, born in April 1998 and then Timothy Paul born in May 1998. Tim's birth also happened to be the day Debbie and Carl were to settle on the townhouse they purchased, so all the papers had to be faxed to the hospital for Debbie's signature. It also would have been my wedding anniversary. Debbie said this would probably give her father another reason not to talk to her.

In 2001, Melanie Elise arrived and completed Deb's family. Her birth was not without excitement. I hurried to their townhouse when I got the call, and off they went to the Seventh Day Adventist Hospital in Takoma Park where her doctor was on staff. Melanie arrived weighing 8 lb. 3 0z. I announced to the boys that they had a new baby sister.

CHRIS' HIGH SCHOOL & COLLEGE GRADUATION, HIS MARRIAGE AND FATHERHOOD

Chris would have graduated from Peary High School, but since it closed in 1984, he went to and graduated from Rockville High instead. Then, he enrolled at the University of Maryland. Having a brother and sister who had already gone through the process made it much easier for him. He had not chosen a career path and took the required core courses and had one elective to fill. After looking through the catalog, he chose "Radio, Television, and Film" to fill the slot. He had always loved making audio tapes for his friends and I was not surprised that he graduated with a Bachelor's degree in that field.

He met Claire Powell at the Orthodox Singles group in 2010 during a crab feast event and two years later on August 18th, they married at St. Mark's. The wedding was lovely, and everyone enjoyed the day. The weather was beautiful, and the bride and groom beamed with joy through it all. They honeymooned in Hawaii and set their sights on the future, hoping to buy a house.

In January 2014, they were able to purchase a house in the Aspen Hill area, close to my house. On February 24, 2014, Caleb Alexander arrived weighing in at 9lbs 0.3 ounces and measuring 21" long. My granddaughter Caroline Adele arrived on December 22, 2016, three weeks early, weighing 8 lbs. 3 oz. At last, Chris has the family he so desperately wanted and deserved. As for me, I have been truly blessed.

TIME HEALS ALL WOUNDS

Time heals all wounds I'm told, but I wonder how much time is needed. Looking back at my life, I know that God must have wanted me to marry Bruce, to have these particular children. But was the breakup of our marriage in God's plan? I couldn't say. Despite all the heartache, I believe that I would still do all the things for Bruce that I had done during our marriage and the crisis.

I know I have grown emotionally and spiritually during this time, and that I'm a much stronger person now than I was before. My favorite bible verse is Roman 8:28 – "We know that all things work together for good for those who love God and are called according to his purpose." In the book *Daily Vitamins for Hurting Hearts: Day by Day with Jesus* by Anthony M. Conaris, there is a paragraph that fits:

> *"The diamond must be cut to bring out its beauty, the gold must be refined to bring out its purity, the vine must be pruned that it may bear more fruit, the clay must be molded that it might become a vessel fit for use and the child of God must be cut and refined and pruned and molded that he might become fit for the Master's use"...*

That covers it all.

Has any good come out of the Iran Hostage Crisis? Definitely, yes! Not everything was bad. During those very trying days, we met some wonderful people who cared a lot about us. Thanks to the parishioners at St. Mark Orthodox Church who supported us through it all, especially my best friends, Sue Petro, Katie Mikuluk, and Margie Johnson. I could not have survived without them or without Father Basil Summer's prayers and spiritual guidance. No Greater Love played a big part in the lives of my children by planning activities where they met celebrities and were able to share their feelings with the other children of hostages. That made the crisis a little easier to bear.

We also heard from many wonderful people who we did not have the pleasure of meeting, but who took time out from their day to write letters of support for our family and our country. Our country came together as one and patriotism was evident everywhere. No matter what happens to this country, we put our differences aside and stick together. You hurt one of us, you must deal with all of us.

Do I harbor resentment, anger, and hate? And whom do I resent and hate? I hated the Iranians for taking my husband hostage and changing the course of my life. I hated Presidential candidate Ronald Reagan and George H. Bush for undermining President Carter's efforts to free the hostages by secretly making deals with the Iranians. An article in the *Washington Post* stated that the FBI found 10 hours of audiotapes in a warehouse at Stewart Airport in Newburg, NY of conversations made during the Crisis between Ronald Reagan and a man said to be Iranian. Nothing was ever done to investigate it or to punish him with treasonable offenses. We were almost at war with Iran! The tapes were said to be "The October Surprise" allegations where the Republicans convinced the Iranians to hold the hostages until after the presidential election. I hated the fact that our Government took away my right to sue the Iranian Government for restitution for the suffering my children and I had endured for 444 days.

As time has gone on, I've learned that not only did my in-laws know what was going on with Bruce's adultery, but also condoned and encouraged it; something I never thought they would do. In 2006 in a telephone conversation with Ben, he mentioned the times that Theresa Hahn would be having dinner with them during our marital problems. If that was so, then everyone knew about the affair. Why didn't they do or say something to stop it? I asked Ben if anyone told Bruce committing adultery was wrong. The only one who said anything was Al, Bruce's stepfather.

I have to admit that I had very definite hatred toward all of these people for many years, but the only person it was hurting was me. The hurt and hatred were festering to such an extent that it was affecting my health, making my life miserable. For God to forgive me, I had to forgive Bruce, his mother, his brother, and his mistress along with all the others I resented. Christ wants us to forgive. That's the hard part! I have forgiven, but have I completely forgiven? After wrestling with that for 35 years, I can finally answer "Yes." I have forgiven them because I don't really care about them as much as I did when I was married. Despite all the heartache, I was cordial to my mother-in-law while she was alive and also to Bruce and his brother, but I haven't forgotten the hurt. I've discussed this with Fr. Gregory Safchuk, who is rector of St. Mark Orthodox Church now, who told me Christ does not ask us to forget – he gave us our minds and those memories don't necessarily go away.

I know that those who have done wrong will answer to God when the time comes. What about me? What will I answer for and what am I guilty of? Could I have done something differently? Maybe so; however, I can look at myself in the mirror without feeling a lot of guilt that I had not done my very best. I tried to shield my children from the terror and hurt that we had endured and the betrayal of their father. Despite all the hardship and stress, they have become wonderful, loving, caring, and successful adults. Had they not had a good foundation; their lives would have been very different.

For me, with God's help I will be able to put it all in the past and go on, but I'm sure I will also have to answer for the hatred I have felt. What does the future hold for me? That is in God's hands and whatever plans He has for me, I must accept them. "Not my will, Lord, but Thy will."

9 781970 157178